300 Years of the French in Old Mines

300 Years of the French in Old Mines

A Narrative History of the Oldest Village in Missouri

MARK G. BOYER

WIPF & STOCK · Eugene, Oregon

300 Years of the French in Old Mines
A Narrative History of the Oldest Village in Missouri

Copyright © 2021 Mark G. Boyer. All rights reserved. Except for brief quotations in critical publications or reviews, no part of this book may be reproduced in any manner without prior written permission from the publisher. Write: Permissions, Wipf and Stock Publishers, 199 W. 8th Ave., Suite 3, Eugene, OR 97401.

Wipf & Stock
An Imprint of Wipf and Stock Publishers
199 W. 8th Ave., Suite 3
Eugene, OR 97401

www.wipfandstock.com

PAPERBACK ISBN: 978-1-6667-2399-1
HARDCOVER ISBN: 978-1-6667-2014-3
EBOOK ISBN: 978-1-6667-2015-0

06/16/21

Dedicated to the memory of those
who came to Old Mines before, with, during, and after
Phillipe Francois Renault,
those whose names are remembered
and those whose names are forgotten,
those who have tombstones in
St. Joachim Parish cemeteries and other grave yards
with their names on them and those who do not,
those who are buried elsewhere,
those who attended St. Joachim Elementary or High School,
nuns, laymen, and laywomen who taught,
priests who ministered,
all past and present parishioners and residents,
and all who have made history for 300 years
in Old Mines, Missouri.

"... [T]he world as we know it is our interpretation of observable facts in the light of theories of our own invention. In other words, we invent our world even while we think we are just observing it and reporting on it."

—Robert F. Taft

"A generation goes, and a generation comes, but the earth remains forever. The sun rises and the sun goes down, and hurries to the place where it rises. The wind blows to the south, and goes around to the north; round and round goes the wind, and on its circuits the wind returns. All streams run to the sea, but the sea is not full; to the place where the streams flow, there they continue to flow. What has been is what will be, and what has been done is what will be done; there is nothing new under the sun. The people of long ago are not remembered, nor will there be any remembrance of people yet to come by those who come after them."

—Ecclesiastes 1:4–7, 9, 11

"... [A] people who do not remember are not a people; they forget their roots, and they forget their history."

—Pope Francis

"Unless we are reconciled with our own history, we will be unable to take a single step forward, for we will always remain hostage to our expectations and the disappointments that follow."

—Pope Francis

Contents

Acknowledgments | ix
Introduction | xi

1. Before the Beginning of Old Mines | 1
2. Beginning of Old Mines | 6
3. After the Founding of Old Mines | 14
4. Old Mines Concession | 18
5. John Smith T | 21
6. The Lamarques: Part 1 | 23
7. St. Joachim Catholic Church and Pastors | 27
8. The Lamarques: Part 2 | 51
9. Rectories, Employees, and Catholic Charities | 57
10. Catholic Cemeteries | 66
11. Schools, Lay Teachers, and Graduates | 70
12. Convents and Nuns | 95
13. Parish Societies and Committees | 106
14. Rural Parish Workers of Christ the King | 115
15. Vocations | 125
16. Knights of Columbus | 130
17. Health Care | 134
18. Public Schools | 138
19. Old Mines Old Baptist Church | 141
20. 250th and 275th Anniversary Celebrations | 143
21. Old Mines Area Historical Society | 149
22. La Brigade a Renault | 153
23. Lead and Barite Mining | 157
24. Old Mines French Language | 163
25. French Customs, Practices, Ways of Life | 169

26 La Guillonee | 188
27 Some Major Events | 195
28 Wars and Soldiers | 202
29 St. Joseph Parish, Tiff, Missouri | 210
30 Old Mines Today (2021) | 215
    Conclusion | 222

    Index | 225
    Recent Books by Mark G. Boyer | 229

Acknowledgments

The writing of this book would not have been possible without the help of many people. Those who spent the most time helping me with this project include Natalie Villmer, a fellow Old Miner, a living historian, who provided food, lodging, and almost three weeks of daily resources through which I searched for material pertinent to Old Mines history. Kathy (Thebeau) Coleman, former St. Joachim School secretary, spent countless hours in school records gleaning lists of eighth-grade and high-school graduates. Joyce (Daugherty) Politte, a former principal of St. Joachim School and current Director of Religious Education for St. Joachim Parish, assisted Coleman with school records and provided page-after-page of critical reflection on the past fifty years of Old Mines history, alerting me to topics that needed to be covered in this book. Also presenting pages of critical reflection was Mary Ann (Politte) Pratt, former and long-time St. Joachim Parish and School secretary, who filled in gaps in the history of pastors, school, personnel, and more. The list of Old Miners who served in the military would not have happened without the assistance of Villmer, Coleman, David Pratt, and Pat L. Nixon, a retired teacher from Potosi R-III. Kris Richards and his staff at the *Independent-Journal* graciously welcomed me to their office, permitted me to research bound volumes of past newspapers, and helped me find numerous stories that I would have missed.

Many others divulged information during in-person interviews. Among those are Joseph Politte, Robert and JoAnn Hahn, Dennis and Linda Boyer, David Pratt, Donald Boyer, Cindy Merx, Donna (Ward) Laramore, Cheryl (Juliette) Boyer, Fran(cis) Pashia, Jeff and Maria (Pashia) Boyer, Angie (Pratt) Mitchell, James Johnston, and Ronald Boyer. Information was also gathered through telephone-interviews from Rosemary Hyde Thomas, Rita (Thebeau) Kamper, Carmen (Coleman) Litton, Regina (Daugherty) Pinson, (William M.) Bill Long, Sister Laura Magowan, CCVI, Sister Rosita Hyland, CCVI, and Sister Doctor Pauline Nugent, CCVI. Still others provided information through e-mail: Dana Boyd, Richard Juliette, Timothy Daugherty, David Politte, and Father Anthony Datillo, pastor of St. Joachim Parish, and Gus, his dog.

I present a big Thank You to Sam (Cassie) Villmer, who cooked delicious meals and served as a dog-sitter and dog-walker (assisted by Coleman and Neva Calvert) for Shelby, my dog.

Acknowledgments

While I owe all of them a hearty Thank You, any mistakes are mine.
Mark G. Boyer

Introduction

FORMER WORDS

On page 2 in the September 1 and 2, 1973, *Historical Program-Pageant Book*, Natalie Villmer wrote words that were appropriate for the 250th anniversary of Old Mines, Missouri, that are also appropriate for the 300th anniversary. Her words begin, "This is a story of people." She continues, "People who had, and have, strong faith in God; people who struggled, and are struggling, to wrest an existence out of the soil of this territory; people who in the midst of poverty enjoyed life with gratitude to God for his gifts; people who kept alive for 250 years a French heritage of culture and customs; people who revere the old but are willing to make room for new ideas and better ways for the future; people who felt that love of God and the family were more important than material goods; people who led simple lives; the story of good people—and some who weren't so good!"

The year before Villmer penned her wise words, on page 2 in the introduction to *History of St. Joachim Parish: 1822–1972; 1723–1973*, I wrote: "Time passes, and we suddenly realize that we are a people with a history. We remember days when we were not, and we marvel at the courage of those . . . who fought that we might become what we now are. Those 150 years of being a parish are closely bound up with those 250 years of founding. And the history is still only beginning because with each new man [and woman] a new history must begin." I continued: "Our history is a history of faith, a history of struggling, a history of service. It is a history of simple people and their beginning search for God. It is a history of a school, a history of a convent, a history of societies." Then, I concluded: "We have grown in faith. We have withstood the wars, the floods, the tornadoes, the elements. We have continued our search for God." I think those words also apply to the 300th anniversary of Old Mines and the 200th anniversary of St. Joachim Parish.

Introduction
NATIVE AMERICANS

However, before we get too caught up in narrating the story about the coming of the French to Old Mines and the establishment of St. Joachim Parish, we need to remember that we were not the first people here. The petroglyphs carved in fixed dolomite rock in Washington State Park's 2,147 acres and in the Cresswell Petroglyph Archaeological Site's 382 acres give proof that Native Americans lived here around 1000 to 1600 CE (AD). Although the elements gradually wear away the figures carved or outlined in stone, it is easy to see the thunderbird, human footprints, snakes, turkey tracks, and symbols of fertility, even though no one really knows the story Native Americans were narrating.

Archaeologists tend to think that the petroglyphs in Washington County, Missouri, were made by mound builders in the Mississippian culture, which thrived along rivers and flood plains across the eastern, southeastern, and midwestern sections of what is now the United States. The culture flourished from 900 to 1700 CE. Washington County's petroglyphs most likely come from the Middle Mississippian period, 1000 through 1400 CE. While no one can be absolutely sure as to what they mean, they remind us that we were not the first ones here.

For the most part of our history, Native Americans and the French enjoyed cordial relations, due in part to the French's willingness to accept Native American culture and way of life. There are plenty of records about Native Americans attacking French explorers, especially when they perceived that natural resources were being abused, some type of cheating was taking place, or their land was being claimed by a foreign power. Native Americans may have led the French to the rich deposits of lead, which the French began to mine. The land known as Old Mines today was part of the hunting grounds of the Osage, the Kaskaskias, and others, later to be joined by the Shawnees and Delawares. These tribes maintained villages, practiced agriculture, and crudely smelted the plentiful lead. All the tribes eventually ceded land claims and moved further westward before the onslaught of European colonization. By the 1830s, most of the Native Americans were gone from the Old Mines area.

OLDEST SETTLEMENT

Ask most Missourians what is the oldest settlement in the State of Missouri, and most will answer Ste. Genevieve. However, that is not true. While Ste. Genevieve is the oldest permanent settlement in the state, Old Mines is the oldest settlement, as the reader will come to understand in the pages that follow. The founding date of Ste. Genevieve is disputed, but many people declare it to be 1751. Old Mines had lead miners as early as 1719 and most likely prospectors long before that. The founding of Old Mines in 1723 coincides with the land grant awarded to Philippe Francois Renault on June 26,

Introduction

1723, to mine lead. Thus, the oldest village in what is now the State of Missouri began as a mining town.

The Frenchmen who came with Renault to mine lead used picks and shovels, because the lead was near the surface of the earth, sometimes even protruding from the earth. After gathering it, the miners brought it to a log furnace smelter. The lead was placed on logs with more logs and more lead piled on top. The logs were set afire. Once the fire burned the logs, while smelting the lead, and everything cooled, the pieces of lead were gathered from the ground, placed in baskets or leather pouches, and carried by horse to Kaskaskia across the Mississippi. From there the lead was shipped to New Orleans, and from there to France, where it was used to make roofs, shot, glass, gutters, pipe, and pewter. Like any other industry, the smelting method was improved over time, roads were built through the woods so carts and horses could cross them, and Ste. Genevieve became a port of shipment for lead that was poured into molds to create small bars, which were easy to package and ship. The processing of lead continued to improve until it came to an end in the 1860s, the same time as the mining of barite, also known as tiff, was beginning. By then, railroads became the primary means of transportation.

HISTORY

As an Old Miner, I am conscious of the history we possess. However, I am also conscious that we do not live in the past; we do not live in a museum. While there are a few log homes left in the Old Mines area, people live in modern homes. Businesses operate out of modern facilities. Buildings no longer useful are razed or burn. No one wants to go back to the pre-industrial days without paved roads, electricity, or appliances. No one wants to have to go out and cut wood for cooking and heating. We don't want to abandon our gasoline cars, propane tanks, or microwave ovens. We could not bear to be without digital TVs, computers connected to the internet, or cell phones. While there is history in an outhouse, no one wants to give up the bathroom.

The purpose of celebrating anniversaries is to remember where our ancestors came from twelve or fourteen generations ago, what language they spoke, and how isolated they were from the rest of the world. We are proud of our French heritage, which we maintain today and keep alive in some form for the next generation. Old Mines is three hundred years old! There is a lot of history here. The data collected and narrated here does not tell the full story, but it is presented to evoke the memories of the past and provide inspiration for today and the future. The people who lived here in the past, and those who live here now, herald no spectacular deeds, no unusually outstanding events, but they disclose the strength of good, hardworking people, who went about their daily lives with faith in God, stopping to chat with each other, assisting each other with domestic chores, consoling each other during sickness and death, telling a story or two, welcoming a newborn to the neighborhood, dancing at a

Introduction

wedding, etc. By reading this book, the reader gets to meet the old and greet the new for a span of three hundred years.

ANNIVERSARIES

The decade of the 2020s is filled with anniversaries to be marked and celebrated in some way. Here is a list of the obvious ones:

- 2021: 200th anniversary of the State of Missouri being admitted to the U.S.
- 2021: 60th anniversary of the priesthood ordination of Monsignor James E. Hanson
- 2021: 200th anniversary of the first log church in Old Mines
- 2022: 100th anniversary of the founding of the St. Ann Sodality
- 2022: 80th anniversary of the founding of the Rural Parish Workers of Christ the King
- 2022: 80th anniversary of the opening of the current St. Joachim Rectory
- 2022: 65th anniversary of Natalie Villmer making final vows as a Rural Parish Worker of Christ the King
- 2023: 300th anniversary of the founding of Old Mines
- 2023: 100th anniversary of the founding of St. Joseph Parish, Tiff, Missouri
- 2024: 100th anniversary of the opening of St. Joachim School with Incarnate Word Nuns (Convent/School)
- 2024: 75th anniversary of the opening of St. Joachim School (current school)
- 2024: 170th anniversary of the enlargement of St. Joachim Church
- 2026: 160th anniversary of the confirmation of the bell in St. Joachim Church
- 2026: 50th anniversary of the priesthood ordination of Father Mark G. Boyer, the first man to be ordained in St. Joachim Church
- 2027: 170th anniversary of the opening of the Lamarque School
- 2027: 170th anniversary of the rededication of St. Joachim Church
- 2027: 50th anniversary of the founding of the Old Mines Area Historical Society
- 2028: 200th anniversary of the establishment of St. Joachim Parish
- 2028: 170th anniversary of the baptism of the bell in St. Joachim Church
- 2031: 200th anniversary of the dedication of St. Joachim Church

Introduction

NOTES

Old Mines in French is *Vielle Mine*, literally Old Mine. Throughout this book, I avoid the use of French as much as possible in order to make the text readable to the standard English reader. Thus, the village's name is Old Mines. Likewise, I have standardized the spelling of names in order to make it easier for the reader to maintain the difference between those named on these pages. For example, Henri has been standardized as Henry. Hopefully, this will avoid confusion. Likewise, I have translated French into English to make reading the text intelligible.

There are many ways to spell a name. However, the earliest French were not literate; they did not know how to spell their names. For example, an Irish pastor did not hear what the French man and woman said when they wanted their baby baptized; the Irish pastor wrote what he thought he heard. Writing a name the way it sounded resulted in many different spellings of names. A German pastor did not hear what the Irish pastor heard. Add the process of anglicization into this and it is no wonder that Osia can also be Oshia, Pashia can also be Pashea, and Mercille can also be Merseal. Once it is written, the spelling of the name usually remains for generations even though one branch of an early Old Mines family may be Duclos and another branch DeClue, Govereau and Govero, or Pratte and Pratt. Thus, throughout this work, I have chosen to use the modern spelling of names unless it is necessary for clarity to use a former version.

This is not a scholarly writing of history; it is a narrative writing of it. While there are no footnotes, the narrative version is firmly grounded in research. At the end of each chapter, the reader will find a paragraph of materials which he or she may wish to pursue further or more in depth. As can be seen by the list, much can be found online with a simple search of the key words. Other reading materials can be found in old books and articles. And *The Diggin's* has become a source for in-depth coverage of specific, historical issues. The narrative in this book progresses from before the beginning to the founding of Old Mines, the Old Mines Concession, and two important people associated with Old Mines (chapters 1–6). With the founding of St. Joachim Parish, the next series of chapters narrate all things associated with the parish (chapters 7–17). After this, the chapter topics turn to things historical in Old Mines (chapter 18–28). After presenting the history of St. Joseph Parish, Tiff (chapter 29), the narrative finishes with a tour of Old Mines in 2021 (chapter 30).

This book contains many lists, such as those for pastors and associates of St. Joachim Church, nuns, graduates from eighth grade and high school, and those who served in the military. Making a list is a dangerous enterprise, because it is easy to leave out someone's name or include a name that should be in another list. The reader will find discrepancies in the list of nuns who taught in St. Joachim School. The lists of graduates from St. Joachim School eighth grade and high school may be incomplete; eighth grade graduation, along with a list of those finishing eighth grade, disappeared

Introduction

during the existence of the high school. The focus was on graduating from high school. There are no lists of eighth grade graduates from 1963 through 1971. What is contained herein are names taken from year books of high school students. It is important to keep in mind that many students left St. Joachim School after finishing eighth grade. The lists of those who served in the military have been gathered from the online Washington County Cemeteries lists (up to December 31, 2016), current St. Joachim Parish death register lists, the plaques carried by St. Joachim parishioners on Memorial Day, names on a list compiled by Pat L. Nixon, names on the Veteran Memorial Wall at Moore and DeClue Funeral Home, and word of mouth. Some lists use middle initials, and some lists do not. Thus, it is impossible to determine if John Boyer is also John P. Boyer, John M. Boyer, or John L. Boyer. To be sure that no one was left out, all variants of John Boyer have been put on the list. If any name in any list needs to be changed, please follow the directions in the next paragraph.

Because of the magnitude of information gathered and presented here, mistakes are easy to make. Even though I had much help in preparing this book, I assume full responsibility for anything in error. If you find a mistake of any kind, please notify me so that it can be corrected in future editions of this book. Either send an e-mail to boyer50@mediacombb.net or write to me at Rev. Mark G. Boyer, 1140 E. Stanford St., Springfield, MO 65807-2058. Please give the page number where the error occurs, and please give a detailed description of the correction to be made.

Introduction
EMBLEM

The emblem on the cover of *History of St. Joachim Parish: 1822–1972; 1723–1973*, on a banner that hung in St. Joachim Church from 1972 to 1975, and on the Old Mines flag that I created for the 250th anniversary in 1973 was slightly modified and adopted as the emblem for the Old Mines Area Historical Society. Originally, the emblem, designed by Father Mark A. Dolan (a priest of the Archdiocese of St. Louis and, at the time of the writing of this book, Pastor of Our Lady of the Presentation Parish, Overland, Missouri), consisted of a shield divided into four sections. The left section displayed three fleurs-de-lis, a flower of France, signifying the French origin of Old Mines. The set of three flowers also paid tribute to the Trinity. The section of the shield displayed a crossed pick and shovel signifying the mining area out of which Old Mines was born. The pick and shovel form an X, which is the Greek letter for Ch in English, the first two letters in the word Christ. Thus, the crossed pick and shovel pays tribute to the Son of God and his redemptive act. The middle section of the shield displayed the dates of the two anniversaries which were being celebrated: 1822–1972, the 150th anniversary of the building of the first log church, and 1723–1973, the 250th anniversary of the founding of Old Mines. The lower section of the shield was left blank, signifying that there is a part of the history of Old Mines and St. Joachim Parish which remained to be made, the future history. The shield was set in front of the outline of St. Joachim Church, representing the importance of the Catholic Church and faith among the French in Old Mines. Since the church grew as the area grew, the history of the church and the area are interwoven and overlapping. The banner under the shield displayed the name of the parish and paid honor to the saint after whom it is named: St. Joachim.

The Old Mines Area Historical Society chose the shield for its logo, but it adapted it in the following way. The twin set of dates that appeared in the middle section of the shield were removed, and that section was left blank. The date of the founding of Old Mines, 1723, was placed in the lower section of the shield, which originally was blank. Both the outline of the church behind the shield and the banner below it were removed. Since that shield continues to represent the history of Old Mines, it is used in this book.

Mark G. Boyer
July 26, 2021
Feast of Sts. Joachim and Anne

1

Before the Beginning of Old Mines

WHO WAS WHO

In 1723, when Philippe Francois Renault, came to mine lead in what is now known as Old Mines, Missouri, Louis XV (1715-1774), known as Louis the Beloved, was king of France. Bordering France was Spain, and its king was Felipe V (1683-1746), the grandson of Louis XIV (1638-1715) of France, who was the father of Louis XV. The pope was Innocent XIII (1721-1724)—he stopped the Jesuits missionary activity in China—who, after a short papacy, was succeeded by Benedict XIII (1724-1730). The Revolutionary War (1775-1783) in the thirteen colonies that would become the United States of America wouldn't begin for more than fifty years. There was no St. Joachim Parish or Church. The superpowers in Europe—France, Spain, and Britain—were sending explorers and laying claim to land in the new world (North America) that would produce wealth and send it back to their home countries. In other words, money was the object of exploitation of the new world discovered by the Portuguese Christopher Columbus in 1492. But before all that took place, Europeans had been exploring what native peoples called Turtle Island (North America).

EARLY EXPLORERS

In 1513, one of those explorers, Juan Ponce de Leon (1474-1521), claimed what is now the state of Florida for Spain. Because this colonization attempt never had a clearly-defined boundary, the land claimed for Spain also included what is today portions of Georgia, Alabama, Mississippi, North Carolina, South Carolina, and Louisiana. De Leon, of course, was looking for gold.

In 1534, another explorer, Jacques Cartier (1491-1557), commissioned by the king of France, Francis I (1515-1547), explored parts of what is today Newfoundland

and Labrador in Canada, along with the Gulf of St. Lawrence and some parts of the coasts. He claimed the land for France, while looking for gold and other minerals to bring back to France. He made subsequent voyages in later years to colonize those areas.

Meanwhile, in 1541, Hernando (Fernando) De Soto (1495–1542), a Spaniard, had discovered the Mississippi River and crossed it. He led an expedition in what is now the states of Florida, Georgia, Alabama, and Mississippi. He was searching for gold, but he found none. He died in 1542 on the banks of the Mississippi River.

In 1603, Samuel de Champlain (1567–1635), a Frenchman, began exploring the territory Cartier had claimed for France. He participated in the settlement of Port Royal, Acadia (now known as Nova Scotia), the first permanent European settlement north of Florida. In 1608, he founded Quebec and New France, which consisted of eastern Canada and the Great Lakes area. He established trading companies that sent goods, primarily furs, to France.

As the seventeenth century continued, the major powers of Europe—France, Spain, Portugal, and England—began to compete for empires in the new world. France, especially, was interested in colonization, which would result in wealth sent back to the home country. With their base in Quebec, explorers began the process of colonization by establishing outposts for trade with Native Americans throughout New France; they were assisted by French Jesuit missionaries, who lent some stability to the outposts through the establishment of Catholic communities of converted Native Americans.

On May 17, 1673, Father Jacques Marquette (1637–1675), a Jesuit priest, and fur trader Louis Joliet (1645–1700) set out on a four-month voyage that carried them thousands of miles through the heart of North America to explore the path of the Mississippi River. After leaving St. Ignace, on Lake Michigan, they crossed what is now Wisconsin and followed the Mississippi River to what is Arkansas. They claimed both sides of the Mississippi River for France, and they opened up new lands for Catholic missionary work. The goal of finding wealth for the home country was coupled with the goal of finding wealth—converting and baptizing native peoples—for God!

In 1682, Rene-Robert Cavelier, Sieur de La Salle (1643–1687), and his lieutenant Henry de Tonti (Tonty) (1649/1650–1704), explored the Ohio River Valley and the Mississippi River Valley, reaching the mouth of the Mississippi, and extended New France to the Gulf of Mexico (including what are now parts of the states of Montana, Wyoming, eastern Colorado, North Dakota, South Dakota, Nebraska, Kansas, Oklahoma, Minnesota, Iowa, Missouri, Arkansas, and a part of Louisiana). La Salle named the territory Louisiana in honor of the French King Louis XIV, the father of Louis XV, who was king when Philippe Francois Renault came to mine lead in what is now known as Old Mines, Missouri, in 1723.

Pierre Le Moyen d'Iberville (1661–1706) sailed from France in 1698. As an official of the French government, he established the outpost of Biloxi (in what is now

Before the Beginning of Old Mines

Mississippi) in 1699. The city was the anchor for French territorial claims not only for the Gulf of Mexico, but for the whole of the Mississippi Valley, called Louisiana and consisting of all French colonies south of Canada.

Father Jacques Gravier (1651–1708), a French Jesuit missionary, interested in converting Native Americans to Catholicism, founded Kaskaskia, Illinois, in 1696. He traveled extensively throughout New France, but on September 8, 1700, he left Chicago for a voyage down the Mississippi River. In a letter dated February 16, 1701, he states that Cahokia, Illinois, had a French trading post. He also writes about the Mississippi River, specifically, the bluffs, mines, wild animals, and other features. On the tenth day of his adventure, he writes about finding the Meramec River, which empties into the Mississippi. He explained that there existed a lead mine about forty-one to forty-five miles from the mouth of the Meramec River; the ore, according to Gravier, yielded three-fourths metal. He did not visit the mine, but merely heard about it from either Native Americans or other Frenchmen. Before modern times, the Meramec River was considered to be what is now known as Big River, in which flows Mineral Fork, and into which flows Old Mines Creek. When Gravier and others after him mention the Meramec, they can be referring to any one or all of those waterways.

Pierre-Charles Le Sueur (1657–1704), a French fur trader, a practical miner, and a mineralogist, came with the Jesuits to Canada before 1683. After returning to France, he came back to New France and ascended the Mississippi River from Biloxi in 1699. On his way to Minnesota, he stopped in 1701 and explored the lead mine reported by Native Americans and noted by Gravier. As word continued to spread, interest in lead kept growing. Small amounts of silver had been found in Louisiana, but the hope was to find more silver.

From Biloxi, in 1702, d'Iberville made a plan to mine lead in Missouri. He wanted the exclusive right to do so. His plan was to protect miners from Native Americans with soldiers, to use slaves, and to exploit the fur trade. He wanted to establish a port at the mouth of the Mississippi, presumably from which to ship lead and furs to France. He asked for the exclusive privilege to work the mines on the Meramec River for twenty years. However, he died before he could put his plan into operation.

However, Antoine Crozat (1655–1738), a wealthy Frenchman, who had become a financier, was made the Marquis du Chatel by the king of France. In 1712, Louis XIV offered him a fifteen-year monopoly in New France, specifically Louisiana. Among his numerous rights were those to open and work mines and to engage in the fur trade. Crozat would have known that small amounts of silver had been found and that lead was there in abundance. Crozat's monopoly did not last long, as he transferred it to John Law (1671–1729), a Scottish businessman, in 1717.

The transference of the monopoly may have had something to do with Antoine de la Motte (Mothe) Cadillac's (1658–1730) appointment as governor of Louisiana in 1710, although he didn't arrive until 1713. He began his life in the new world as an explorer and adventurer in New France in 1683 in Acadia. He was also a trapper and a trader of alcohol and furs. After making a trip home to France in 1712, he convinced Crozat to invest in Louisiana (see above). In 1715, like many explorers before him, he traveled up the Mississippi in search of silver mines, which he had been deceived into thinking existed in Upper Louisiana. When silver was not found, he explored for lead. Cadillac directed some lead mining, leaving his name on the mine known as Mine La Motte in northern Madison County, Missouri. He may have brought in slaves to work at the mine; lead was important for ammunition used in Louisiana and the colonies. Cadillac mined some silver and lots of lead, which could be found very near the surface of the earth.

From 1717 to 1718, a series of French royal edicts were issued by King Louis XV. After Illinois became part of Louisiana, a new capital at New Orleans was established in 1718. Law, to whom Crozat had transferred his monopoly in 1717, created the Company of the West (later called the [Royal] Company of the Indies, and often referred to as the Mississippi Company), was put in charge of the economy for Louisiana. He had success at running finances as director-general of the Royal Bank of France. His future was dependent upon the vast lead he hoped to mine and the fur trade he hoped to exploit. Moreover, between 1717 and 1719 there were a number of explorers, who, under the auspices of the French royal government, came to Upper Louisiana in search of silver. Sieur de Lochon, a Parisian smelter and mineralogist, was sent by the Company of the Indies in 1719 to look for silver on the Meramec, but he probably never got beyond the mouth of the Meramec River; he may have visited the Mine La Motte region. Native Americans showed him where he could mine lead, but after smelting it, it was determined to be an inferior quality. Without the proper equipment, even if he had found silver, Lochon soon returned to Paris.

Also in 1719, Charles Claude Du Tisne (Dutisne) (1681–1730), a French Canadian, was sent by the governor of Louisiana, Jean-Baptiste Le Moyne, Sieur de Bienville, into Missouri to find a route to establish trade with the Spanish colony in Santa Fe, New Mexico. After his first attempt failed because of Native American hostility, his second attempt brought him below Ste. Genevieve where he took the Osage Trail through Washington County, Missouri. He followed the trail to below the Missouri-Kansas border, where he found pieces of lead ore. After several visits to other Native American villages, he continued work on the frontier until he was named a captain and given command of Fort de Chartres in Illinois.

Thus, from 1600 to 1719, from Canada to the Gulf of Mexico the French sought new-world wealth in terms of silver, lead, and furs. They sought silver and lead in mines located on the Meramec River (Big River, Mineral Fork, and Old Mines Creek). They sought furs in the forests that carpeted the country. What they didn't know was that they were in the earth's greatest known concentration of lead, both surface deposits and underground. That would change in 1720.

FRANCE EXPANDS

Thus, by the beginning of the 1700s, the French had established what was named New France, the area of the St. Lawrence River and the Great Lakes. For administrative purposes, they divided New France into five colonies: Acadia, Canada, Hudson Bay, Newfoundland, and Louisiana. Acadia was made up of what is now New Brunswick, Nova Scotia, and part of the State of Maine. Acadia, as we will see, was conquered by the British during the War of the Spanish Succession (1702–1713) and ceded by France to Britain with Newfoundland and Hudson Bay according to the 1713 Treaty of Utrecht. Explorers continued to claim more lands, as noted above, for France, ultimately from Canada to the Gulf of Mexico.

In this work, the term Acadia refers to those French expelled by the British from New Brunswick, Nova Scotia, and part of the State of Maine in the mid-1700s. Many of those French, migrated to Old Mines. However, the term Acadia is also used to refer to the regions of North America which today are associated historically with the lands, descendants, and culture of the former French region. Those French brought with them their roots, language, and culture and deposited them all along the Mississippi River to Louisiana on the Gulf of Mexico.

For Further Reading: Wikipedia: Antoine de la Mothe Cadillac, Jacques Cartier, Samuel de Champlain, Antoine Crozat, Claude Charles Du Tisne, Jacques Gravier, Illinois Country, Louisiana (New France), Pierre-Charles Le Sueur, and New France. Kansas Genealogy: Charles Claude Du Tisne. French in American—New France Colonies, *The Diggin's* 22:3. *Historical Program-Pageant Book, 250th Anniversary, Old Mines, Missouri*, Natalie Villmer.

2

Beginning of Old Mines

RENAUDIERE

Philippe de La Renaudiere (1690–1728/1734), an employee of the Company of the Indies, is listed on the November 15, 1718, roll of people onboard the Comte de Toulouse as Clerk of the Company and Conductor of Mines. Also on the ship's roll are a few miners, soldiers, tobacco workers, concessionaires and their people, and unspecified others. Renaudiere's name appears in two records of baptisms—he was the godfather in one and the father of the child in another—in Kaskaskia in 1721. The recorder noted that he was the Director of Mines of the Company of the West in the one entry, and that he was the Commissioner of Mines for the Company of the West in the other entry. In 1723, while in New Orleans, he drafted an account of his mining. He had visited La Motte's mining area and the mines on the Meramec (including Big River, Mineral Fork, and Old Mines Creek). He described the mines, located 190 miles from the mouth of the Meramec River, as being rich in lead. This would place Renaudiere's digging and mines at the headwaters of the Mineral Fork and Old Mines Creek in Washington County, Missouri.

He must have built a small community of huts or cabins, in later documents referred to as cabins of Renaudiere, for his miners. This may have been the beginning of Old Mines. It is clear that Renaudiere had worked mines sometime between 1719 and 1720, but because he had no men who knew how to build a smelting furnace, he abandoned the mines. Unless the lead was smelted, it was not economical to transport it through the woods—there were no roads—with horses to the Mississippi River, where it would be shipped elsewhere for smelting. He seems to have lost his title of director/commissioner of mines and been assigned to the newly-formed Provincial Council of the Company of the Indies (1722).

Beginning of Old Mines

While his name appears in church registers in Fort de Chartres, Illinois, in 1723 and 1724, in 1724, he is listed as a member of the Provincial Council—a demotion with serious impact upon his career—and described as a mining engineer. His name appears in church records of Fort de Chartres in 1725, in the census of 1726, and in Fort de Chartres records of 1727. After that he is back in New Orleans in 1728. And after 1728 his name disappears. Thus, between 1719 and 1720 Renaudiere was looking for and mining a minimal amount of lead in Old Mines. While he found the area rich in lead, his operations were short lived and most likely very primitive in terms of lead mining.

RENAULT

At about the same time as Renaudiere was demoted as Director of Mines, Philippe Francois Renault (Renau, Renaud, Renaut) (1686–1755) was named Director of Mines. Renault was the son of Philippe Renault, a wealthy iron founder at Cousolre, France, and a stockholder in the Company of the West (Royal Company of the Indies). Philippe the younger was a French politician, businessman, explorer, metallurgist, a forge-master, and a favorite courtier of King Louis XV of France. He left Picardy, France, in 1718, for the Illinois Country and Louisiana and arrived in 1719. According to tradition, he came with two hundred miners and workers with the purpose of exploiting the lead mines and finding silver and maybe gold. In the same year, he was granted a mining concession in the Illinois Country. In 1720, he discovered a thick vein of lead on the Meramec River, but nothing resulted from his discovery. He made a trip to Saint-Domingue (Dominican Republic), where he bought African slaves for labor in his mines. Then in 1722, he opened a new mine on the Meramec River, about thirty miles from Fort de Chartres. To protect himself from attacks by Native Americans (Fox), he was granted a land concession upon which he built a small fort, named Fort Saint-Philippe, on the road to the mine. The fort contained four houses, a store, and a timber-framed church. It also contained Renault's stone house, built between 1722 and 1723.

To declare that Renault had connections is an understatement. His father was a stockholder in the Company of the West. Under that company, the younger Renault formed a subsidiary Company of Saint-Philippe to finance his operations in Louisiana. He had learned smelting from his father, while becoming one of King Louis XV's favorite companions and advisors in attendance at his court. So, it would come as no surprise that on June 14, 1723, Pierre Duque de Boisbriant (1675–1736), commander of the Illinois Country at Fort de Chartres, and Marc Antoine de La Loire des Ursins, Clerk of the Company of the West, granted him several large tracts of land, one which included the land upon which was located Mine La Motte and one which contained the huts or cabins built by Renaudiere in Old Mines, for the purpose of lead mining. The concession, which includes the Meramec River, Big River, Mineral Fork, and

Fourche au Renault mentions a tributary of the Meramec River upon which Renault had built a smelting furnace at a place called the Great Mine. The tributary was Old Mines Creek and the smelting furnace was located in Old Mines. In the months following his receiving the concession, Renault contracted with a number of day laborers for a year to work in his mines with payment to be made in cash from the company storehouse.

Near Fort de Chartres on the Illinois side of the Mississippi River, he was granted a parcel of land about three-and-one half miles wide by seven miles long along the Mississippi River for a huge garden. The parcel was located about three miles north of Fort de Chartres. Renault established a settlement, which he named St. Philippe. There he raised provisions for the men who worked in the settlements in his mines. Taking advantage of the rich, black soil, he grew enough food not only for those working his mines, but he was able to sell some of it to others as far away as New Orleans. The settlement also served as Renault's basis for operating his mines.

In 1724, Renault delivered 20,000 pounds of lead to repay the loans to the Company of the West which he had used to pay his workers' salaries. By 1725, Renault was producing 1500 pounds of lead a day. However, in late 1725, Renault seems to have abandoned some of his mining operations due to hostilities from the Native American Fox. He was in Fort de Chartres in 1725, serving as a godparent at a baptism. In 1726, he is listed as managing the farm on a concession of land owned by Boisbriant and des Ursins. He owns twenty slaves. In the same year, he builds a barn for Joseph Adams. In 1728, Boisbriant loses his status as commander of the Illinois Country, and des Ursins loses his position as Clerk of the Company of the West—both may be due to Renault's political connections in Louisiana, the Illinois Country, and France. While Boisbriant's and des Ursins's farm is sold, Renault reactivates his own land concessions, especially that named St. Phillipe, and purchases other lands from their owners. In 1728 and 1729, he is still described as Director of the Mines, but that title disappears three years later in 1732, when the Company of the West is dissolved.

With the dissolution of the Company of the West, Renault's financial backing disappeared, and without that his mining operations, which could not support themselves, began to dwindle. In 1732, in a census, Renault's village of St. Philippe lists twenty-three black slaves, two Native American slaves, twenty-eight oxen, forty-two cows, 163 pigs, twenty-five horses, two mills, nine houses, seven barns, and five stables. The number of men and women is not given, but with seventeen children listed, there were probably around forty men and ten women, along with twenty-five slaves working 211 acres. In 1733, Renault is surveying land, functioning as an engineer, metallurgist, a mill-site appraiser, and director of the St. Philippe concession (village). By 1733, he could not supply the lead for consumption in Louisiana, and he was in substantial debt. He remains in the area, most likely engaged in some mining and directing the affairs of St. Philippe, until he was forced to return to France in 1742. He seems to have been a man of many talents, but in the new world he was unable to use them to make a lot of money!

Renault's mining operations foundered because of attacks by Native Americans. In the 1720s, he had to deal with the Fox; he constructed Fort de St. Philippe near the mouth of the Meramec River to protect his upstream mining operations. There is no doubt that in 1741 Native Americans were exploiting a mine that had once been worked by Renault. In 1743, it was the Fox and Sioux. In 1774, the Osage attacked Mine La Motte and killed a number of Frenchmen. While no tribe had a permanent settlement in the whole of the mining region, various tribes visited the area seasonally for hunting and gathering. Their seasonal presence was enough to cause Renault to abandon his mines.

One such story, which occurred during the early days of lead mining, is told about Henry Padgett (alias Henry Fry), who settled at Big River Mills. The story demonstrates that as late as 1759, Native Americans were attacking settlers. As the story goes, Padgett was engaged to Elizabeth Baker, who lived in his neighborhood. Because there was no church or judge in the area, they decided to travel to Ste. Genevieve with their attendants to have their marriage witnessed by the Catholic priest there. The wedding party brought with them the food they would need for a meal after the marriage ceremony. The whole group, consisting of the bride and groom, five or six bridesmaids and five or six groomsmen set out on horseback. On the way, they were stopped by a band of Kickapoo Native Americans, who took their food and clothes and let them go on their way. Once they got near Ste. Genevieve, they called to a Frenchman, who saw their distress signal, talked to the bridegroom, and went into the village to find clothing, which he brought back to them. Once all were fitted with ill-fitting clothes, they went to the church, where the marriage took place as planned.

Renault also suffered from the lack of financial resources. The cost of salaries, food, equipment for miners, clothing, building cabins, and shipment of the lead to New Orleans led to the collapse of the Company of St. Philippe and the Company of the West which sponsored it. The system that had been established by Law required a rapid return on investment, and Renault was not able to accomplish that. He began well, but could not maintain the business momentum required to satisfy investors. In the end, not only did the Company of St. Philippe collapse, but so did that of the Company of the West and, ultimately, Law's financial system.

TRADITIONAL RENAULT

According to tradition, Renault brought two hundred skilled miners with him from France to work in the lead mines. That seems to be a good example of what happens to a story as it is passed on verbally: It continues to expand! The record of the ship, Comte de Toulouse, lists only fourteen men, four of whom have wives, and some of whom have three children. This is why in 1723, after receiving the land concession to mine lead, Renault is found contracting with day laborers to work in his mines. It can be inferred easily that he probably did not bring two hundred miners with him. The cost of feeding, clothing, shelter, and mining tools would have prohibited so many; furthermore, most ships at that time could not carry two hundred passengers. At the height of his mining operations, he may have had two hundred employees—including those who worked in St. Philippe—but many of them were Frenchmen already in the Illinois Country, Louisiana, or they had come recently to the area looking for work in the mines. In reality, Renault probably had about thirty Frenchmen working in the mines in 1723.

Tradition also holds that Renault bought two-hundred or five-hundred slaves in San Domingo to work in his mines. However, like the number of miners, these numbers seem to be exaggerated. At St. Philippe, he had eighteen black adult slaves and five children slaves in 1732. That number seems in keeping with the number of slaves owned by men of his stature. Unless he sold all the two hundred (which may be the same number of miners) or five hundred (while not impossible, but improbable), there would be more than twenty-three slaves left in the area in 1732. Furthermore, no census records show the existence of that many slaves in all of Louisiana. And after several generations, there would be countless numbers of descendent slaves working in the mines. And such records do not exist.

Another tradition is that Renault brought fifteen thousand bricks, each stamped with his name, with which to build smelting furnaces. While it is reported that one such brick was discovered on the Fourche a Renault—where one of Renault's furnaces was located—in Washington County by a surveyor, one brick represents .006 percent of fifteen thousand. A fourche is a fork, a branch, or a tributary. Transporting fifteen thousand bricks on a ship from Paris to New Orleans, and then from there to Fort de Chartres, and then from there to the Meramec River and its tributaries would have been a project beyond the means of any human being in 1719 and 1723. The weight of the bricks could have sunk the ship across the Atlantic Ocean. And even if that had not happened, how would Renault have gotten them up the Mississippi from New Orleans? There were no roads; the river was the only means of travel through the forests. Likewise, even if the bricks had made it to Kaskaskia, how would Renault have gotten them from there to Old Mines? There were no roads. Thus, no carts could have been used. And it would have taken hundreds of horses with saddle bags full of bricks to get them through the woods.

The reader must also keep in mind that smelting was accomplished using a log heap furnace, which needed no stones nor bricks. Later, the log furnace was used, but its hearth was easily built from stones on the slope of a hill. A more likely scenario is that the bricks were made of mud and straw at the sites where Renault's furnaces were built; the molds may have featured his name or his initials or a brick maker may have marked a brick to indicate that a stack of bricks were designated for Renault. Mud and straw, even if baked, deteriorate in the elements. That is why only one brick has ever

Beginning of Old Mines

been found, if such a find ever occurred. By the time the ash furnace and the scotch hearth furnace appeared on the smelting scene, Renault was back in France. Thus, it is highly unlikely that he brought fifteen thousand bricks with him from his home country. More information on the furnaces used for smelting lead can be found in chapter 23 on Lead and Barite Mining.

The lead that Renault smelted had to be taken to the Mississippi River and sent to New Orleans, where it was put on ships and brought to France. There it was used primarily as a roofing material. A tour of any ancient European building, especially cathedrals, displays the huge sheets of lead on roofs. It was used—even though huge roof joists had to be put in place and the walls had to be supported by buttresses to keep the roof from pushing the walls apart—because it withstood the elements for many years. The tradition that at his two main mining operations—Mine La Motte and Old Mines—that after the lead was smelted it was cast into horse-collar shaped pieces and placed around the necks of horses does not cohere with equine physiology. Not only would the smelted lead have to have gone through a difficult casting process, but a horse is not made to carry weight on its neck; rather, weight is placed on the horse's back. Furthermore, once the lead would have made it to Kaskaskia, it would have had to be recast into bars, ingots, or sheets before it could have been sent on barges in transport to New Orleans. Because there were no roads and only trails through the woods, the most likely scenario is that Renault had the lead smelted, gathered it from log heap furnaces or from log furnaces and maybe cast into small bars, placed them into leather bags, loaded the bags on pack horses, and led them over trails to Kaskaskia and/or Fort de Chartres.

Since Ste. Genevieve was not founded until 1752, and by then Renault was back in France, Ste. Genevieve could not have grown originally as a port of shipment for the lead! There may have been a small village there as early as 1732 or 1735, but it was not large enough to serve as a port for shipping lead down the Mississippi. The census of 1752 lists only twenty people, including children and slaves, living there. Thus, Renault's lead bars were packed on horses and transported from the smelting furnaces to the Mississippi River. There, it was loaded onto river boats, which took it to Kaskaskia, Fort de Chartres, or maybe even St. Philippe, where Renault's office was located, and then put on a river boat or barge heading to New Orleans. Later in history, once trails became roads, the lead mined by Renault's successor miners was hauled in two-wheel carts. And eventually Ste. Genevieve grew large enough to serve as a port of shipment.

Renault's mining operations in Louisiana, more specifically, Old Mines, was short lived. From 1723 to 1742, Renault had established mines and settlements on the Meramec River, Big River, Mineral Fork, Fourche a Renault, and Old Mines Creek. By 1743, the mine at Old Mines was being operated by a few volunteers and eighteen or twenty people who were serving a sentence for dissolute living; it was a primitive type of penal colony. Residents of Old Mines were most likely seasonal, living there between the latter part of spring and the latter part of fall, or, if they were farmers, from the end of the harvest to before the winter began. The rest of the time they moved to Kaskaskia, Fort de Chartres, St. Philippe, or, once it was founded, Ste. Genevieve.

OLD MINES AREA

Instead of thinking of Old Mines as a single mine with a smelting furnace and cabins in its vicinity, it is better to think of Old Mines as an area encompassing many different villages of a mine and several cabins about a quarter- or a half-day's horse ride from each other. Eventually, the villages of Richwoods, Racola, Shibboleth, Cannon Mines, Kingston, Cruise, Tiff, Barytes, Fertile, Bellefontaine, Cadet, Mineral Point, etc. were established. The men working in the mines, their wives, and children didn't think of themselves as founding a town. Rather, they thought that they were merely making a living by mining, hunting, gardening, and gathering. Once enough log cabins were built in an area, it was not long before a general store appeared; in it could be purchased tools and foodstuffs and other supplies that were not available otherwise. At a later date, log churches would be constructed, meeting halls built, taverns opened, one-room schools erected, etc. Even though Renault went bankrupt, many of those who had accompanied him stayed to mine lead; it was a lucrative way to supplement their incomes when not growing food or hunting. Active and enterprising miners would take possession of a mine, and, over the course of a few years, possession would become ownership. While the mining was seasonal, the presence of the French in the Old Mines area was continuous.

The continuity of the human presence in Old Mines is verified by the notation in the registers of St. Anne Church in Fort de Chartres in 1748. On September 28 of that year, Pierre Vivarenne, who was born in Picardy, France—Renault's hometown—and his wife, Marie Anne Rondeau, present their daughter for baptism. The priest records that they are from the village of the Mines. Because no church had yet been founded in Old Mines, anyone desiring baptism had to travel to Fort de Chartres or Kaskaskia for ministration by the Jesuit priests who were missionaries in both the Illinois Country and Louisiana. This fact does not rule out the fact that some of the Jesuits probably visited Old Mines from time to time to minister to the Catholic population there. However, in 1748, Catholics would have wanted baptism for their child a few days after birth because of the high mortality rate and the church's teaching that non-baptized children would end up in limbo—and not heaven—if they should die!

La Renaudiere's cabins or huts for lead miners in Old Mines became Renault's aggressive mining and smelting community. For a time, it may have served as a type of penal colony for the Illinois Country and Louisiana. Ultimately, Old Mines became an area composed of multiple villages founded by Renaudiere and Renault in 1723 and forever known as Old Mines.

For Further Reading: Wikipedia: Philip Francois Renault. *The Diggin's*: There's More to a Name than a Word, 8:3; Excerpts from History and Customs, 6:1; 275 Years

Beginning of Old Mines

of the French in Washington County, 4:2. A History of Missouri from the Earliest Explorations and Settlements until the Admission of the State into the Union, Louis Houck. Parallel Lives: Philippe de La Renaudiere and Philippe (de) Renault, Directors of the Mines, Company of the Indies, Elizabeth Shown Mills, *The Natchitoches Genealogist* 22:3–18. The Enduring French Creole Community of Old Mines, Missouri, Walter A. Schroeder, *Historical Geography* 31:43–54. Photos of Saint Joachim Church, in Old Mines, Missouri, Rome of the West, Mark S. Abeln, February 21, 2008. II. The Old Mines Community and Its People in *It's Good to Tell You*, Rosemary Hyde Thomas. *Historical Program-Pageant Book, 250th Anniversary, Old Mines, Missouri,* Natalie Villmer.

3

After the Founding of Old Mines

After Philippe Francois Renault went bankrupt and returned to France in 1742, mining, trapping, fur trading, and homesteading continued in Old Mines. The inhabitants of the village grew in number even though it was isolated from the rest of the world for the most part. Travel between the smaller villages that comprised Old Mines and travel to Fort de Chartres, Kaskaskia, and Cahokia in the Illinois Country also continued. What had once been Renaudiere's and Renault's Old Mine (*La Vieille Mine*) gradually became many surface lead mines. A lot was about to change in twenty years, however. The world powers of Europe—England, France, and Spain—were at war with each other; these almost eternal on-again, off-again enemies/allies would treat their new world acquisitions like pieces on a chess board all in the hope of making lots of money or settling debts as a result of war!

FRENCH AND INDIAN WAR

From 1756 to 1763, in what is known as the Seven Years' War in the British colonies (referred to as the French and Indian War in the U.S., and referred to as the War of the Conquest in Canada), the major players were Britain and France, and later Spain. It is called the Seven Years' War in the British colonies because the British fought the French and their Native American allies for seven years in Europe, even though the conflict lasted for nine years in what is now the U.S. In the U.S., it is named the French and Indian War because the French allies were Native Americans—the Algonquin, Abenaki, Huron, and others. Canada calls it the War of the Conquest because Quebec fell to the British. This does not mean that no Native American tribes allied themselves with the British. On the contrary, throughout New England and New France, various tribes for various reasons inter-tribally and extra-tribally formed alliances with each other and with Britain and France.

AFTER THE FOUNDING OF OLD MINES

In the British colonies, which would declare independence in a few years, the war lasted for nine years. It began in 1754 with the conflict between Britain and France as the British tried to expand their territory beyond the colonies into that claimed by the French in what was known as New France. Likewise, the French were looking for ways to expand their territory into what had become the British colonies. On June 16, 1755, the British assaulted Acadia and expelled its French settlers; some of those French traveled down the Mississippi River to the French mining settlements on the west side of the river—one being Old Mines—while others traveled to what is now the state of Louisiana, where they become the Cajuns.

In 1756, the British suffered a series of defeats against the French, but in 1759, the British defeated Quebec—the capital of New France—and the French capitulated; by 1760 the British had expelled the French from Canada. Spain entered the war as an ally of France in 1761, but that did not stop the British from ultimately defeating France in North America. France's last attempt occurred in 1762; French forces attacked St. John's, Newfoundland, but they were ultimately defeated by British troops in this final battle of the war in North America. It forced the French to surrender to the British, who now controlled most of North America.

SPANISH RULE

In the Treaty of Fontainebleau in 1762, France ceded Louisiana west of the Mississippi River to Spain in compensation to Spain's loss of Florida to Britain in the war. Thus, in 1762, Old Mines, Missouri, became a part of Spain. In the Treaty of Paris—which ended the war in North America—in 1763, France ceded its territory—Illinois—east of the Mississippi River to Great Britain. In order to escape British government, many French settlers from Fort de Chartres, Kaskaskia, Cahokia, and elsewhere crossed the Mississippi River to Missouri, thinking that they would find territory governed by France only to discover that they had entered Spanish territory! The British, who now owned the territory to the north, west, and south of their thirteen colonies, had removed their European rivals from the new world.

UNITED STATES BORN

While the British thought they had everything under control in North America after 1763, the thirteen colonies there decided that they had had enough of British government. The thirteen colonies, responding to excessive taxation from the home country, formed the First Continental Congress to boycott British goods in 1773. In 1775, the Second Continental Congress created an army, and on July 4, 1776, issued a Declaration of Independence. War, which had existed from 1775, ensued in earnest from 1776 to 1781. Even after 1781, some fighting took place through 1783 between Britain and France and Spain. In 1778, France, seeing an opportunity to weaken their British enemies and establish a new trading partner independent of them, declared war on Great Britain. In 1779, Spain, likewise, declared war on Great Britain. In 1782, King George III of Britain recognized U.S. independence, and in 1783, the Treaty of Paris was signed between Great Britain and the U.S. with its French and Spanish allies.

FRENCH INDEPENDENCE, LOUISIANA PURCHASE

While the U.S. was basking in independence, in 1789, the populace of France began the French Revolution in order to gain its independence from King Louis XVI (1754–1793). The social and political chaos that began in France and its colonies in 1789 did not end until 1799. After Louis XVI was beheaded, periods of political turmoil followed. In 1793, Spain, ruled by Charles V (1788–1808), declared war on the French Republic. In 1795, France defeated Spain, and in 1800 regained Louisiana; the transfer does not occur until 1803 in New Orleans. Meanwhile, Napoleon Bonaparte, a brilliant military leader, rose through the ranks during the French Revolution and orchestrated a coup in 1799 which made him First Consul of the French Republic. Before becoming the First Emperor of France, Bonaparte (1804–1814) sold Louisiana to the U.S. in 1803 for fifteen million dollars three weeks after it's official transfer from Spain. The treaty, dated April 30, 1803, was signed May 2, 1803.

Thus, from 1763 to 1803, Old Mines was under the Spanish government. In 1800—confirmed in 1801—it was again under the French government, but sold in 1803 to the relatively new United States of America. On March 9–10, 1804, in St. Louis, which had been founded in 1764 as a fur-trading village and established as the Spanish seat of government the same year, Spain officially transferred Louisiana to France, which then officially ceded it to the U.S. The day all that took place was called Three Flags Day. People living in Old Mines were now U.S. citizens.

During Spain's government of Louisiana, the territory was divided into five administrative districts under the Spanish lieutenant governor in St. Louis. Each district was overseen by a commandant. Old Mines was in the Ste. Genevieve District. However, there was little change that occurred in Old Mines other than officially switching from French to Spanish rule. Because the population remained French and the village was isolated in the interior of Missouri, Old Miners continued to mine lead—seasonal and through the year—trap, engage in fur trade, and homestead. In other words, not much changed, except that the French were resentful of Spanish rule! Thus, the Spaniards who came to Missouri were those who held military positions or governmental posts; little to no immigration occurred, even though Spain fostered it. During and after the Revolutionary War, more people came to the area after it became a U.S. territory. Mills, bridges, roads, stores, and churches were built and cemeteries were opened. The French enjoyed a common pasture—there were no fences—and common woods.

After the Founding of Old Mines
POTOSI

During the Spanish years of government, the only major discovery in the Old Mines area was in 1763: Rich lead ore was discovered six miles south of Old Mines in what is today called Potosi. Francois Azau, commonly known as the Breton (because he was from Briton) discovered the outcroppings of lead while, according to tradition, hunting a bear with a Peter Boyer. Azau was probably one of those who had come with Renault and stayed once Renault went bankrupt. Named Mine a Breton (Burton), it was a very productive lead mine. Many Old Miners moved to the location, later laid out as a town and named Potosi by Moses Austin, to make a living at the mine digging and smelting the lead ore. At its beginning, miners lived in temporary shelters in camps because most mining was seasonal. Lead was taken by horse or cart or wagon to Ste. Genevieve for shipment to New Orleans.

For Further Reading: A search on the internet for any topic mentioned in this short chapter will provide a number of in-depth articles on it.

4

Old Mines Concession

Under Spanish rule, Old Mines was in the Ste. Genevieve District. The commandant was Francois Valle I. After noticing that more and more people—Americans—were coming across the Mississippi River from the east to escape British rule and that little had changed since Spanish rule began in 1763, the inhabitants of Old Mines petitioned the Spanish governor, Hector, Baron de Carondelet (1748–1807), in 1796 to recognize their land grants that they had mined and cultivated since Renault in 1723. Up to this point in time, there was little competition for land, and the French were not overtly concerned about who owned what tract of property. When they did not get a response from Carondelet, who in 1797 was appointed elsewhere, they appealed their petition to Valle, who was a Frenchman appointed by the Spanish government.

Around 1800, the Native American Osage, roaming in the Old Mines area, caused an evacuation of the area. The French, living in Spanish territory, merely retreated, and, once the Osage were gone, at least twelve French families returned. After Bonaparte sold Louisiana to the U.S. with a treaty dated April 30, 1803, and signed May 2, 1803, the French in the territory knew that this change in government would bring a change in land ownership. Many people living in Old Mines did not have a title to the land upon which they were living.

Thus, on May 25, 1803, Valle wrote another petition and sent it to Carondelet's successor in St. Louis: Carlos Dehault Delassus (1764–1842), the last Spanish governor (1796–1804), who just happened to be Valle's friend. In preparing the petition, Valle sent his agent, Nicholas Boilvin, to Old Mines to gather signatures on the petition. No one knows how Boilvin went about doing that. Even though the U.S. now owned the territory, Delassus issued instructions on June 5, 1803, that the thirty-one tracts in Old Mines mentioned in the 1796 petition were to be surveyed. Thomas Maddin completed the survey. Delassus had instructed Maddin to conduct a drawing of lots to determine ownership beginning with the longest resident of Old Mines and continuing with others in the order of their length of residence. The population of the village is noted as thirty-one heads of families, thirteen women, seventy-two children, and eighteen slaves. Valle most likely bribed lame-duck Delassus, who had no authority to act; this explains why it took only ten days to get Delassus to order the survey, whereas it had taken years to get the petition advanced to this point.

The names on the plat recorded by Maddin, including the lot numbers, are as follows: 1. B[asil]. Valli, 2. [Aug(us')t Valli, 3. M[anuel]. Blanco, 4. Jean Portell [John Porter], 5. Pierre Martin, 6. Jacob Boisse, 7. Alex[ander] Duclos; 8. Cha[rle]s. Robert, 9. Jos[h]. Pratte, 10. T. Maniche, 11. Amable Partenay, 12. Jos. Blay, 13. Jean Robert, 14. L[ouis]. Boyer, 15. B[apt]. Placet, 16. Widow Col[e]man[t], 17. Jos[eph]. Boyer, 18. C[harlene]. Boyer [Boze], 19. A[ntoine]. Grouvinay [Govereau], 20. N. Bo[i]lyin, 21. Thos. Rose, 22. L[ouis]. Lacroix, 23. T [Francois]. B[te]. Valle, 24. I [Francois]. Milhomme, 25. J. Guibo[u]rd, 26. Fr[ancois]. Thib[e]ault, 27. A[mable]. Pa[s]tenut[t]e, 28. I. [Jos.] Be[c]quet[te], 29. B[ernard]. Col[e]man[t], 30. Hypolite Robert, and 31. Pierre [Bte.] Boyer. Three other plots intruding upon the first to the eighth grants are recorded as belonging to Peter Boyer, Elias Bates, and August P. Chouteau. On the list of signatures on Valle's petition of May 25, 1803, there appear two more names: James Roxe and P. Charles. Nevertheless, out of the 31 land owners, twenty-three were poor residents of Old Mines who lived in cabins. Eight were wealthy residents of Ste. Genevieve and other places who wanted to reap some of the profits of the lead mines.

Each of the thirty-one people who were awarded land grants received about 340 acres. The whole concession was plotted as a rectangle, about 10,548 acres, three and one-third miles wide by five and two-thirds miles long. All of the thirty-one grants along with the other three that intrude upon them have rights to Old Mines Creek, which flows in a curve through all of them. The long strips of land, rather than rectangles, gave everyone water rights and meant that villagers were not too far away from each other.

After Maddin's survey and lottery, those people receiving a grant had title to land, approved by the governor. All that a commandant or the lieutenant governor could do was grant a land concession. Miners living in Old Mines needed to raise food for themselves and their families. Their gardens were fenced with wooden rails to keep out domestic animals, like cattle or pigs. The Spanish government did not issue land grants or concessions to miners; it did, however, award land to private owners for the purpose of agriculture. It considered miners to be transient, but those engaged in agriculture were considered to be permanent. This would insure settlement and economic and social development of the area.

On February 3 and 4, 1804, after the Louisiana Purchase, the boundaries of the concession were surveyed again. Keep in mind that people had been living on land before the lottery occurred. Residents objected to the lottery procedure because it was highly unlikely that they would draw the lot number of the land upon which they had a cabin, a garden, and a fenced-in area. Therefore, once the lottery was complete, Old Mines residents continued to live where they were living no matter what lot they had drawn. In fact, because many had no intention of living on or using their assigned lot, they sold them. By 1812, the French in Old Mines had sold eighteen of the twenty-three lots assigned to them.

On March 2, 1805, Thomas Jefferson, president of the U.S., signed into law an act for ascertaining and adjusting the titles and claims to land within the Louisiana Purchase. The act stated that anyone who on October 1, 1800, was a resident of Louisiana and possessed a duly registered warrant or order of survey for lands lying within it would be confirmed in his claim. The same act allowed for two presidential appointees as land commissioners who, along with the recorder of land titles, would ascertain the rights of claimants under either French of Spanish grant. When Old Mines residents heard about the Board of Land Commissioners, they became concerned that the land they lived on probably would not be confirmed because they were not living on their assigned tract. So, they began claiming settlement rights to gain ownership. However, the Board of Land Commissioners was also instructed by congress not to confirm any land with lead; congress considered the mineral to be a national resource. Thus, lead-bearing land was to be in the public domain and leased to miners. Since the whole Old Mines Concession was lead-bearing, no claims to the land were confirmed. In 1833, the restriction on private ownership of lead-bearing land was lifted, and the Old Mines Concession was confirmed in 1836.

Thus, what had been the land where Renaudiere and Renault mined lead became the Old Mines Concession. It sits in Townships thirty-eight and thirty-nine of the rectangular systems of townships, ranges, and sections adopted by the U.S. government. When surveyors encountered a boundary of the Old Mines Concession, they stopped, skipped over the land grants of the concession, and picked up on the opposite side. Thus, surveyors did not interfere with the boundaries of the Old Mines Concession, which is askew of the surrounding rectangular land holdings. It is to be noted that the first white child born on the Old Mines Concession was La Plant Boyer in 1801.

In 1887 or 1888, some names on the list of the original land grantees had changed. The plot numbers are not listed, but the names are the following: P.P. Boyer, William C. Carr, John B. Portel, Pierre Martin, Jacob Boise, A. Diclos, Charles P. Robart, Joseph Pratt, B. St. Gemme, Widow Coleman, Joseph Boyer, Charles Boyer, Nicholas Bouelvian, F.B. Valle, Jacque Gibbourd, Joseph Bequette, and Bernard Coleman. Most likely, this list reflects the owners of the tracts in 1887 or 1888 and not the tracts drawn by lottery in 1803. Throughout the years, the tracts were sold or subdivided and sold, some being subdivided again and again and sold.

For Further Reading: *Historical Program-Pageant Book, 250th Anniversary, Old Mines, Missouri*, Natalie Villmer. *The Diggin's*: The Old Mines Land Concession of 1803, Walter A. Schroeder, 13:3; Public Lands, No. 9, Old Mines Concession, 16:1; List of Characters of the Old Mines Concession, 16:2; Ribbon Farms, Pat Moore, 21:4.

5

John Smith T

One of those Americans coming to Old Mines to buy many tracts of land upon which to mine lead was John Smith T. According to tradition, this Tennessee native added the T to his name to distinguish himself from all other John Smiths! He came to Old Mines sometime in 1804, and he bought land in the Old Mines Concession: tracts seven, eight, fourteen, seventeen, and others. There are other records of him buying acres of land in the Ste. Genevieve District in 1805 and 1808, totaling around 2,500 acres. He began lead mining at Shibboleth and Bellefontaine on 845 acres he bought from Jacques de St. Vrain. He is often described as a bold and daring land speculator. By 1811, his Shibboleth mine had produced 3,125,000 pounds of lead from 5,000,000 pounds of ore. In 1819, from underground shafts he was mining 1,000,000 pounds of lead from stiff red clay and 2,700,000 pounds of lead from surface mining. He had 240 miners employed. From his Old Mines and Bellefontaine Mine, twenty miners were producing forty-five thousand pounds of lead.

Smith T is known as a duelist. He had two black slaves making firearms in his gunsmith shop. He was recognized as a gunsmith himself. In 1819, he dueled with Lionel Browne, whom he shot in the center of the forehead and killed. In 1821, Smith T was indicted for murder in the Washington County Circuit Court. Smith T thought that Richard Rose was trying to lure away some of Smith T's slaves, so he shot and killed him.

By 1823, Smith T had erected a three-story brick home—razed around 1910—to replace his log home in Shibboleth, where there was a store operated by his company. He was a very wealthy owner of lead mines, but he was conspicuous because of his duels and attained notoriety. He was often described as an adventurer, land speculator, bully, and desperado! He had a brother, named Thomas A. Smith, who made his way in the army to become a general, from Essex County, Virginia. Smith T disappeared from Old Mines around 1825, after selling his mines and real estate, and went to

Mississippi to establish a plantation. Before he went, he sold the house he built in 1818 south of what is now St. Joachim Church to Etienne and Marie-Louise Lamarque.

For Further Reading: A search on the internet for John Smith T will present a number of articles and books about the life of this interesting character.

6

The Lamarques: Part 1

Etienne (Stephen) Lamarque (LaMarque) (1785–1851) was a native of France. His wife, Marie-Louise (1799–1868), was the daughter of Louis Bolduc, a merchant, lead miner, and land owner in Ste. Genevieve, Missouri. Born in St. Marie Doleron in the Lower Pyrenees in France, Lamarque was the son of Bernard Lamarque and Josette Mari. Marie-Louise Bolduc, born March 1, 1799, in Ste. Genevieve, was the daughter of Louis Bolduc II and Marie-Louise Ste. Jeme Dit Beauvais.

Louis Bolduc II (1769–1804) was a fifth-generation Bolduc, a descendant of Pierre Bolduc, who was King Louis XIV's apothecary. He came to Ste. Genevieve with his father, also named Louis I, around 1765 as a refugee from the French and Indian War in which Quebec was captured by the British. His father married Agathe Govereau on January 28, 1765, in Ste. Genevieve. After her death, his father married Marie Courtoise on January 28, 1775, in Ste. Genevieve.

Etienne Lamarque had made his way to Ste. Genevieve either by traveling up the Mississippi from New Orleans or coming down the Mississippi from Canada. He married Marie-Louise Bolduc on September 28, 1815, in Ste. Genevieve Church, Ste. Genevieve, Missouri. Before the wedding, he signed the articles of agreement, today known as a prenuptial agreement. In his day, the articles of agreement were prepared only for the upper class. The articles declared that after they were wed, Lamarque and Bolduc would hold all real and personal estate and property in community. Neither would be responsible for debts incurred by the other before the wedding. In case of the death of one of the spouses, the surviving spouse would inherit all real estate and personal property belonging to both of them. Furthermore, Lamarque would provide a dowry of two hundred dollars, and Bolduc would retain the right to divorce him and repossess all the estate for herself and any children born of the marriage. Such articles of agreement were signed and recorded to protect the real estate, personal property, and other wealth of Marie-Louise Bolduc, who was but seventeen years old at the time of the marriage.

Bolduc's father, Louis II, died on February 4, 1804, and her mother remarried in 1811. Her uncle, Paschal Detchemendy, was appointed guardian for her and her brother, Louis III, to be sure each received their share of their father's estate. Their inheritance was no small sum considering the wealth that their father, Louis II, amassed, along with their father's own inheritance from his father, Louis I, and that from their Ste. Jeme Dit Beauvais and LaCroix ancestors. Thus, Marie-Louis Lamarque and Louis Bolduc III represent the heirs of the merger of several families' fortunes into one, making them two of the wealthiest families in the Louisiana Territory. Lamarque had little of value; it was his marriage to Marie-Louise that made him wealthy.

Louis Bolduc I, Marie-Louise's grandfather, was a merchant, trader, and lead miner. He ran a general store out of his home, selling groceries, meats, dry goods, hardware, shoes, stationery, glasses, fiddle strings, and real estate. He had built his home in 1770, but enlarged it considerably in 1785 to accommodate his business. He furnished the house with the best of furniture, silverware, mirrors, fireplaces, a chest of drawers, and a cherry sideboard; only the wealthy could afford such luxuries as a chest of drawers and a sideboard. He was paid in salt, pelts, and lead. He bought and owned land in Old Mines in 1802, section nine of the Old Mines Concession. After his first wife died in 1774, his wealth was estimated to be well over twenty thousand dollars a year.

However, it was lead that made him rich. He traded merchandise from his store for lead, then he shipped it down the Mississippi River to New Orleans. In partnership with another Ste. Genevieve businessman, he owned three-fourths of a horse-powered flour mill. He owned the Saline Salt Works. And he owned many parcels of land in Ste. Genevieve.

Bolduc I owned slaves, which only the wealthy could purchase. They labored in the salt works and prepared lead for shipment; they took care of the gardens, grape arbor, and orchard. Inside the house, they prepared meals and took care of the children. As was the custom, they took Bolduc's name when they were baptized.

Louis Bolduc II was born January 30, 1768, in Ste. Genevieve. As he grew, he inherited the expertise of his father in the nineteenth-century world of business. At eighteen years of age, he was buying and selling real estate. And, like his father, he owned slaves. At twenty-nine years of age, on August 29, 1797, he married Marie-Louise Ste. Jeme Dit Beauvais in Ste. Genevieve. She was the granddaughter of the wealthiest man in the Illinois Country, Jean-Baptiste Ste. Jeme Dit Beauvais I, who had married Marie-Louise LaCroix at Fort de Chartres in the Illinois Country in 1725. After moving to Kaskaskia, his father-in-law, Francois LaCroix, who was a voyageur, merchant, and very wealthy, got him involved in the merchant business there. When LaCroix died in 1755, he left his son-in-law and daughter everything he had, including land, slaves, horses, and other animals.

Beauvais I got involved in the trade and lead mining in Ste. Genevieve, even though he continued to live with his wife in Kaskaskia. When he died in 1773, he

The Lamarques: Part 1

owned much land, six lead smelting furnaces, a water mill, salt works, and more. In marriage to Marie-Louise LaCroix, he had six children. The son named Jean-Baptiste Ste. Jeme Dit Beauvais II married Therese Boucher de Mont Brun Sieur de La Seaudrais on January 29, 1770, in Kaskaskia. By 1790, they had moved to Ste. Genevieve, where they built a very large house and furnished it with the best of furniture. Part of their compound included quarters for their slaves, barns, stables, and more. The slaves worked in the lead mines, maintained a huge garden and orchard, and provided domestic services inside the home. Wealth in the eighteenth century was calculated by the personal property people possessed. Beauvais II was considered to be the wealthiest man in the Louisiana Territory.

To the union of Jean-Baptiste Ste. Jeme Dit Beauvais II and Therese Boucher de Mont Brun Sieur de La Seaudrais were born six children. One of them was Marie-Louise Ste. Jeme Dit Beauvais, who married Louis Bolduc II on August 29, 1797, in Ste. Genevieve. Louis Bolduc II was the wealthiest man in the Louisiana Purchase. His wife was the granddaughter of the wealthiest man in the Illinois Country. To this union, three children were born, one of them being Marie-Louise Bolduc, who married Etienne Lamarque. Marie-Louise Bolduc, along with her one surviving brother, Louis Bolduc III, were the heirs of the merger of the wealthiest families in the Louisiana Territory.

Marie-Louise Bolduc was in Old Mines before her marriage to Etienne Lamarque. The pre-nuptial agreement indicates that the signing of the articles took place in the house of Jean Fouquier Von Pretre, Marie-Louise's step-father. After her father's death on February 5, 1804, her mother married Jean Fouquier Von Pretre on April 7, 1811. After the wedding, the couple with Marie-Louise and Louis III moved to Old Mines. Thus, it was there that the articles of agreement were signed on September 28, 1815, and the couple traveled to Ste. Genevieve to have the ecclesiastical marriage witnessed by the pastor of the parish there. As yet, the parish of St. Joachim in Old Mines had not yet been founded. The civil marriage took place on July 20, 1816, and the pre-nuptial agreement was recorded the same day in the Deed Record Book in the Court House of Washington County, Missouri. At this time in history, the ecclesiastical wedding did not suffice for the legal contract; thus, a civil ceremony also had to be held. Often these occurred on the same day or subsequent days; sometimes months and years intervened.

At some point between September 1815 and before July 1816, Etienne and Marie-Louise Lamarque were living in Old Mines. Not only were they close to her family, but, like her father before her, they were interested in lead mining. Jean-Baptiste Ste. Jeme Dit Beauvais, Marie-Louise's grandfather, had received a land grant in Old Mines in 1803. Likewise, her grandfather, Louis Bolduc I, had not only been buying and selling land in Old Mines in 1802, he also traded for lead and shipped it from Ste. Genevieve down the Mississippi River to New Orleans. By 1815, the Old Mines village was growing; supplies were accessible from Ste. Genevieve; people like the wealthy Lamarques were interested in more wealth which could be obtained through the mining of lead.

In order to mine lead, they needed to buy land, and that is what they began to do. As early as 1822, they were purchasing land. In 1822, they purchased land and the home John Smith T had built in 1818 in Old Mines. Over the course of the next forty-five years, the Lamarques bought a minimum of thirty-three tracts of land for which they paid twenty-six thousand dollars and sold tracts of land receiving over fifty-one thousand dollars. These tracts of land do not include that given to the Bolduc nieces and nephews nor that given to the Catholic Church. They owned at least two lead-smelting furnaces in partnership with another lead miner. They loaned money with interest to others to purchase land and a smelting furnace. Other documents declare that Marie-Louise Lamarque retained the rights to mines on land she leased.

The Lamarques operated what might be described as a French plantation. They had a farm, an orchard, and a garden. Their many slaves provided the necessary labor on the farm, in the orchard and garden, and in the lead mines, along with domestic tasks in the Lamarque home. Some slaves were brought from Ste. Genevieve, and some slaves were acquired after the Lamarques settled in Old Mines. There are multiple church records of baptisms, marriages, and burials of slaves and their offspring all bearing the last name Lamarque. Over ninety slaves are recorded in church records bearing the name of Lamarque. Thus, with their land buying and selling, their lead mining, and their plantation home all operated with slave labor, the Lamarques, although French, were equal to any southern aristocrats in wealth and manner of living.

Because the Lamarques professed Catholicism, as did the majority of the French in Old Mines and Ste. Genevieve, they brought that faith with them. As will be seen, they became instruments for the planting of the Catholic Church in Old Mines on a very firm foundation. At this time, Old Mines was a village, located on lots four, five, and six of the Old Mines Concession along Old Mines Creek. Those who lived there had a cabin, a small fenced clearing, and a garden. There were paths and cart trails connecting cabins. The name given to the area was the village at the Old Mine. Moses Austin, the founder of Potosi (Mine a Breton), had a road built from Old Mines to Potosi to link the two settlements.

Even though the French King Louis XV's decree about black slaves of 1724 had long been replaced by the Louisiana Purchase, the Lamarques, along with others, continued the practice of having their slaves instructed in Roman Catholicism and baptized Catholics. They also made sure that their baptized slaves were married in the Catholic Church and buried in the Catholic cemetery.

For Further Reading: The Lamarques in Old Mines: 1815–1868, Mark G. Boyer.

7

St. Joachim Catholic Church and Pastors

PRE-PARISH VISITATION

Until 1815, when Louis William Dubourg was consecrated bishop of the entire Louisiana Territory, Old Mines had been visited intermittingly by Jesuit priests from Fort de Chartres and Kaskaskia. As early as 1700, Jacques Gravier had written about the vast deposits of lead in the area. A Jesuit missionary priest, Philibert Francis Watrin (Vattrin), from Kaskaskia, had visited Old Mines as early as 1734 in order to celebrate some marriages. On September 28, 1748, Pierre Vivarenne and his wife, Marie Anne Rondeau, living in the village of the Mines, travelled to Fort de Chartres to have their baby baptized in the Church of Ste. Anne. Thus, the Jesuits knew about the Catholics living in the interior of Missouri west of the Mississippi and made infrequent trips to visit them.

HENRY PRATTE

Once Ste. Genevieve was founded, grew, and established a church, priests from there began visiting the Catholics in Old Mines. Tradition states that three log churches were built in the Old Mines village before the brick church was begun. In a letter dated January 25, 1792, a Father Joseph de Granada states that he has been chaplain in Vegia Miniere (Old Mine). From 1796 to 1814, Father James Maxwell traveled to Old Mines Village from Ste. Genevieve several times a year to minister to the Catholics living there. Father Henry Pratte, pastor of Ste. Genevieve from 1815 to 1822—the first native-born Missouri priest, ordained in 1815, a Vincentian—was appointed pastor of Old Mines in 1816 by Dubourg and celebrated the first Mass. Pratte, who continued to visit Old Mines every three months, built the last of the log churches in Old Mines in 1820 and named it St. Joachim Church. After this, he visited Old Mines almost weekly.

The log churches had to be constructed bigger and bigger to hold the growing number of Catholics there. Records indicate that by 1825, there were two hundred families in the Old Mines area.

Undoubtedly, the Lamarques influenced the erection of the last of the log churches. Coming from Ste. Genevieve, they would have known Pratte, and he would have known the Bolduc and the Ste. Jeme Dit Beauvais families in Ste. Genevieve. The Lamarques, the Bolducs, and the Ste. Jeme Dit Beauvais families were the major contributors to the church there. Their financial and social influence was also felt in Old Mines.

For example, Pratte recorded the oldest baptism of a white child in Old Mines on April 20, 1820: Edward Robert, who had been born December 2, 1819, to Louis Robert and Eloise Coleman. The godparents for the child were Francis Coleman and Marie-Louise Lamarque. A few days later, on April 23, 1820, he recorded the baptism of Guillaume, born May 24, 1819, a slave born of a slave named Frosine, who belonged to Baptiste Micheau. The godparents were Pierre Boyer and Hyacinthe Placet. He baptized Andre Jacques Scott on April 27, 1820; the godfather was Etienne Lamarque. On June 13, 1821, he witnessed the marriage of Francois Auge (Osia), son of Francois Auge and Therese LaPlante, to Marie Milhomme, daughter of Louis Milhomme and Catherine Gagnon. In Old Mines, the Lamarque name appears throughout Pratte's records.

Pratte died of a fever on September 1, 1822, in Ste. Genevieve. He was replaced there by Father Francis Xavier Dahmer, another Vincentian (the other name for members of the Congregation of the Missions). Dahmer continued Pratte's practice of making regular visits to the Catholics in Old Mines. He was there on October 27, 1827, to witness the marriage between Francois, a slave belonging to Etienne Lamarque, and Ester, a negress belonging to Joseph Moreau, in the presence of Jacques Bone, Felix Boyer, Paul Boyer, Jean Baptiste Villmere, and others. That was the first slave marriage recorded in Old Mines. Dahmer continued to go to Old Mines until 1828.

JOHN BOULLIER

Meanwhile, in 1826, Rome established the Diocese of St. Louis, and, in 1827, Joseph Rosati, a priest of the Congregation of the Missions, was named and consecrated its first bishop. Now, Old Mines was in the Diocese of St. Louis. In 1828, Rosati named Father John Boullier, another member of the Congregation of the Missions, as pastor of St. Joachim Church in Old Mines. Boullier, who had been ordained March 11, 1826, set to work on establishing St. Joachim Parish because that had not yet been done. In a letter to Rosati, he explains that he has taken charge of St. Joachim Parish as its first permanent pastor as of July 25, 1828. In a March 1, 1828, letter he sent from New Orleans before getting to Old Mines, he wrote about his battlefield now being the village and so named Old Mines because of the large number of lead mines there.

St. Joachim Catholic Church and Pastors

He also mentions that the population was growing, that the villagers had never had a resident priest, and that there was only a small log church in the main village. All residents were French.

By 1828, the log church erected by Henry Pratte was too small to hold the increasing number of Catholics in Old Mines. So, Boullier began construction of the current St. Joachim brick church; it was to be bigger than the previous log church. Under the direction of Obadiah Freeman (Ferguson), a stone mason and architect from St. Louis, bricks were made from clay found on the property of Adrian Coleman, one of the original land grantees in the Old Mines Concession, by members of the village. The cornerstone—placed above the double front doors—was laid November 9, 1829. On the large block of sandstone is carved: D. O. M. (abbreviation in Latin for *Deo Optimo Maximo*, meaning "to the greatest and best God" or "to God most good, most great"), *In Memoriam Sancti Joachim* (Latin for "in memory of St. Joachim"), *B.V.M. Patris* (abbreviation in Latin for *Beata Virgo Maria*; and *Patris*, meaning "father"; thus identifying St. Joachim as "father of the Blessed Virgin Mary"). Then, there are three biblical verses in English: (1) "This is no other but the house of God" (Gen 28:17); (2) "My house shall be called the house of prayer" (Isa 56:7, Mark 11:17); and (3) "How lovely are thy tabernacles, O Lord of hosts" (Ps 84:1). On January 12, 1831, Boullier wrote to Rosati and informed him that the church was not yet finished because the men worked slowly.

In the same letter, Boullier narrates some of the history of Old Mines. He notes that there had been people living in the Old Mine permanently fifteen or twenty years before 1801. He calls their habitations mining camps, which were occupied in good weather, but left during bad weather, when miners went to Ste. Genevieve or Kaskaskia. He estimated the Catholic population in the area to be around two thousand.

This first brick church was rectangular in structure with Palladian (classical temple architecture of ancient Greeks and Romans) detail; it was thirty feet wide and one hundred ten feet long. A five-sided apse on the building's west end formed the sanctuary, marked off from the rest of the church by a communion rail. Behind the apse was a three-sided sacristy displaying a window to the north and a window and door to the south; the sacristy was connected to the apse with a double (French) door. A small chimney emerged through the roof of the sacristy to vent a stove inside. Chimneys on the north side of the church vented the smoke from the two wood stoves that were used to heat the building. It had a steeple that rose fifty feet. Each of the windows consisted of eighteen panes of clear glass of equal size with a cross etched across each pane. The roof was made from wooden shingles.

It had double doors at the main entrance, facing the east, and maybe a side door facing south. Inside, it was filled with box pews with doors or gates. Each pew had a divider down the middle with a door or gate at each end which was locked. A family paid annual pew rent, which was used for the upkeep of the church. Depending upon where the pew was located, rent could be a few dollars to four or five dollars a year.

The walls of the church were frescoed over which was erected a barreled wood ceiling. In the apse at the west end was a simple stone altar carved by Angelo Oliva, a stone cutter and a lay member of the Vincentians living at St. Mary Seminary, Perryville, Missouri.

For a short time from 1829 to 1830, Boullier was in France; Father Philip Borgna, a Vincentian, took his place and oversaw some of the construction of the church. Boullier returned from France to Old Mines early in 1831. Borgna liked being in Old Mines. On May 9, 1837, he sought permission from Rosati to stay there.

On October 1, 1831, Rosati left Perryville, the site of the Congregation of the Missions headquarters and seminary, on horseback with Fathers Francis Cellini, Francis Xavier Dahmer, John Odin, Louis Rondot, John Timon, Philip Borgna, Angelo Mascaroni, Regis Loisel, and Benoit Roux—all Vincentian priests—along with seminarians Louis Tucker, Frederick Laucier, Hilary Tucker, George Hamilton, and John Shannon. They rode to Fredericktown, and from there to Old Mines, where on October 9, 1831, they dedicated St. Joachim Church and placed relics of saints and martyrs—Sts. Pius V, Venuste, and Honoree—in the altar before dedicating it. Timon preached a sermon in English, and Rondot preached one in French. A large number of Catholics attended the service.

Soon after the church was dedicated, Boullier set to work building a rectory. See chapter 9 on Rectories, Employees, and Catholic Charities for more information.

The twenty acres of land in the Old Mines Concession, upon which St. Joachim Church was built, was donated to Rosati on March 29, 1830, by John Smith T for the sole purpose of building a Catholic Church. This was only a verbal agreement, because by 1830 the church was well on the way to being constructed and the corner stone had already been placed the year before. The verbal agreement needed to be recorded legally on paper; otherwise, Smith T had control of the church property. Thus, on April 4, 1836, Rosati donated the church property to John Timon and John Boullier, both Vincentian priests. This made them trustees of the property; legally, they owned it for the church. Trusteeism was a system in which clergy or lay persons could administer church property after consulting with the bishop. It became a controversy in the eighteenth and nineteenth centuries, when a rogue trustee could do what he wanted with church property without seeking the bishop's approval. Trusteeism was abolished in 1860. In this case, the trustees were Timon and Boullier; Timon was assisting Boullier in Old Mines at this time. In other words, they were joint tenants of the twenty acres of church land.

Even before the legal paper of ownership was signed, Boullier had been using church property and income to make investments. In March of 1834, he wrote to Rosati to inform him that he had lost three thousand dollars in an investment. In that letter, he also mentions other losses that have left him short on cash! In August of the same year, he wrote to Rosati again, describing another monetary failure regarding a contract for lead for the church; only a few bars of lead could be smelted. Odin, a Vincentian, writes in a September 18, 1837, letter that Boullier sold ten acres of land at Old Mines to a Mr. Reed for $330; this sale took place after Boullier had been transferred to another parish!

Besides all that, on June 2, 1832, Boullier wrote to Rosati, telling him that the past two weeks in Old Mines had been filled with sorrow, pain, and grief for him. He felt that it was impossible for him to stay there much longer. He even feared getting ill! So, he sought permission to travel to New Orleans. In March of 1833, he again wrote to Rosati and petitioned him to let him go to New Orleans, where his presence was demanded to take care of several affairs. Because he was lonely in Old Mines, he asked Rosati in several letters to send another priest to live with him.

Thus, Rosati sent Borgna, Timon, and Roux, while Boullier was pastor from 1828 to 1836. However, in the fall and winter of 1833–1834, he had as his guest Father John Saint-Cyr, who was on a tour of the area seeking funds for his struggling church in Chicago. He was preparing to build the first Catholic Church there in what is now downtown. It was known as St. Mary of the Assumption; it was begun in 1833 as a wooden structure, moved in 1836, and razed in 1971. In a letter to Rosati on June 4, 1833, Saint-Cyr stated that he thought Chicago would one day become a great city of commercial importance!

JOHN BRANDS

On January 1, 1836, Rosati transferred Boullier out of Old Mines and replaced him with Father John Brands, a Vincentian priest. He also sent Father Peter J. Doutreluingne, another Vincentian, to assist him. As early as May 1837, Doutreluingne recommended removing Brands from Old Mines as soon as possible. Later in June that same year, Brands expressed his discontent at staying there. He must have gone back to Perryville, because on September 18, 1837, Father John Odin states that Doutreluingne had grown very unpopular in Old Mines during Brands's absence. The reason given for Doutreluingne's unpopularity was his attempt to preach in English to French-speaking residents, who could not understand his long sermons! One thing Brands did accomplish was the formation of the Holy Rosary Society on September 8, 1836. See chapter 13 on Parish Societies and Committees for more information.

At this time, along Old Mines Creek there were several stores, blacksmith shops, and grist mills, where cereal grains were ground into flour, in Old Mines Village; usually, grist mills were powered by a water wheel. One grist mill on Old Mines Creek, owned by the Higginbotham family, was operated for a time by James Jullerate, who came to Old Mines from France in 1823. Another was located on Mineral Fork near Kingston, and another one on Mill Creek near Tiff, operated by the McClanahan family; it was later known as Bust's Mill.

From 1839, when both Brands and Doutreluingne leave Old Mines, there are four Vincentian pastors within five years. They are: Fathers Bart Rolando, 1839–1841;

J.M. Mignard, 1840–1841; J.B. Tornature, 1841; and Joseph de Marche, 1841. It is assumed that they continued to minister to the Catholics there: performing baptisms, marriages, anointings, and burials. On December 2, 1841, Rosati appointed Father John Cotter as the first diocesan pastor of St. Joachim Parish, Old Mines.

JOHN COTTER

Cotter continued the ministry that Boullier had begun and others who followed Boullier to Old Mines. Cotter was trained at the Vincentian-run seminary in Perryville. While a student there, he worked in the infirmary, where he acquired some knowledge of medicine. He was known in Old Mines for traveling the roads and byways and bringing corporal along with spiritual assistance to his flock. From 1842 to 1845, he was assisted by Father Joseph V. Wiseman, and in 1844 by Father Louis Tucker. Cotter began a Society of the Scapular in 1842, a Society of the Blue Scapular, and the Confraternity of the Red Scapular in 1866. See chapter 13 on Parish Societies and Committees for more information.

On June 5, 1851, at 1:45 p.m., while making a trip from Old Mines to Perryville in the company of Vincentian Father Francis Barbier, Cotter was killed when his horse shied and threw him against a tree and then to the ground near Ste. Genevieve. In his obituary, he was described as a devoted priest, whose death disturbed many. He was like a father to his children (parishioners), a sincere and self-sacrificing man admired by Protestants as well as Catholics. Saint-Cyr, who was then the pastor of Ste. Genevieve Parish, buried and entombed him in the sanctuary of St. Joachim Church on June 7, 1851. The priests who assisted Saint-Cyr included Fathers Theodore Burke, James Fox, and John Rosi. Later, when Father James Fox finished enlarging the church and slightly raising the height of the sanctuary, Cotter's brick and cement tomb became the resting place for a large floor joist! Until 1995, when a bronze plaque was placed on the floor in the sanctuary of St. Joachim Church, no one knew where his tomb was located.

All through this time, Boullier and Timon held legal title to the church property. On November 10, 1849, during Cotter's pastorate of St. Joachim Church, Boullier and Timon sold the church property to Thomas Burke and John Lynch, Vincentian priests, for five hundred dollars. Thus, as of November 10, 1849, the brick church, the rectory, and the land upon which both were built no longer belonged to the resident pastor, the trustee, of the church in Old Mines. It belonged to the Vincentians in Perryville; they were the new trustees. Within three years of the sale of the church property, Boullier had left the country and made his way to the city of Tours, France. When notice of the sale reached Peter Richard Kenrick, who had been appointed the second bishop of St. Louis in 1843 and the first archbishop of St. Louis in 1847, he and Cotter contacted Burke and Lynch and persuaded them to return the property to the care of Cotter. Kenrick purchased the property in his own name for one dollar on May

1, 1850. However, Kenrick failed to file this transfer as a legal sale. Thus, Burke and Lynch remained the legal owners of the church land, even though they thought they had sold it to Kenrick! And Kenrick believed that he owned the land because he had received it from Burke and Lynch. The legal loop-hole remained undiscovered until 1854.

After Cotter's early death, Father John C. Fitnam served as pastor of St. Joachim Church from June 15, 1851 to April 11, 1852. While Fitnam was the pastor, Father Louis Rosi, pastor of St. Stephen Church, Richwoods, had the privilege of burying Etienne Lamarque, who died on November 10, 1851, at the age of sixty-six, after having received the last rites of the Church. Lamarque was buried and entombed in the old cemetery (Cemetery 1); a grave-sized chiseled marble tomb cover gives his name, identifies him as a native of France, gives the date of his death, and presents his age when he died. In 1852, Father James Fox, who had been pastor of St. James Parish in Potosi, was named pastor of St. Joachim Parish by Kenrick.

JAMES FOX

Once Fox got to Old Mines, he wasted little time making a liaison with Marie-Louise Lamarque to enlarge St. Joachim Church. As the number of people continued to grow, so did the need for additional space grow. Born in County Wicklow, Ireland, and having studied for the priesthood at Carlow, Fox came to St. Louis in 1849 and was ordained a priest by Kenrick on June 9 of that year. After a very short time at Corondolet Seminary and St. John Church in St. Louis, he was appointed pastor of St. James Parish, Potosi. After Cotter's death, he was named pastor of St. Joachim Parish in 1852; he held that office for sixteen years.

With funds supplied by Marie-Louise Lamarque, now a childless widow, he began work on enlarging and renovating the brick church that Boullier had built in 1831. Kenrick sent Father John Hogan, whom he ordained April 19, 1852, to Old Mines to assist Fox in ministering to slaves during Fox's first year; later, Hogan, a native of Bruff, County Limerick, Ireland, was named pastor of St. James Parish, Potosi, and, ultimately, was named the first bishop of the Diocese of St. Joseph, Missouri, on March 3, 1868, and the first bishop of the Diocese of Kansas City, Missouri, on September 10, 1880.

To the rectangular building, Fox added wings measuring eleven and one-half feet so that the building became cruciform in shape. He used large steel pipes as pillars (two on each side) to support the walls he removed in order to add access to the wings, thus creating three Roman arches on either side. In the south wing of the church, he placed four pews for the African American slaves in the parish. The four original windows, two on each side, displaced by the wings were moved to the ends—the ends of the arms. He replaced the wood shingles. Inside the frescoed ceiling of the sanctuary was painted. The simple stone altar was enlarged when the stone was covered in wood, which was stained to look like marble. Three French oil paintings—one above the altar and one on each side of the church—were added. Fox states that Lamarque paid for the paintings, which may have been a part of a collection sent at one time by a French king for churches in the Louisiana Territory or from a group purchased by John Mullanphy when he acquired the crucifixion scene which hangs in the Old Cathedral, St. Louis. Whatever the case, they hung in St. Joachim Church until the 1920s, when they disappeared. The one of the Blessed Virgin is displayed in the Old Mines Area Historical Society archive building in Fertile, Missouri. It was found in the rectory garage among tools in the 1970s; it had undergone considerable damage.

When Fox was finished, the enlarged and renovated church measured one hundred twenty-four feet long and thirty-six feet wide with eleven and one-half feet wings or arms. On November 12, 1854, the enlarged and renovated church was blessed and placed under the invocation of the Blessed Virgin Mary and her father, St. Joachim, by Father A.S. Paris, pastor of the (now Old) Cathedral of the Archdiocese of St. Louis. On July 20, 1847, the Diocese of St. Louis was elevated to an Archdiocese. Paris was assisted by Fathers J. Caffrey and S. Grugan with many people of Old Mines attending the ceremony. Fox records that the enlargement of the church, its renovation, and the paintings were paid for by Lamarque.

Fox may have also installed a large wood-burning stove in the north arm of the church. At one time, there was also a chimney in the sacristy, where most likely there was a wood-burning stove to provide heat for the priest and altar servers as they were preparing for Mass during the winter months.

While Fox was enlarging and renovating the church, Burke and Lynch in 1854 discovered that they still owned the church, the rectory, and the parish property because Kenrick had never filed the legal claim to it. They informed Kenrick that as the legal owners, they had decided to sell it and file a legal record of the sale. Kenrick immediately purchased the land from Burke and Lynch for four hundred dollars on October 18, 1854. By a special agreement between Fox and Lamarque, money for the purchase was given to Kenrick by Lamarque. Finally, after eighteen years, the archbishop of St. Louis owned the property upon which sat St. Joachim Church and rectory.

JOHN JAMES CAFFREY

It was in the oldest section of Cemetery 1 that Father John James Caffrey was buried by Fox, assisted by S.A. Grugan, pastor of St. James Parish, Potosi, on February 17, 1856. Caffrey was pastor of St. Stephen Parish, Richwoods, Missouri, about twelve to fifteen miles from St. Joachim Church. Like Cotter before him, his horse shied and plunged him into the Meramec (Mineral Fork) River in which he drowned near the Virginia Mines while going to anoint someone near death and to say Mass at a place near there. After his body was found, Fox and Grugan conducted his funeral Mass and buried him along an east-west axis instead of the north-south axis of all other graves. His tomb stone was erected by the priests of the Archdiocese of St. Louis; it states how and why he died at the age of forty. "The good shepherd lays down his life for the sheep" (John 10:11), appears at the bottom of his grave marker, along with the Latin phrase: *Requiescat in pace* (Rest in peace).

FOX AND LAMARQUE

Fox began the Society of the Scapular of Mount Carmel on July 16, 1856. See chapter 13 on Parish Societies and Committees for more information.

On November 15, 1857, James Duggan, who had been ordained the coadjutor bishop of the Archdiocese of St. Louis by Kenrick on May 1 of that same year, traveled to Old Mines to reconsecrate the enlarged and renovated St. Joachim Church. Duggan had immigrated from Ireland in 1842, studied at St. Vincent Seminary, Cape Girardeau, Missouri, and was ordained a priest in 1847. Ultimately, he became the fourth bishop of Chicago in 1859. Earlier in 1857, Fox had opened a school, built with funds from Lamarque; more on this can be found in chapter 11 on Schools, Lay Teachers, and Graduates in Old Mines.

Even after the church was reconsecrated, Fox had more plans to accomplish with the funding provided by Lamarque. After extending the height of the steeple of the church in Greek Revival style (some of the wood shingles of the previous tower remain under the one Fox built), he ordered and installed a bell weighing 960 pounds and costing $351.30. The bell was cast by the J.G. Stuckstede Bell Foundry Company in St. Louis in 1866. On it is embossed in Latin: *Maria Mater Dei Immaculata* (Mary, Immaculate Mother of God). In his January 12, 1831, letter to Rosati, Boullier had mentioned a bell, but he didn't describe it or say for what it might be used. The bell, paid for by Lamarque, was installed by Fox before September 6, 1858, because on that day he blessed it. Before Vatican Council II (1962–1965), a bell was treated like a person; this means that it was baptized and confirmed. Thus, when Fox baptized the bell, he gave it the name Mary; Francis Portais was its godfather, and, of course, Marie-Louise Lamarque was its godmother. On September 22, 1866, when Kenrick was in the village to celebrate Confirmation for ninety-seven parishioners, he confirmed the bell with the name of Mary; the sponsors were Adrian Coleman and Justine Detchemendy.

On February 3, 1863, Fox recorded that he had interred the remains of Henry B. Murphy in a free-standing vault—the only one that exists—in St. Joachim Cemetery 1. Fox records that the vault was erected by Murphy's father, T.C. Murphy. Murphy was one of seventy to one hundred people killed or injured on February 28, 1859, onboard the steamboat Princess, which was traveling the Mississippi River with four hundred passengers from Vicksburg to New Orleans. Near Baton Rouge, all four of the Princess's boilers exploded at once on the four-year-old steamer, killing many immediately, scalding others, and, eventually, sinking the riverboat of passengers on their way to celebrate Mardi Gras. Murphy, who is listed as a resident of St. Louis, was temporarily buried in Baton Rouge while the vault was erected in Old Mines. Four years later, the body of the twenty-three-year-old was brought to St. Joachim Cemetery 1 and placed in the roofed sandstone vault after being contained in a steel sarcophagus. Later, several other members of his family were placed in the vault. Vandals and grave robbers caused the door to the vault to be sealed.

In November 1866, Fox opened the first lending library in Washington County, Missouri. With money from Lamarque, he purchased 196 books and established rules for the Catholic Lending Library. Books could be checked out and returned on the first Sunday of the month after High Mass. If a book was not returned when it was due, twenty cents was charged to the person who had borrowed it. Lamarque, of course, was one of the first borrowers of books.

Later in the 1860s, barite, known in Old Mines as tiff—from the word *tuff*, a local French word for waste—was discovered to be saleable. Those who mined lead found the barite with the lead in red clay and tossed it aside. In the late 1860s, a use was found for the soft, white, non-metallic mineral. Not only was it a long-lasting white pigment, but it could be used in paint and oil-drilling as a lubricant. From it could be extracted barium. It was used as a filler in plastics, paper, and rubber. Tiff was used in producing chemicals, refining beet sugar, manufacturing cosmetics and in x-raying the digestive system. The more than two hundred uses for barite brought a new boon to the economy of Old Mines. It had already been dug from the earth, although there was more in the earth; it just needed to be gathered, washed, crushed, and sent to market. More about tiff can be found in chapter 23 on Lead and Barite Mining.

Marie-Louise Lamarque did not see the development of the tiff industry. On July 3, 1868, she died at the age of sixty-nine. After burying her on July 5 of that year, Fox recorded that her home was the house of the priest, indicating that he spent time there with his benefactor. Her home was located just south of the church, across the creek, and on the next hill. Fox explains that she used her wealth for the cause of religion in charitable acts too numerous to mention. All Fox writes is that the enlargement of the church was primarily due to her, its paintings were paid for by her, and the school was erected by her. Because she and her husband, Etienne, had no children, this brought the Lamarque era—at least fifty-seven years—to an end. Only one act remained: the probation of her last will and testament. That story is told in chapter 8 on The Lamarques: Part 2.

Marie-Louise Lamarque was buried and entombed next to her husband, Etienne, in St. Joachim Cemetery 1. Her grave-sized above ground box tomb matches that of her husband. Both are made of marble. However, her cover stone (lid) is extensively carved. The first two lines in Latin are a quotation from the Book of Wisdom: "The souls of the righteous are in the hand of God, and no torment shall touch them" (Wis 3:1). There follows: This tomb, erected over the remains of Marie-Louise Madame

St. Joachim Catholic Church and Pastors

Lamarque, silently reminds all who visit this sacred spot to pray for the repose of her soul. During life, she was eminently munificent toward the sustaining and propagating of religion and zealous for the instruction and sanctification of souls. The prayers of those, to whom she contributed, edify by her holy life, and assist by her unfeigned charity, are all she asks in death. She died on the third of July 1868 at the age of 69 years, four months, two days. May she rest in peace. Amen. In the 1930s, the sides of both Lamarque tombs were taken down due to cracks in the marble—and danger of falling over—and placed under the cover stones (lids). Kent Bone restored the box tombs in the 1990s. A few days after he buried Lamarque, Fox was transferred from St. Joachim Parish. For the continuation of the Lamarque story, see chapter 8, The Lamarques: Part 2.

NEXT FIFTY YEARS

After Lamarque died and Fox left St. Joachim Parish, the buildings and other things on the property were viewed as being arranged around the church. Behind the church was what used to be called Cemetery 1, which was moved before the convent/school was built in 1924 to the cemetery donated by Lamarque, now considered to be Cemetery 1. To the right of the front doors of the church was the Lamarque school. To the left of the front doors of the church was the cistern for collecting and storing water, and to the left of the cistern was the wooden rectory built by Boullier. Behind the rectory was a three-part structure housing the wash house (laundry), the tool shed, and a storage shed. Opposite the three-part structure on the right was the grape arbor, out house, and garden. Behind the garden was the sheep lot. To the left of the three-part structure was the garage, and to the left of it was the well house and the hog house, and behind them were the chicken house and barn. Up on the hill to the far left was Cemetery 1. Thus, with Fox's sixteen years of improvements, funded mostly by Lamarque, the church property was left in excellent condition.

That helps to explain why the next fifty years are best characterized as care-taker years by the pastors who come to St. Joachim Church. They did not stay very long, and they accomplished no major improvements. They came and celebrated the sacraments of Baptism, Eucharist, Penance, Anointing of the Sick, and Marriage, and buried members of the parish who died. In those fifty years, the following priests served as pastors of St. Joachim Parish, Old Mines: Father Edward J. Shea (July 1868–1869), Father Myles W. Lobyn (September 10, 1868–December 1, 1868), Father P.J. Clark (February 1, 1869–November 4, 1869), Father John I. Quinlan (November 4, 1869–May 26, 1870), Father Thomas G. Daly (March 26, 1870–May 1874), Father Andrew M.J. Hynes (May 1874–November 1878), Father Francis P. Gallagher (December 4, 1878–1881), Father P.F. Cooney (December 3, 1881–December 11, 1881), and Father P.A. Trumm (December 11, 1881–January 3, 1883).

After he got to Old Mines, Trumm announced that there was going to be a ball and supper in the Temperance Hall, which had been built in the village, for the benefit of the church. He gave young people permission to attend what must have been a New Year's Eve dance. He did not permit round dance between ladies and gentlemen. Trumm also announced that Zeno Troke had established a shoe shop in the village, and he encouraged parishioners to patronize his business. In 1882, Trumm wrote about there being economic hard times. In exchange for parishioners' contributions, he asked the men of the parish to plow his garden with their mule teams. The Temperance Hall was also used as a school.

NAZARENO ORFEI

After Trumm, Father O.J. McDonald from St. James Parish, Potosi, was pastor (January 3, 1883–April 22, 1883). He was followed by Father Nazareno Orfei (Nazaveno Ovfei) (April 22, 1883–July 1, 1885), who on August 5, 1883, began the Society of St. Joseph for male parishioners and the Society of the Children of Mary for young ladies. See chapter 13 on Societies and Committees for more information.

On May 25, 1885, Orfei had an article on the history of St. Joachim Parish in Old Mines printed in the *Western Watchman*, a weekly Catholic journal (newspaper) published in St. Louis from 1869 to 1933. In the article, Orfei gives the date for the laying of the cornerstone of the church (1828), when it was finished being built (1830), and when it was consecrated (October 9, 1831) under the invocation of the Blessed Virgin and St. Joachim by Rosati of St. Louis with the assistance of ten priests. Among those ten, he only mentions Father John M. Odin, who afterwards was named the Archbishop of New Orleans. Later, he states that Father John Timon was named the bishop of Buffalo, New York, and John Joseph Hogan was named bishop of Kansas City.

He explains that the church was built in the form of a Latin cross; this is Fox's enlarged church, which was reconsecrated on November 15, 1857, by Bishop James Duggan, Coadjutor Archbishop of St. Louis, assisted by Father Patrick John Ryan, who became the Archbishop of Philadelphia, and six other priests. He also states that the church had an interior porch—vestibule—in which was located the baptismal font. He mentions what used to be the two side chapels, one in each arm of the cross. He writes about priests coming from Ste. Genevieve to Old Mines to visit French families as early as 1793, thus making St. Joachim Church the second oldest in the Archdiocese of St. Louis.

He recounts the history concerning Pratte and Boullier, as narrated above. Then, he indicates that the parish was served by the Lazarist Fathers, another name for the Vincentians or the Congregation of the Missions. From 1841 to 1885, he mentions that twenty-five pastors and associate pastors, all diocesan priests, served the parish. He became the pastor on April 22, 1883, and on March 3, 1885, celebrated his Silver Jubilee of ordination to the priesthood.

St. Joachim Catholic Church and Pastors

In his article, Orfei narrates that Ryan came to St. Joachim Church on August 19, 1883, to confirm four hundred people, one hundred of them being older adults. He indicates that on the same day the Society of St. Joseph was formed for men along with the Children of Mary for young ladies. In 1884, a society for the married women was begun; it was called the Sacred Heart of Mary. He also narrates that the Society of the Most Holy Rosary had existed since 1836. See chapter 13 on Parish Societies and Committees for more information.

The area covered by the parish is estimated by Orfei to be fifty to sixty miles. The 1885 census he took indicated five hundred families with over two thousand people. However, even though there were so many people in his parish, Orfei notes that while they are good and practicing Catholics—attending services and participating in processions—they are very poor and are barely able to meet the needs of one pastor. They speak French, but he states that English is quickly taking hold, and it will not be long before their mother tongue will die.

Orfei was assigned to another parish in July of 1885.

PASTORS AND ASSOCIATE PASTORS 1885-1916

After Orfei, Kenrick appointed the following pastors: Father William Noonan (July 1, 1885–June 21, 1887), Father E.T. Gallaher (September 19, 1887–July 1, 1889; August 10, 1889–February 2, 1893), Father Louis Napoleon Larche (January 31, 1893–April 13, 1899). In 1895, Bishop John J. Kain (1895–1903) was appointed as the third bishop and second archbishop of the St. Louis Archdiocese. He named the following pastors of St. Joachim Parish: Father E.T. Gallaher (April 20, 1899–September 16, 1901), Father Luke J. Kernan (September 17, 1901–August 24, 1912). In 1903, John J. Glennon (1903–1946) was appointed the fourth bishop and third archbishop of the Archdiocese of St. Louis. He sent Father J. McMahon (June 28, 1904–March 18, 1905) to assist Kernan. Father C.J. Kane became pastor (September 1, 1912–1915) and was assisted by Father Louis O. Adrian (1914). He was followed by Father Phillip Maher (July 1915–November 1915), who was assisted by Father Joseph A. Gimon, a Redemptorist (Congregation of the Most Holy Redeemer) priest. Father Joseph A. Beil followed Maher as pastor (December 1915–February 1916), then Father John P. Daly (March 1, 1916–1928).

JOHN P. DALY

Daly had a brother named Patrick, to whom he leased for a hundred years a small parcel of church property to the southeast of the church. Upon it, Patrick built a small home and a general store out of which he sold a variety of foods, beverages, and hardware to the people of Old Mines. The Daly home was raised in 2018, and the store was raised in 2019, after it was hit by cars two different times. Father Daly served as pastor of St. Joachim Parish for twelve years, reestablishing longer periods for pastorates. It is also to be noted that Patrick Daly had a son named John, who was ordained a priest for the Archdiocese of St. Louis. After a number of years, he was laicized in 1968 and married. The most important accomplishment of Father Daly was the erection of a convent for nuns and new school rooms in the same two-story building. Most likely, he also had the school built by Lamarque moved from its original location on the north side of the church to behind the church so that it was more accessible as a classroom. That narrative is found in chapter 11 on Schools, Lay Teachers, and Graduates.

Daly also oversaw the removal of the etched glass windows from the church, and, with the assistance of donors, had colored glass windows with painted designs in their upper parts installed. Windows were donated by the Cannon Mines People, the Semar Family, S. Thebeau & Paul & Francis Robart, John & Margaret Clancy, S.S. Paul, Walter & Mary Casey, John Z. Coleman, the St. Joseph Society, Henry Bourisaw, the Altar Society, P[ete].S. & Emma Coleman, The Parish, Anthony Koch, and Daly himself. Two windows were given in memory of deceased loved ones: Lucy & Zeno Pashia and Elisha & Anne Boyer. The two windows in the sanctuary present a eucharistic theme with grape vines displaying abundant clusters of grapes. In the upper part of the north window is painted a chalice, and in the upper part of the south window is painted a monstrance. One of the seventeen windows displays no donor nor was it given in memory of anyone. Both the upper and lower fourth of each window was hung with hinges and chains so that their clasps could be pulled and the window would swing open. Once air conditioning was installed in the church, the chains were removed from the inside and the windows were covered with a layer of protective glass on the outside.

In 1918 or 1919, Daly had a new shingle roof put on the church. Then, he employed a professional painter from St. Louis, who fresco painted all the sanctuary and around all the windows. The sanctuary ceiling looked like the blue sky with white clouds and golden stars.

Daly also had two wood-burning furnaces installed in the basement of the church. In 1980, Lawrence Z. Pashia remembered how much wood they burned when he fired them. Ultimately, the wood furnaces became coal-burning furnaces, then propane-burning furnaces. Until the last century, two outdoor chimneys remained on the north side of the church; one-by-one the brick chimneys were removed, as was the chimney in the sacristy, when they were no longer needed.

In 1922, Daly began the St. Ann Sodality for the women of the parish. See chapter 13 on Parish Societies and Committees for more information.

Pashia also remembered how Daly gathered tiff from Cemetery 1 to sell to help pay parish bills. In 1980, Pashia stated that the usual procedure for the tiff-rich Cemetery 1 was to shovel the tiff back into the grave after a burial. Daly asked grave diggers to leave the tiff on the bank, from where he would have it gathered and sold. He also had pieces of it on top of the ground over a grave gathered so that grass would grow over the grave; a few people thought that he was digging in graves, which, of course, he was not. Using buckets, the tiff was carried to a sled pulled by a horse. After the sled was loaded with barite, it was taken to a tiff mill and sold.

JOHN F. WALSH

Following Daly, Father John F. Walsh became pastor (1928–1940). In 1929, Archbishop Glennon came to St. Joachim Church, where he confirmed 247 people. On June 5, 1934, Bishop C.H. Winkelmann confirmed 333 people in St. Joachim Church. By October 19, 1937, Walsh had removed the old outbuildings that had been in place for almost a hundred years. On January 6, 1938, a fire started in the garage; not only was the garage destroyed, but Walsh's 1937 Chevrolet sedan went up in flames, too. Walsh was followed by the Redemptorist Father Roy C. Kalter (1940–1941).

VINCENT L. NAES

Glennon appointed Father Vincent L. Naes as pastor on July 21, 1941; he remained pastor of St. Joachim Parish until May 1948. While in Old Mines, he had the assistance of three other priests: Father Richard Reichling (January 1942–April 1942), Father Francis P. Donovan (April 1942–January 1947), and Father Bernard A. Suellentrop (January 1947–May 1951). While he was pastor of St. Joachim Parish, Naes, like Fox before him, began a program of renovation.

In the sanctuary, he removed the white wood tabernacle with its baldachin for the small metal crucifix sitting under it. He replaced the tabernacle with a large bronze round one. The stone altar—that had been covered with wood and made to look like marble—had two steps installed on either side of it for candles at two different levels. Over the altar he erected a baldachin, and from it hung a purple curtain from its top to the back of the altar, placing a large decorated-on-the-ends cross with a crucified Jesus on it in front of the purple curtain. He painted the sanctuary walls using an intricate design of large circles with XP (the Greek abbreviation for Christ) and small circles with a fleur-de-lis in them. The color scheme was red, blue, and beige.

In the body of the church, the box pews were replaced with long wood pews on both sides, like double columns of printed text on a sheet of paper. The ends of the pews had spirals carved into them, and on the back were clasps under which men's hats could be attached. The prints of the fourteen stations of the cross that Boullier had installed were replaced with plaster reliefs of all fourteen stations painted in bright colors. The wood floors were covered in linoleum tiles. Along the lower part of the walls, plaster was used to simulate large gray foundation stones. The barreled wood ceiling, from which electric lights were hung, was covered with acoustical tiles. The two clear glass windows in the sacristy were replaced with blue colored glass.

As soon as he got to Old Mines, Naes began work on replacing the over one-hundred-year-old rectory with a modern building. See chapter 9 on Rectories, Employees, and Catholic Charities for the narrative about funding and building a new one.

Naes also removed buildings that Walsh had left but were now no longer used or needed on the property. The grounds were planted with maple trees evenly spaced in rows. Thus, as one approached the front doors of the church on the walkway from the east, after going through the double iron gates and up three steps, a person walked under a canopy of trees. When Naes was reassigned in May of 1948, he left a parish plant in the best of working order.

EDWARD A. BRUEMMER

After Archbishop Glennon was named a Cardinal in 1946 and died, he was replaced by Joseph E. Ritter (1946–1968) as the fifth bishop and fourth archbishop of St. Louis. Ritter assigned Father Edward A. Bruemmer (1948–1954) as pastor of St. Joachim Parish, Old Mines. In addition to Suellentrop, who was still there, he was assisted by Father Joseph J. Ryan (1951–1952) and Father Joseph Helfrich (1952–August 1955). Bruemmer's contribution to the St. Joachim Church campus was a new school; those details can be found in chapter 11 on Schools, Lay Teachers, and Graduates. Because he had a devotion to the Infant of Prague, he placed a large statue of the Infant on a pedestal in the sanctuary and an even larger white one on a pedestal near the front door of St. Joachim School. Bruemmer began the St. Joachim Conference of the St. Vincent de Paul Society on January 15, 1950; see chapter 13 on Parish Societies and Committees for more information. Bruemmer also began the Confraternity of Our Mother of Perpetual Help on March 24, 1950, with 329 members; this was the beginning of the Tuesday evening Mother of Perpetual Help Devotion.

ALPHONSE H. HOORMANN

Bruemmer was followed by Father Joseph Bartin (October 1954–June 1955). Then Ritter appointed Father Alphonse H. Hoormann (June 1955–May 1962) as pastor; he was assisted by Father Joseph A. Capizzi (August 1955–May 1961) and Father Anthony J. Jansen (May 1961–June 1969). Hoormann inherited the debt for the school that Bruemmer had built. He began work on a Debt Reduction Campaign on March 11, 1957. In the St. Joachim Campaigner, a flyer produced for the program, Hoormann wrote, "With all parishioners, united and with a singular goal of success in mind, this major debt reduction campaign cannot and will not fail." He invited people to participate in this investment in their future. The general chairman of the campaign was Vincent Paul, assisted by Francis Bone. Memorial gifts were handled by Edward Nephew, who was assisted by Lawrence Pashia. Friends' gifts were handled by Bernard Coleman, assisted by Raymond Boyer. There were seven teams with a captain and an associate, whose responsibility was to canvas the parish and solicit pledges from parishioners. On April 5, 1957, Hoormann wrote to the parishioners that the campaign had been a success. While the final report remained to be filled, he offered his gratitude to all officers, captains, and workers, and to all who contributed in any spiritual and financial manner.

BERNARD A. SUELLENTROP

In May 1962, Ritter appointed Father Bernard A. Suellentrop as pastor (May 1962–April 1970). Suellentrop had served as assistant pastor in St. Joachim Church during the last year of Naes's pastorate and four years of Bruemmer's pastorate. Suellentrop was very much like two of his predecessors: Fox and Naes. In the years following Vatican Council II (1962–1965), the church needed to be renovated to conform to the directives of the council. During his eight years as pastor, Suellentrop renovated the interior of the church. After removing the communion rail, which had been installed by Boullier or Fox, he rounded the steps leading into the sanctuary and laid a gold-colored carpet on them. Fox's white wood altar stained to look like marble was covered in stained wood by Edwin Politte. The baldachin's supports were enlarged along with the top front and all wood was stained. Naes's purple curtain was changed to gold, and the large corpus on the fancy cross was placed upon a simple wooden cross in front of the gold curtain.

A new wood altar was constructed to sit upon the steps so that the priest would face the people when celebrating the Eucharist. The pews installed by Naes were removed and their lightly-stained, solidly-built-out-of-wood replacements complimented the rest of the wood in the sanctuary. The sanctuary was painted using a light blue to match the walls of the body of the church. The lower section of the walls was covered in one-inch square white tiles streaked with gold. The old, dark tile floors were replaced with beige tiles. The confessionals installed by Fox in both arms of the church were removed and new, light-stained wooden ones were made to replace them. Even the sacristy was renovated. The old dark wood vestment closets and drawers were replaced with a center counter with drawers underneath, cabinets above, and vestment closets on either side.

The heavy wood doors at the main entrance were replaced with aluminum and glass doors; likewise, the heavy wood side door was replaced with an aluminum glass door to let in more light. A handicapped walkway was added to the side door, and a new brick and cement porch with light fixtures on either side was added to the front of the church. The roof was replaced with rosy asphalt shingles, and the bell tower was completely rebuilt and painted and its roof recovered in tin. The large cross topping the bell tower was removed, remade, replated with gold, and blessed by Jansen before it was reinstalled. The bell that Lamarque had bought was left in the steeple, but it was deemed too dangerous to ring. A new electric carillon with its speakers located in the bell tower and its large metal control cabinet located in the sacristy was donated in memory of Homer and Dorothy Politte. The system featured a tape deck which played the sound of recorded bells projected through the speakers.

After repeated repairs, in 2003, the St. Ann Sodality raised funds to replace the carillon with a new electronic semiconductor digital system costing $8,100. All new cable from the sacristy to the four new speakers in the bell tower was installed. At some point before 2019, an electrical power surge destroyed that system. However, the St. Ann Sodality went to work again and raised $9,000 to purchase the Verdin Sonata Digital Carillon, a computer system. The amplifier was replaced along with the main processor and the speakers in the bell tower. That system continues to ring bells at the time of the writing of this book.

During Suellentrop's pastorate, sidewalks around the church and the rectory were enlarged. A statue of St. Francis of Assisi standing in a birdbath was placed in the back yard. A flag pole was erected near the church so it could also be used by the school. The outside walls of the brick church and the outside walls of the brick school were sandblasted to remove years of dust and dirt. And a new convent was built for the nuns; that narrative is found in chapter 12 on Convents and Nuns. The Lamarque school was moved to the west of the school built by Bruemmer; that narrative is found in chapter 11 on Schools, Lay Teachers, and Graduates.

In Cemetery 2, Suellentrop had a statue of the pieta installed on a stand with a roof built on four pillars covering it. In Cemetery 3, he installed a crucifixion scene on an altar-like stand. In the middle was Jesus on the cross. Two standing figures represented Jesus' mother, Mary, and St. John; a kneeling figure represented St. Mary Magdalene.

During Suellentrop's pastorate, the Parent Teacher Association became St. Joachim Home and School Association. The purpose was to develop a deeper appreciation for the aim and ideals of Catholic education, develop a closer relationship between parents and teachers, and assist the school to provide adequate facilities for physical, social, and moral development of students. More on the Parent Teacher Association can be found in chapter 11 on Schools, Lay Teachers, and Graduates.

On March 12, 1967, Suellentrop officiated at the formation of the Washington County Council Number 5936 of the Knights of Columbus. See chapter 16 on the Knights of Columbus for more information.

In 1966, Suellentrop was named the pastor of St. Joseph Parish, Tiff, Missouri, in addition to continuing as pastor of St. Joachim. He was assisted until 1969 by Jansen, mentioned above. In June 1969, Jansen was replaced by Father Edward J. Schramm (June 1969–1973), who served as Suellentrop's associate for the last ten months of his pastorate. Suellentrop's remodeling, renewal, and reconstruction project touched every building on the St. Joachim Church and School campus and cemetery. Suellentrop also brought a dog onto the St. Joachim campus; she, a collie, was named Princess

Fawn. Like Fox and Naes before him, he left a parish plant in excellent condition for the next pastor: Father Richard H. Suren (1970–1975).

RICHARD H. SUREN

During Suren's term as pastor, the poplar trees on the parish property west of the garage were dying, and he had them removed. They were replaced with maple trees planted by volunteer men in the parish. Princess Fawn, left by Suellentrop, died. Also, after he closed St. Joachim High School in 1972 (see chapter 11 on Schools, Lay Teachers, and Graduates for more information), he had some of the fixtures from the home economics room moved to the rectory, where they were installed in the kitchen.

Suren was the pastor for the sesquicentennial (150th) celebration of the founding of St. Joachim Parish in 1972, and the sestercentennial or semiquincentennial (250th) celebration of the founding of Old Mines in 1973. Likewise, Suren was pastor when native Old Miner Mark G. Boyer was ordained to the transitional diaconate in 1975; this was the first ordination to occur in historic St. Joachim Church. See chapter 20 on the 250th and 275th Anniversary Celebrations for more on the parish and area celebrations. Also, see chapter 15 on Vocations for more on the diaconate ordination of Mark G. Boyer. Suren was transferred to another parish by John J. Carberry, who had become the sixth bishop and fifth archbishop of St. Louis in 1968 and named a Cardinal in 1969.

THE NEXT THIRTY-EIGHT YEARS

Carberry sent Father Theodore Brug to St. Joachim Parish in 1975. He was assisted by Father James Moll, who came to Old Mines in 1974 and stayed until 1977, when Father Robert Rosebrough replaced him as associate pastor. In April 1978, Brug and Rosebrough sponsored the sesquicentennial (150th anniversary) celebration of the beginning of the building of St. Joachim Church in 1828. They invited former pastors and associate pastors to return to the parish and give retreat talks. The celebration began with Suellentrop addressing parishioners on Sunday, April 16, 1978. He was followed by Father Mark G. Boyer, who was ordained in the historic church in 1975 and 1976, who spoke on the faith of the ancestors of those now living in Old Mines. Jansen returned on Tuesday, April 17, 1978, to give a presentation, and Suren returned to speak about the faith of people in that year. The vision of tomorrow was the topic for Schramm's and Moll's presentation on Wednesday, April 19, 1978. Special guests were invited to join Brug and Rosebrough celebrate Mass on Thursday, April 20, 1978, with a reception that followed in the school auditorium. The week of spiritual renewal culminated with the celebration of Confirmation on Friday, April 21, 1978, by Auxiliary Bishop of the Archdiocese of St. Louis John Wurm.

The late 1970s was a time of implementing many of the reforms of Vatican Council II. Brug and Rosebrough further developed the parish council, finance council, and choir, among other things. Carberry transferred Brug in 1979 to another parish and sent Father Bernard Schloemer as pastor of St. Joachim Parish. With the help of Father James Moll, who had been assigned associate pastor in 1973, and Father Robert Rosebrough, who replaced Moll in 1977, Schloemer got to work getting people more involved in St. Joachim Church and School.

Because he was a caring and organized person, Schloemer related well with parishioners. He picked up where Brug left off implementing the reforms of Vatican Council II. During his two years as pastor, a ten-member parish council was formed, the St. Ann Sodality, the Home and School Association, and the St. Vincent de Paul Society were reinvigorated, choir musicians grew to nine and the choir itself numbered over twenty, an education committee of seven people was formed, a finance council of five people was developed, a group of five people provided ministry to shut-ins, seven men formed a maintenance committee, while four people formed a joint St. Joachim-St. Joseph youth committee, and seven people served as Scout leaders. Schloemer also formed a committee for parish activities and family life. In two years, Schloemer with the help of Rosebrough attempted to bring together the approximate 350 families in St. Joachim Parish. Under Schloemer's leadership more people took responsibility for their parish. The introduction of RENEW International, a small-group Bible-study program, helped bring together parishioners and give them a sense of responsibility.

Because of the growth in the size of the choir and musicians, Schloemer moved them from the choir loft to the right (north) arm of the church after several pews located there were removed. One of his missions was to have a good choir to lead the singing during Mass. As a result, both adult and children's choirs were formed. For many years, Natalie Villmer, a Rural Parish Worker, served as choir director to help fulfill Schloemer's mission which came from Vatican Council II.

During Schloemer's time as pastor and Rosebrough's as associate pastor, lots of Little League baseball games were played on the four diamonds in the large field to the west of Cemetery 3 on Saturday mornings. Rosebrough even headed an adult softball team.

Carberry was succeeded in 1980 by John L. May, the seventh bishop and sixth archbishop of St. Louis. May transferred Schloemer in 1981 and replaced him with Father Robert Johnston, who was assisted by Rosebrough (1977–1984), Father John Bolderson (1984–1987), and Father Larry Gerst (1987–1988). Johnston had the wood paneling in the rectory pained white and book shelves installed in both the pastor's and the associate's pastor's rooms. He also built a handicapped-accessible ramp from the parking lot to the basement/cafeteria of the school; more information on the ramp can be found in chapter 11 on Schools, Lay Teachers, and Graduates. Johnston inherited Schloemer's work, and he continued to guide parishioners in implementing the reforms of Vatican Council II. In 1987, May transferred Johnston to another parish and assigned Father Theodore Pieper, who had returned from serving in a parish in Bolivia for seventeen years, as pastor in June 1987.

THEODORE PIEPER

Pieper was assisted by Father Larry Gerst until January 1988 (about eight months), when Gerst was assigned to another parish by May. Gerst became the last associate pastor in St. Joachim Parish up to the present. Pieper remained pastor from 1987 to 2013, when he retired from active ministry in a home he bought south of Potosi. A few years later in October 2017, he died and was buried in St. Joachim Cemetery 3. However, before that took place, Pieper was known in at least four different ways.

First, he was a hard-working maintenance man. In the summer, he could be found with the person hired to mow the three parish cemeteries. Pieper did all the trimming and cleanup of the cemeteries and the parish grounds. Often, he could be found on the tractor hauling loads of soil to the cemetery or raking leaves in the front church yard. He continued after he retired to help with upkeep around the parish until he died. Likewise, even though the parish employed a school maintenance man, Pieper did all the repair work in the school. When a bathroom was installed in the church, Pieper was found outside digging a ditch for the pipe and a hole for the septic tank. He was known for using lots of duct tape and bailing wire for maintenance purposes!

Second, he was a pastor who provided sacraments to the people of the parish. He baptized, witnessed marriages, celebrated the Eucharist, heard confessions, visited and anointed the sick in their homes, and said funeral Masses for those who died. While he rode a motorcycle as transportation in Bolivia, he had a country car for visiting the sick and shut-ins in Old Mines and a city car for trips to St. Louis; both cars displayed duct tape. He maintained those old cars with the help of Al Veach, a parishioner. While he was dedicated to visiting the sick and elderly, he also celebrated Mass for the prisoners in the Potosi Correctional Center and visited patients in Potosi Manor and Georgian Gardens Nursing Home.

Third, Pieper was known as a humble man who gave a lot to the parish. While he did not have many friends in the parish due to his stubbornness about not spending money, it was through his efforts that the parish got out of debt and saved some funds for the future. Out of his own inherited funds, he gave money to the parish. However, as a result of not spending money on upkeep, the parish buildings entered into a state of disrepair during his pastorate.

Fourth, Pieper facilitated an increase in the number of lay leaders and lay participation in parish life. Liturgies and worship were vibrant with abundant lay liturgical ministers. The choir shifted from performance to leading the congregation in song. Pieper even made an Advent Wreath for the church and climbed a ladder to hang it from the ceiling.

In 1995, Pieper, with the help of others, removed the two layers of wood that had been placed over the original altar by previous pastors. First, the stained wood, expanded baldachin, and gold curtain from Suellentrop's pastorate were removed. Second, the wood that was stained to look like marble from Naes's and Fox's pastorates was removed. As all the wood was removed, the cabinets that had been placed behind the altar by Naes were moved intact to the sacristy to serve for storage. Once all the wood was taken away, all that remained was the original 1828 stone altar with Naes's brass tabernacle sitting in the middle of it. Steps that had once led to it were removed to provide more room in the sanctuary; the removal of the steps revealed that the altar was built through the floor joists. In other words, the altar sits on the ground beneath the floor and the floor beams run through it; it was built around the floor joists after they were installed. Above the floor, the altar is made of limestone slabs on three sides; the back is made of bricks, which have been plastered to look like a single block of stone. The top is a single slab of marble, which may have come from France in the early 1800s. LaDonna Hermann, a Rural Parish Worker, and Janie Skiles, a parishioner, restored the altar by bringing the gold leaf and stippled decoration back to its original state. The cross that had hung from the baldachin and in front of the gold curtain was mounted on the wall behind the altar.

Now that there was more room in the sanctuary, a new altar, ambo, credence table, and hand rails for entering and leaving the sanctuary were designed and made by Fran(is) Pashia, a cabinet maker parishioner. Pashia also made cabinets for the choir and several multi-use cabinets found in the church. The altar that faced the people, installed by Suellentrop on the sanctuary steps, was removed to make way for the new church furnishings.

Six burnished silver candelabra chandeliers, each holding six bulbs, replaced the lights that had been installed when electricity had been added to the church in the 1930s or 1940s.

In the front of the church inside the vestibule, two side, swinging doors once permitted entrance to the church without having to open the two very large doors that led directly to the center aisle. In the alcove to the south (left) had been located the baptismal font, which was moved to the south (left) arm of the church. In its place, Pieper installed a reconciliation room, where penitents had a choice between celebrating the sacrament of Penance behind a screen or face to face. After that was finished, he removed the two confessionals, one located in each arm of the church, that had been installed by Suellentrop. In the alcove to the north (right) under the steps to the choir loft, he installed a bathroom.

During Pieper's twenty-six years as pastor of St. Joachim Parish, Justin F. Rigali (1994–2003) had succeeded May as the eighth bishop and seventh archbishop of St. Louis. In turn, Rigali had been followed by Raymond L. Burke (2004–2008), the ninth bishop and eighth archbishop of St. Louis. In 2009, Robert J. Carlson (2009–2020) was appointed the tenth bishop and ninth archbishop of St. Louis, and in 2020, Mitchell T.

Rozanski (2020–present) was appointed by Pope Francis as the eleventh bishop and tenth archbishop of St. Louis.

ANTHONY DATTILO

Carlson accepted Pieper's request for retirement in June 2013, when he appointed Father Anthony Dattilo (2013–present) as pastor of St. Joachim Parish. Datillo inherited parish buildings that for the most part had received little upkeep for over twenty-five years. He began by seeking volunteers who had expertise in skills needed in various area. People volunteered to cut the grass. After daily Mass, parishioners were invited by Dattilo to join him for a cup of coffee; during those coffee sessions he got to know people who could help with repairs or know others who could help with repairs.

In 2015, Dattilo commissioned Fran(cis) Pashia to build a larger altar to replace the one he had built in 1995. In that same year, new carpeting was installed in the sanctuary. In 2017, new roofs were placed on the church, the rectory, the garage, the school, and the convent. In 2018, the church steeple was repaired, rebuilt, repainted, and covered with copper under the direction of J.V. Contracting. In 2018, the Daly House was deemed unfit for occupation, and it was razed. In 2019, after being hit by cars on two different occasions, the Pat Daly Store was razed; more about this can be found in chapter 22 on La Brigade a Renault. About 90 percent of the cost for such repairs to buildings and removing old ones was donated, and much of the labor was volunteered by parishioners.

One major project that Dattilo accomplished was the renovation of the convent building in 2016 into the Incarnate Word Center. The second floor became the parish offices with space for storage of records in addition to a room for children's liturgy; children were dismissed from the 10 a.m. Mass and led by a volunteer catechist to their room for their own service of readings. The first-floor kitchen was remodeled, and the space designated for gatherings and meetings. More information on the renovation of the convent can be found in chapter 12 on Convents and Nuns.

Dattilo also renovated the rectory. The details concerning that work can be found in chapter 9 on Rectories, Employees, and Catholic Charities. Dattilo brought to the parish his ability to allow parishioners to work toward beautifying and upgrading the parish buildings and grounds. He formed a Building Committee to guide the rehabilitation of parish structures for which he found the needed funding.

Future projects will include repair of a section of the north wall of the church which contains a bulge identified by men tuckpointing the church three years ago. Also, volunteers are waiting for the coronavirus to subside to replace the bathroom tile on the lower part of all the walls, put there by Suellentrop, with wooden panels.

Dattilo has a dream of the parish growing spiritually. He hopes that parishioners will return to Mass after not attending due to COVID-19 and fill the church again. He stated that he knows that they live in a very secular time, when the practice of the faith is not a big priority, but he believes that Jesus is the center of St. Joachim Parish, especially in the Eucharist. He hopes that the 200th anniversary of the parish will spiritually reignite parishioners so that they will continue to grow into God's loving family and continue to serve one another and neighbor in their communities.

8

The Lamarques: Part 2

At some point between September 1815 and before July 1816, Etienne and Marie-Louise Lamarque were living in Old Mines. Etienne died on November 10, 1851, and Father Louis Rosi buried/entombed him in Cemetery 1 on November 12, 1851. Marie-Louise lived for almost another seventeen years, dying July 3, 1868. During the almost seventeen years between her husband's death and her own, she monetarily supported the ministry of Father James Fox as he enlarged the church, bought a bell, built a school, procured title to the property, began a lending library, enlarged the cemetery, and more.

On August 23, 1865, three years before her death, Lamarque issued her last will and testament. At the time of her death, her estate was worth fifty-four thousand dollars. Because she died childless, she specified that twenty-eight thousand dollars be allocated to nieces, nephews, her brother, half-sister, half-brothers, and a cousin. The remainder of the estate was willed to Peter Richard Kenrick. On July 10, 1868, seven days after her death, Fox and Adrian Coleman, who had witnessed her will, brought it to the County Court in Washington County, Missouri—the county in which Old Mines is located—to have it probated. Erastus B. Smith, Clerk of the County Court, admitted the will to probate. In the will, Lamarque had named co-executors: Peter Richard Kenrick and George B. Cole. Most likely Fox informed Smith that Kenrick declined to serve as co-executor; thus, Cole was appointed by Smith to serve as the sole executor.

And all would have been fine, except on August 5, 1868, Louis Bolduc, Lamarque's brother, and others named in her will as heirs contested the will being admitted to probate on the grounds that the funds left to Kenrick violated the Constitution of the State of Missouri. Article 1 of Section 13 of the 1865 constitution stated any money or land bequeathed to any minister of any kind for personal support or to support any religion was void. Lamarque thought that she could evade that clause by simply naming Kenrick without his title of archbishop. Her brother, Bolduc, stated that everyone knew Kenrick was an archbishop, and this was an attempt by his sister to sidestep the Missouri Constitution. What could not be done directly could not be done indirectly, according to Bolduc.

Nevertheless, the County Court admitted the entire will to probate on August 6, 1868, except for the tenth clause on the grounds that the bequest to Kenrick was void because it was in violation of the Missouri State Constitution. The court declared that Lamarque had died intestate as to all estate monies and property not specifically addressed in the other nine clauses of her will. The remainder of her estate that was designated for Kenrick was to be distributed by the executor of her will to her heirs.

Kenrick, most likely represented by Fox, appealed the decision of the County Court to the Circuit Court on October 4, 1868. On November 6, 1868, the case was heard, and the Circuit Court overturned the order of the Washington County Court, declaring it to be vacated and annulled. On November 7, 1868, Bolduc, who was determined to get more than the one thousand dollars his sister left him, filed a motion for a new trial on the grounds that the Circuit Court's decision was not based on witnesses, and no evidence had been presented. He stated that the will purporting to be Lamarque's may not have been executed by her. Bolduc held that the Circuit Court had not considered all the next of kin to Lamarque in the case, that there was no provision for appeal from the County Court to the Circuit Court provided by law, and, thus, the Circuit Court had no jurisdiction in this case. In other words, Bolduc argued that the Circuit Court did not have the authority to accept Kenrick's appeal. On November 10, 1868, the Circuit Court dismissed Bolduc's motion to set aside its verdict and judgment in favor of a new trial. That, however, did not stop him. On November 14, 1868, he filed an appeal to the Second District Court, and the appeal was granted.

The Second District Court heard Bolduc's appeal on February 8, 1869. He argued that the Circuit Court should have dismissed Kenrick's appeal because it had no jurisdiction over the case. He also stated that the Circuit Court had rendered a judgment contrary to the law of the State of Missouri. Kenrick, of course, appealed the Second District Court to uphold the judgment rendered by the Circuit Court. The case was heard on February 11, 1869. Two days later, it affirmed the judgment of the Circuit Court; this meant that Kenrick could now receive what Lamarque wanted to give him. The judge, William Carter, wrote an opinion stating that Bolduc's argument about the tenth clause of the will being unconstitutional was extraordinary; it was a gift to Kenrick. He also added that the proof that the will was Lamarque's had been ascertained by Smith, when he admitted the will to probate.

Bolduc was not yet finished. He appealed the decision of the Second District Court to the Supreme Court of the State of Missouri which was at that time meeting in St. Louis. His appeal was granted, and the Supreme Court heard his case in the October Term of 1869. His appeal was the same as before, namely, that the Circuit Court had no jurisdiction to hear the case, that is, to appeal the probate of a will. The Supreme Court upheld the decision of the Washington County Court. In writing his opinion, Judge Philemon Bliss (1868–1872) stated that the County Court had jurisdiction when it came to probate wills, and there was no allowance for an appeal. Thus, in agreement with the other justices on the Missouri Supreme Court, Bliss declared that the case came to it in error. The case should not have been heard by the Circuit Court, as that was against the law. The judgment of the District Court was reversed, and Bolduc's appeal was dismissed. However, Bliss also stated that Bolduc still had other avenues to pursue.

Next, the case returned to the Circuit Court where Kenrick's appeal had been accepted. On April 15, 1871, the Circuit Court ordered Cole, Lamarque's executor, to file an answer to Kenrick's appeal thirty days before it began its next session. So, on September 8, 1871, he presented his findings to the clerk of the Circuit Court. For some unknown reason he denied that Lamarque had bequeathed the remainder of her estate to Kenrick. He testified that the tenth clause of her will was not a part of the original will he had witnessed. Also, he stated that the clause was added to her will when she was not of sound mind. Cole also stated that Fox, who was Lamarque's advisor, had forced her to add the tenth clause. He called it an undue influence by Fox, and that curtailed her freedom to write her will. Cole advised that the court uphold the Washington County Court's decision to probate the will except for the tenth clause. He estimated that the Lamarque estate was worth one hundred thousand dollars. Since Kenrick was not related to her, the remainder of her estate should be distributed only to her heirs.

On June 3, 1872, Kenrick filed a motion to have part of Cole's testimony removed. He argued that Cole used irrelevant, superfluous, and redundant words and phrases that had nothing to do with evidence. The court overruled Kenrick's motion.

Thus, on June 6, 1872, Kenrick filed his reply to Cole's answer. He denied having any knowledge that her estate was worth one hundred thousand dollars. He denied knowing that the remainder of the estate was worth twenty-five thousand dollars. He also denied that Fox had influenced Lamarque to write the tenth clause; it was her free act. He stated that naming him as an individual and not as an archbishop was not Lamarque's attempt to sidestep the law. Her gift to him was for his personal use as a private citizen.

Cole filed an amended answer to Kenrick's reply on June 19, 1872. Besides what he had already written, he added that Lamarque had made previous wills before the July 4, 1865, adoption of the Missouri Constitution, and in those previous wills she had named Kenrick, the archbishop of St. Louis, as the heir to the remainder of her estate. He also declared that after the Missouri Constitution had been adopted, she changed the tenth clause, which had indicated that she wanted the funds left to Kenrick to be used for educational purposes and for the repair of St. Joachim Church in Old Mines, by naming Kenrick as the inheritor of the remainder of her estate while not referring to him as archbishop of St. Louis. On the same day, Kenrick filed a motion to have parts of the Cole's amended answer removed from the record. Because the court made no immediate decision in the case, both Bolduc and Kenrick filed for a change of venue from the Circuit Court of Washington County to the Circuit Court of St. Louis County. The change of venue was granted.

Thus, on June 17, 1873, the Circuit Court of St. Louis County, Eighth Judicial Circuit, heard the case. Cole filed an amended answer to Kenrick's last amended reply. The jury of the Circuit Court of St. Louis County rendered a decision on January 5, 1874. It declared that the tenth clause of Lamarque's will was not in the original will. Kenrick filed a motion for a new trial on February 13, 1874, but that motion was overruled. However, on March 9, 1874, the Circuit Court of St. Louis County permitted him to appeal it during its general term. At the appeal Doctor William Evans, Lamarque's physician, testified that before her death she was feeble, suffering from rheumatism and other diseases. She had not been able to leave her home to go to church; even walking to the table was difficult for her. She could not be left alone. Cole testified that as executor of Lamarque's will, her total estate was wroth somewhere between sixty-five and forty-seven thousand dollars. He added that she was feeble and she did not live alone; two other ladies lived with her. Her mind was not impaired, but she was old. Kenrick was not a relative, and he had seen Fox at her house on occasion.

Kenrick's defense read a deposition that Fox had made before he died in 1873. The deposition had been taken in St. Louis on September 29, 1871. Fox declared that he had witnessed Lamarque sign her will. Before the last one, she had made three previous wills. The last one had been made after the latest Constitution of the State of Missouri had gone into effect. The last will did contain the tenth clause in which she gave the remainder of her estate to Kenrick. Fox also stated that for five years before her death, Lamarque had been in poor health, but her mind remained clear. He testified that he was well acquainted with her, visited her often, sometimes every day, while he was pastor of St. Joachim Parish in Old Mines.

In his deposition, Fox declared that the funds left to Kenrick were for educational purposes, principally for educating children in Old Mines, and for repairs to St. Joachim Church. Then, he presented some evidence concerning Lamarque's intention in making her last will; it was to avoid litigation under the law in the Missouri Constitution. Furthermore, Fox declared that she had asked Bolduc in his presence not to interfere with the probate of her will, and he had promised to abide by her wishes. Fox's testimony concurred with Bolduc's, namely, that she had written the last will not naming Kenrick as an archbishop with the same intention she had when she had written the one before it naming him as an archbishop. Also, in the deposition, Fox reported that he had notified Kenrick after Lamarque's death concerning the tenth clause in her will, and he had said that he would defend her intention to leave funds to him as an ordinary citizen.

Next, Alex J.P. Garesch, who wrote Lamarque's wills, stated that in a previous will Lamarque had left funds to Kenrick for St. Joachim Church, Old Mines, for charitable and educational purposes, and to him personally. After the adoption of the Missouri

Constitution, she realized that the clause excluding gifts to clergy was aimed primarily against the Catholic Church and its ownership of property; he rewrote her third will removing Kenrick's title, reasoning that he could inherit as an individual citizen.

Finally, Kenrick testified on his own behalf. He stated that he had never made any promises to Lamarque, but he knew that in her previous wills that she had expressed three intentions: Masses said for her after her death, care of the poor in Old Mines, and education of seminarians in St. Louis. Kenrick stated that he had told Fox that he wanted to receive Lamarque's bequest under the Missouri Constitution, and that he would adhere to Lamarque's intentions.

After the Circuit Court of St. Louis County heard all the evidence, it ruled that the tenth clause of the will could not be probated because Lamarque's intention in her fourth will was the same as it was in her third will: to leave money to Kenrick, who was the archbishop of St. Louis, contrary to the law in the Missouri Constitution. Kenrick moved for a new trial, but his motion was overruled. On March 25, 1874, Kenrick filed for an appeal to the Missouri Supreme Court, and that appeal was granted to him.

In its January 1876 term, the Missouri Supreme Court heard the case. Judge David Wagner delivered the opinion of the court. He stated that the tenth clause of Lamarque's will was made for the illegal purpose and intent to evade the prohibitions of the Missouri Constitution. It was an attempt to do indirectly—give money to a clergyman without naming him so—what was directly forbidden—giving money to a clergyman. He explained that Kenrick could have had the property for his own personal use, but he had testified that he would carry out Lamarque's wishes. Such a move would place some of Lamarque's property in the possession of the Church in defiance of the constitution. Thus, the judgment of the Washington County Court was affirmed, and the case that had moved through the courts for ten years was dismissed.

As executor of the Lamarque will, Cole had been making settlements according to the other nine clauses in Lamarque's will. After he dispersed the $28,500 specifically designated for Lamarque's heirs and settled any other claims made to her estate, he was left with $54,247.24; those funds intended by Lamarque for Kenrick were divided among her heirs. Before he was dismissed on November 17, 1876—having fulfilled his responsibility as executor—Cole had made seventeen settlements for the Lamarque estate. Thus, the Lamarques, who had supported the Catholic Church for over fifty years, were unable to leave anything to it because of the Missouri Constitution. Neither Kenrick nor St. Joachim Church in Old Mines received a penny of the estate of Marie-Louise Lamarque! The irony is that the family wealth, which enlarged and renovated the church, built a school, opened a lending library, donated property for a cemetery, and more, could not be willed after death to the institution it supported during life. Nevertheless, the munificence of Lamarque is still remembered by the people of Old Mines.

The side-by-side graves of the buried and entombed Etienne and Marie-Louise Lamarque attest to their wealth. The funeral custom of the wealthy French was burial in the ground with a large vault/tomb above. In Ste. Genevieve, the vaults for the Bolduc and Ste. Jeme Dit Beauvais families attest to their wealth. In all of Old Mines, there are only a few such vaults in Cemetery 1: one is over the grave of Etienne Lamarque, and the other is over the grave of Marie-Louise Lamarque.

For Further Reading: The Lamarques in Old Mines: 1815–1868, Mark G. Boyer.

9

Rectories, Employees, and Catholic Charities

FIRST RECTORY

After St. Joachim Church was dedicated on October 9, 1831, Father John Boullier set to work on building a rectory for himself and the pastors who followed him in which to live. On December 19, 1833, he wrote to St. Louis Bishop Joseph Rosati, informing him that the priest's house in Old Mines was finished, and that he had been living in it for about two months. The rectory was a multi-room wood structure with a pointed tent-like roof made of metal. The steep French hip roof's architectural ancestry came from Canada and Louisiana by way of Normandy, France, where it was called a pavilion roof. Before metal, the roof was made of thatch, then wood shingles. The outside walls were clapboard, before that they were daubed with mud and whitewashed. Both the front and the back of the house had porches or galleries that stretched the length of the house. Around the house were windows, swinging on hinges, for ventilation, and through the roof rose a large chimney to vent the fireplace inside.

Inside, the front section of the rectory contained two large bedrooms, one on each end with an office in the center. To the back of the office was the dining room, and to the south of it was the kitchen. To the north was a large room for the housekeeper, and further north was the small room for the young, male servant who was responsible for pumping water and filling designated containers for washing, bathing, and cooking. A large tank in the attic also had to be filled; gravity fed it to all the places it was needed. The hot water tank stood next to the wood stove in the kitchen; a pipe from the tank ran through the firebox, then back to the tank. The male servant was also responsible for pumping water for the farm animals. He fed the horses, cows, sheep, hogs, and chickens.

The structure of the first rectory looked like many of the old houses seen in Ste. Genevieve today. Boullier's rectory served as the priest's house for over a hundred years, from 1833 to 1941.

SECOND RECTORY

Father Vincent L. Naes, pastor from 1941 to 1948, supervised the razing of the rectory built of wood by Boullier in 1833 after building a two-story one made of brick with a basement behind the first one. He called a parish meeting on July 20, 1941, and 175 parishioners came to the church. Ten men—five appointed by Naes and five elected by the parishioners—formed a committee to build the new rectory. Naes appointed Lawrence Pashia from Racola; Kernan Paul from Happy Hollow; Pat Daly from Old Mines, A.H. Long from Cadet; and Pat DeClue from Tin Can; those men represented some of the smaller villages comprising the Old Mines area. The five men elected were Bernard Politte from Old Mines; Morgan Ronquest from Bellefontaine; Fred Politte, Sr., from Frog Town; Marvin Politte from Fountain Farm, and Earl Bequette from Shibboleth. Roy J. Boyer volunteered to represent the Bliss District. The eleven men were responsible for delivering pledge cards to people living in their respective areas and asking each family to pledge or donate ten dollars toward the cost of the new rectory.

On September 2, a meeting was held with the eleven men. Earl Bequette had died. He was replaced by Cecil G. Schmidt. Other things discussed at that meeting and others held on October 20, November 3, and December 1, 1941, included bricks, nails, and digging the basement, which was done later by Henry Hartzel. Lumber bids were examined, and J.B. Boyer and Son won. Chapman prepared the concrete foundation at the cost of $835. Brick was purchased from Jackson for $16.50 per thousand; twenty thousand face brick, five thousand backing brick donated by Ernest Peace saving eighty dollars, and 4,500 tiles were used. Steel cost $177, and J.B. Boyer and Son's bid for mill work was accepted at six hundred dollars.

Electrical supplies cost $223. Rock wool insulation from J.B. Boyer and Son cost $59.50. Plastering by Armbrusters cost $228 with the plastering material supplied by J.B. Boyer and Son for $166.75 and the laths that went under the plaster for $223. Plumbing fixtures cost $88 per bath room (there were four) and installation cost $184. Asphalt tile flooring cost $420, while rubber covering for the stairs from the first floor to the second cost ninety cents per step. After water samples had been taken from the two wells on the property and analyzed, the one found closest to the new rectory was condemned. Thus, it had to be drilled deeper. When the drilling was finished, it was 124 feet deep and the casing had been set at sixty-five feet.

After the basement was excavated, eighty-five sacks of cement were used for the footing; sand, mixed with the cement, had cost eleven dollars. The complete basement required 320 sacks of cement at a cost of $208. J.B. Boyer and Son supplied the asphalt roofing for $178. Perritt of Bonne Terre was chosen to do the electrical work for $22, a Mr. Schmelig donated the electrical fixtures along with wiring, saving $225. South Iron Company installed the heating system (a coal furnace) for $691.50. Finish work was done by a Mr. Williams at eighty cents per hour, and painting was done at a total cost of $165.

On November 3, 1941, pledges amounted to $1,457, and expenses had been $1,237. The Assistant General Manager of National Lead Company—a Mr. Hofstetter—had donated four hundred dollars. By December 1, 1941, the pledges amounted to three thousand dollars out of which $1,664 had been used to pay bills.

When the project was finished, April 20, 1942, the rectory was forty-five feet long and twenty-seven feet wide. The contractors had been Fred Politte Sr., Charles F. Boyer, and Noah E. Politte, all carpenters in the parish; their helpers were paid thirty-five cents an hour and thirty cents an hour for manual labor. They followed the plans which had been prepared by a friend of Naes in St. Louis. In the basement, space was provided for laundry, storage, and meetings. On the first floor was the large main door for entering the rectory with steps leading to a porch and it. Inside, to the left there was a door which opened to the pastor's two rooms (office/sitting room and bedroom) and on the right was a secretarial/records/religious articles/counselling room. Towards the back door on the right was the kitchen and to the right of it was the dining room, access to which was through a plaster barreled ceiling from the aisle connecting the front door to the back door, made of wood with glass window panes. A wood staircase led to the second floor, where the associate pastor's two rooms (office/sitting room and bedroom) were located immediately above the pastor's rooms. To the left was the housekeeper's room, and across the hall a guest room and at the end of the hall another guest room. The pastor's, associate pastor's and housekeeper's rooms each had a private bathroom attached; the upstairs guest rooms shared a bathroom located between them.

The April 20, 1942, meeting was held in the rectory, which was blessed by Naes assisted by his associate pastor, Father Francis P. Donovan. The members of the committee agreed to get some help to finish concrete sidewalks around the new building and to raze the old wooden one. The driveway was widened and the gravel was oiled.

From 1941 to 2013, not much was done to the building except for routine maintenance, namely, painting the walls, replacing the carpet, cleaning windows, etc. During the pastorate of Father Bernard Suellentrop (1962–1970), a bathroom was installed in the basement for use by the quilters, who worked there, and others, who met there. Also, the sewer system was improved and replaced and the back porch was enclosed and fitted with windows on three sides. After the high school was closed, Father Richard Suren (1970–1975) had the metal kitchen cabinets removed from the home economics room in the school and installed in the rectory kitchen. During the pastorate of Father Robert Johnston (1981–1987) central air conditioning was added, new carpeting installed, some walls were paneled, and bookshelves were added. Also, Johnston created an office for Catholic Charities in the basement.

During the pastorate of Father Theodore Pieper (1987–2013), the rectory began to need repairs. Pieper had moved his rooms to the two upstairs guest rooms with the bathroom between them. The downstairs two rooms (office-sitting room and bedroom) that had been the pastor's rooms were turned into the secretary's office. Two secretaries worked there; thus, there were two desks, two computers, filing cabinets, and chairs. Upstairs, the two rooms that had been the associate pastor's office-sitting room and bedroom became the guest quarters for visiting priests. The live-in housekeeper's room was used for storage.

During the summer of 2004, while Pieper was on vacation, the secretary, Mary Ann (Politte) Pratt, cleaned and scrubbed the kitchen with her sister's help. Then, they painted the kitchen walls, the dining room walls, and the hallway walls, and they shampooed the carpets. Nothing else was done to the rectory until 2014.

RENOVATED RECTORY

One of the first things Father Anthony Dattilo (2013–present) did after he got to St. Joachim Rectory in July 2013 was to make plans to renovate it in the summer of 2014. The kitchen was completely renovated and remodeled. New appliances—stove, refrigerator, dishwasher—donated by the St. Ann Sodality were installed. New kitchen cabinets were made and installed by Fran(cis) Pashia. All the walls were painted, new flooring was installed in the downstairs rooms and the upstairs pastor's rooms. Rooms with carpet received new carpet. The parish offices were moved out of the rectory to the Incarnate Word Center; see chapter 12 on Convents and Nuns for more information. What had been the pastor's rooms, then the offices, became guest rooms. What had been the secretarial/records/religious articles/counselling room became a guest office. Upstairs what had been the associate pastor's two rooms became the pastor's two rooms. The guest rooms connected by a bathroom that had been Pieper's rooms were restored to guest room status. And the former housekeeper's room was kept as a storage room. Outside the rectory a handicapped-accessible ramp was built for entry to the back porch and through the back door.

The whole house was electrically rewired by Ronald Boyer, while Burgess Barton and James Bourisaw took care of the plumbing. A new sewer system was also installed. The heating and air conditioning systems were updated. And in 2019, a pavilion was built between the rectory and garage to facilitate outdoor dining and/or serve as an outdoor meeting place. Once the rectory became a home in which to live, Dattilo set his sights on other neglected buildings on the parish campus. In 2022, the current rectory marks its eightieth anniversary of use.

Rectories, Employees, and Catholic Charities

EMPLOYEES

Closely associated with the second rectory, because they worked in it or out of it, are four parish employee positions: housekeeper, secretary, maintenance, and Catholic Charities Director.

Housekeeper

When Naes built the new rectory in 1942, he included a room with a private bathroom for a live-in housekeeper. The first person to occupy that position was Helen Camel (Campbell), who served as Father Edward A. Bruemmer's housekeeper (1948–1954). When he was transferred to a parish in St. Louis, she went with him. The second person to occupy the position of live-in housekeeper was Rose Ellen Pratt, born October 24, 1908, the daughter of John Thomas and Mary Margaret (Ackerson) Pratt. She was hired by Father Alphonse H. Hoormann, shortly after he became pastor (1955–1962). In her earlier years, Pratt worked in the housekeeping department in Kenrick Seminary, Shrewsbury, Missouri, with her sister Adeline. Pratt's responsibilities in St. Joachim Rectory were centered mainly on cooking meals, making beds, and answering the telephone when needed. She was assisted at various times with laundry and other housekeeping chores by Adeline Pratt, Margaret Kite, Margorie Maness, and Judy Coleman. After serving as housekeeper for over twenty-five years, Pratt retired in 1981–1982, during the pastorate of Father Robert Johnston (1981–1987). After retirement, she moved to the Georgian Gardens Nursing Home, Potosi, and died May 28, 1992, at the age of 83. She was buried in St. Joachim Cemetery Number 3 next to her sister Adeline Pratt, who died in 1971.

After Pratt retired in 1981–1982, Agatha Bequette came to the rectory to cook meals until 1987, but she did not live there. For a few years during Father Theodore Pieper's pastorate (1987 to 2013), Mary Politte came to the rectory to do laundry and some cleaning. In 2013, Father Anthony Dattilo hired his sister, Mary Dattilo, to cook, clean, and do laundry one day a week.

Secretary

Until Father Anthony Dattilo moved the parish offices out of the rectory to the Incarnate Word Center in 2017, the secretary's office was located in the rectory. Records indicate that Janet Bone worked part-time as secretary from 1966 to 1968. Mary Ann (Politte) Pratt became full-time secretary in 1968, after graduating from St. Joachim High School. She held that position until 1975, when her sister, Cathy (Politte) Portell, took the job. Portell left the position in 1977, when Mary Catherine Portell became parish secretary. The latter Portell retired in 1991. Angie Bouse was secretary from 1991 to 2003. She was assisted part time by Jeannie Ramsey from 1993 to 2003, when both Bouse and Ramsey resigned their jobs. Mary Ann (Polygone) Pratt was hired again in 2003 and continued to 2017, when she retired. Beginning in 2006, Vicki (Pratt) Thurmond was hired to help Pratt part-time until 2010, when she became the full-time accountant; she retired in 2018. Meanwhile, Debbie (Pratt) Miller was hired as secretary in 2017, and Angie (Pratt) Mitchell was hired in 2018 as full-time accountant.

Maintenance

Neil Thebeau, born December 4, 1913, was hired as the maintenance man, usually referred to as the janitor, by Father Vincent L. Naes (1941–1948). Before being hired to work for St. Joachim Church, Thebeau worked for the Civilian Conservation Corps (CCC), a work relief program that operated from 1933 to 1942 hiring unemployed, unmarried men ages eighteen to twenty-five. As a part of President Franklin D. Roosevelt's New Deal, the CCC provided manual labor jobs related to the conservation and development of natural resources in rural lands owned by the U.S. federal, state, and local governments during the Great Depression. Thebeau helped to build the rock wall in Arcadia, Missouri. After he left the CCC, he worked for two years in the Brown Shoe Company, Potosi, Missouri.

When he was hired in the late 1940s, Thebeau had the daily responsibility in the winter time of shoveling coal—delivered by Bernard Koch and Norman Wilson—into the furnaces in the church, school, convent, and rectory at noon and between midnight and 1 a.m. daily. He also rang the 6 a.m., 12 noon, and 6 p.m. angelus bell from the church's choir loft by pulling the rope that was attached to it in the bell tower. On a regular basis he cleaned the church and the school, for which he was also responsible for unlocking every morning during the school year. He also painted, did yard work, and showed grave diggers where to prepare graves. Before phones came to Old Mines, it was not unusual for someone from the parish to knock on Thebeau's door in the middle of the night to request help with a maintenance issue or problem. In other words, Thebeau was on call day and night. After working for St. Joachim Church for over thirty years, he retired in the mid-1970s, and died December 28, 2002, at the age of 89.

During his many years as the maintenance man, he was assisted by Marion Govero, Bernard Thebeau, Richard Villmer, and Albert Battreal, who lost his life and home in 1957, when, after a huge rainstorm, a dike burst and flooded his property along Old Mines Creek. More on that event can be found in chapter 27 on Some Major Events in Old Mines. In the summer, Thebeau was assisted by Larry Sansoucie and other high school students.

After Thebeau retired, Michael Coleman was hired to replace him. Michael Sansoucie was hired to replace Coleman. By the time Sansoucie was hired, the coal-burning furnaces had been converted to propane and a carillon had taken over ringing the angelus bell. Once Sansoucie left, the following were hired as school custodians: Judy Buchanan, Irvin (Ervin) Bollefer, John Boyer, Christine Henson, and Maria McCauley. Some of those also helped to cut the grass in the summer. Once Datillo became pastor, all building maintenance and grass cutting was done by parishioner volunteers. At the time of the writing of this book, Ray Thebeau holds the part-time position of maintenance man for the school and the parish; he began this job in 2018.

Just as an aside, the former coal bin in the church was converted to the Catholic Charities Food Pantry; the coal bin in the rectory became a pantry closet; the coal bin in the school was converted into storage space. One can still find the school's coal bin shoot in the concrete slab behind the school below the women's restroom.

Before Thebeau was hired as the maintenance man, Max J. Villmer, who had a job at H(iginbotham) & P(olitte) Mining Co., rang the church bell every day at noon and 6 p.m. for the angelus. During Naes's pastorate and Suellentrop's pastorate, Villmer was part-time maintenance man, tuckpointing the church and making repairs. He transported Redemptorist priests from DeSoto to St. Joachim to say Mass on Sunday when needed. He was known to drive a school bus on Pat Daly Road and Arnault Branch Road to pick up parishioners for Mass and children for religious instructions between Sunday Masses.

Catholic Charities

During the pastorate of Father Robert Johnston (1981–1987), Catholic Charities of the Archdiocese of St. Louis established a Parish Outreach Center (POC) in the rectory basement. The POC, opened in January 1983, was intended to assist rural parishes in Washington County with social services that were available through Catholic Charities to St. Louis City parishes but were not easily accessible to rural areas of the archdiocese. Johnston and the Rural Parish Workers of Christ the King were instrumental in bringing the Outreach Center to St. Joachim Parish, which provided at no cost office space in the rectory basement. While the POC was located in St. Joachim Parish, its immediate scope also included St. Stephen Parish, Richwoods; St. James Parish, Potosi; St. Joseph Parish, Bonne Terre; St. Joseph Parish, Farmington; and Holy Martyrs Parish, Sullivan.

Donald Boyer was hired as the original coordinator of the program and served in that capacity from January 1983 to July 1987. He was succeeded by Marvin J. (Joey) Politte from August 1987 through September 1997, when the program came to an end. The original duties of the coordinator were to identify existing services at both the county and state levels and to make referrals to these services when applicable and to identify needs that were not being met with the existing services. Local social service organizations included the East Missouri Action Agency, the Division of Family Services, the Rural Parish Workers of Christ the King, St. Vincent de Paul Societies at each of the local parishes, and the Washington County Knights of Columbus Council.

Some of the basic needs that were not being met included food, financial assistance with utility bills, emergency financial assistance for medical bills, transportation, greater educational opportunities, and access to legal services.

One of the first needs to be addressed was food with the establishment of a Food Pantry in the basement of St. Joachim Church. Resources for the Food Pantry, established in what had once been the coal bin, were obtained from the St. Louis Area Food Bank, the Boy Scouts of America Annual Food Drive, various corporate donors throughout the region, and the local St. Vincent de Paul Society. The Food Pantry worked in coordination with other food relief efforts within the county. In some instances, corporate donors would announce a surplus of product—like produce, bakery goods, bread, eggs, ice cream, butter, peanut butter, and other short shelf-life products—that needed to be brought to the pantry and distributed within a short time. Often, such items were made available after Sunday Masses in the school auditorium.

Direct financial assistance for help in paying utility bills was done through the Catholic Charities office in conjunction with the Rural Parish Workers and the local St. Vincent de Paul Societies.

Assistance with transportation needs came with the acquisition of a 1976 Dodge fifteen-passenger van, obtained through a joint venture with Catholic Charities and the Cardinal Ritter Institute. The van was used to transport the elderly and others to doctors' appointments and specialty health services in the St. Louis area and as far as Columbia, Missouri, and Cape Girardeau, Missouri. One day a month, the van transported eight to ten senior women to the grocery store, various locations for errands, lunch, and to enjoy the company of their peers. By using the van that way, the women were more self-sufficient and less dependent on others for their transportation needs. The van was also used to pick up and deliver supplies for the Food Pantry and meet other transportation needs when necessary. Eventually, the 1976 Dodge was replaced with a 1987 Ford fifteen-passenger van.

The POC made the van available to a group of men who had lost their employment due to an economic downturn that was experienced county wide. A private business school in the St. Louis area offered short-term computer programs that ranged in duration from nine to eighteen months. The school provided financial assistance through Pell grants and student loan programs, and the POC provided the van and covered all costs for transportation to and from the business school for the men who enrolled in the evening courses. Upon completion of the program, the business school assisted the men with job-placement opportunities.

A GED program was also established to meet an additional educational need in the area. Many people had not completed high school and needed to obtain a GED in order to meet minimum educational requirements for employment. The GED program was organized in conjunction with Jefferson College and met in St. Joachim School auditorium one night a week. Upon completion of the program, students would take their exam on the Jefferson College campus. Many who completed the

GED program continued their post-secondary education by participating in additional programs offered at Jefferson College.

In conjunction with the East Missouri Action Agency and the POC, free legal services were provided by Legal Services of Eastern Missouri. The POC provided the initial screening with clients who needed legal services and set up appointments with a representative of Legal Services at the POC office in St. Joachim Rectory.

Thus, for fifteen years, the Catholic Charities Parish Outreach Center program served the needs of people in Washington County. It established a Food Pantry, a means to offer financial assistance with utility bills, transportation for a variety of needs, a GED program, and free legal services. It also assisted battered women, those suffering from alcohol abuse, and those needing medical care. The POC, functioning from the rectory basement, impacted many lives during its fifteen-year existence.

For Further Reading: *History of St. Joachim Parish:* 1822–1972; 1723–1973, Mark G. Boyer.

10

Catholic Cemeteries

CEMETERY 1

Because the Catholic custom was to bury the dead as close to the church as possible, it didn't take long for the first cemetery, which was located immediately behind the current church—where there is now a parking lot and school—to fill. That cemetery was moved during the pastorship of Father John Daly (1916–1928). The graves were opened, and the caskets removed and loaded onto the parish spring wagon. Joe Portell hauled the caskets to what is now Cemetery 1, where they were reburied.

Another cemetery was opened before 1830 (as there are grave markers with that date on them) to the south of the church across what is now known as Pat Daly Road and up the hill. That approximate two-acre space was directly north of what would have been the road to Marie-Louise Lamarque's orchard. Today, Murphy's Mausoleum is located on the south side of where the road would have been.

This cemetery was divided in two parts by a hearse lane or road that ran south to north from the road to Lamarque's orchard through iron gates—located further south on the hill than where they exist now—and across the creek to Pat Daly Road. It is highly likely that part of this section of Cemetery 1 was used for burials at about the same time as the parish was founded (1828) or even before that; Catholics who died in Old Mines had to be buried some place. Likewise, Catholic slaves had to be buried somewhere. Some graves were marked with wood, which deteriorated long ago. Some were marked with sandstone, which dissolves in the elements. Some graves were marked with only hand forged iron crosses made by village blacksmiths. And some graves were never marked in any way.

On January 1, 1856, Lamarque donated (legally sold for one dollar) two and a half acres of land to Kenrick for the purpose of a cemetery. Those two and a half acres of land in lot six of the Old Mines Concession expanded Cemetery 1, originally in lot seven, to the south by two and a half acres. At the time of that donation, a road to Lamarque's orchard ran across the hill east and west in front of where the Murphy Mausoleum sits today. To the north of the road was the original pre-1856 cemetery with a hearse lane running through it from south to north. Sometime after 1900 and after the road to Lamarque's orchard was closed and used for graves, the southern part of the cemetery was slightly enlarged to the east and very much enlarged to the north to the creek over which was built a log and then a concrete bridge. Iron gates, which had been located further up the hill (south)—indicating where the original boundary had been—were moved north (down the hill) to the new boundary south of the creek. In recent times, a split rail fence was erected along the cemetery's northern boundary to replace the wire fence that had been there. Thus, the approximate four- to five-acre cemetery, which was expanded several times, is known today as Cemetery 1. When it was decided in the twentieth century (early to mid-1920s) to build a convent/school behind the church and move the Lamarque school from its location north of the church to behind the church where the first cemetery used to exist, the graves there were exhumed and the bodies were moved to Cemetery 1 or Cemetery 2 (see below). Thus, what had been the original cemetery immediately behind the church was completely eliminated, and a new Cemetery 1 took its place.

In 1992, Kent Bone, a member of the Old Mines Area Historical Society, began restoration of Cemetery 1. Ninety of the two hundred iron crosses—with their various tips on bars and crossbars indicating the blacksmith who made them—which had fallen over, been collected, and stacked along the fence line in the cemetery, were restored to grave sites and set in concrete on graves. Because there was no way of knowing which cross went on which grave, Bone looked for depressions in the ground, which indicated where a wooden coffin had rotted and the earth had settled (the way people were buried before the invention of metal caskets and vaults); he placed an iron cross at the head of those depressions. Likewise, eighty footstones and ten headstones needed to be returned from the fence line to their former positions in the cemetery. The footstones were easy to replace; all Bone needed to do was match the initials on the footstones with the names on the tombstones. The ten headstones needed to be replaced presented a tougher problem to solve.

Because there is no surviving plat of the cemetery, Bone made one based on tombstones and interviews with local people. The oldest grave markers go back to the 1830s, but people undoubtedly were buried there before then. Some graves were unmarked; some that were marked with sandstone slabs or grave markers dissolved in the elements and became unreadable. Many of the plots in Cemetery 1 were sold as eight- or twelve-grave sections. Bone estimated room for four thousand graves in Cemetery 1 as it now exists. As of the writing of this book, Bone's project is a work in progress, as he continues to collect information that designates where someone may be buried. Today, one digs a grave in Cemetery 1 at his or her own risk; there is no way of knowing if an unmarked place has anyone buried in it unless a surviving family member knows for sure.

It was into the original Cemetery 1—after it was enlarged, but before burials had begun in it—that Father James Fox buried Father John James Caffrey on February 17, 1856. See chapter 7 on St. Joachim Catholic Church and Pastors for more information on Caffrey's death and burial.

CEMETERY 2

In the 1930s, most likely during the pastorate of Father John F. Walsh (1928–1940), additional property was acquired for a cemetery to the south and west of St. Joachim Church in lot seven of the Old Mines Concession off what is now Pat Daly Road. That approximately two acres, which had been part of Lamarque's land, became Cemetery 2. During the pastorate of Father Bernard Suellentrop (1962–1970), Benedict Thebeau erected the pieta shrine that sits near the entrance to this cemetery. After the deaths of Neil and Helen Thebeau, St. Joachim Church bought, in 2010, from their descendants the over-four-acre property which adjoins Cemetery 2 on the west and south boundaries in order to expand Cemetery 2. Buildings on the property were removed. At the time of this writing, trees are awaiting removal from the property that needs to be platted for cemetery use. A flagpole used to display the U.S. flag was erected in Cemetery 2 in 2017. The flagpole initiative was the work of George Wall, facilitated by Carissa Skiles, On November 12, 2017, veterans from around the area gathered for the dedication of the flagpole, which cost $7,000, raised by people of the area.

At one point in time, about sixty acres of property bordering Cemetery 2 were used for wood. Trees were felled and cut, and the wood was brought to St. Joachim campus to be burned to supply heat for the church, convent/school, and rectory. Later, the wooded acres were divided into small parcels of land for home sites.

CEMETERY 3

Cemetery 3, located in lots seven and eight of the Old Mines Concession, can be found on the north side of Pat Daly Road behind (west of) St. Joachim Church. It is accessed by a hearse lane off Pat Daly Road that bisects the cemetery north and south or by a hearse lane that extends Crest Road past the church, rectory, and garage and bisects the cemetery east and west, intersecting with the hearse lane from Pat Daly Road in front of the crucifixion shrine depicting St. John, St. Mary Magdalene, and the Blessed Virgin Mary at the cross. During the pastorate of Father Bernard Suellentrop (1962–1970), Benedict Thebeau erected the shrine behind which are buried members of the Rural Parish Workers of Christ the King and in front of which is buried Father Theodore Pieper.

A small section of Cemetery 3 located in the southwest corner and bordered on the west and north by the St. Joachim ball and soccer field was opened during the pastorate of Father Vincent L. Naes (1941–1948) for individual burials. The rest of Cemetery 3 was opened at the same time, the first section being in the northwest corner. Father Francis P. Donovan, associate pastor from 1942 to 1947, planted the cedar trees along the fence dividing the cemetery from the baseball and soccer fields to the west. After the northwest corner was opened, the northeast corner followed, then the south east area. During the pastorate of Father Richard Suren, the south west area was opened. Father Theodore Pieper expanded the cemetery to the east on both sides of the hearse lane that extends Crest Road through the cemetery. With the help of Benedict Thebeau, who had constructed the stone pillars and gate marking the eastern boundary of Cemetery 3, the pillars and gate were moved further east, thus expanding the boundary of Cemetery 3 east towards the church and providing room for several rows of burials. Later, Pieper again expanded the eastern boundary of the north east section beyond the stone pillars to the east toward the church to allow for four more rows of burials.

The additional space in Cemetery 2 and Cemetery 3 was needed to accommodate the large number of people desiring to be buried in Old Mines.

For Further Reading: *The Diggin's*: Ancient Cemetery Restoration Project, Kent Bone, 1:1, 2:1, 16:2; Murphy's Tomb, Natalie Villmer, 23:2; Baton Rouge, LA: Steamboat Princess Disaster, GenDisaster.com; *History of St. Joachim Parish:* 1822–1972; 1723–1973, Mark G. Boyer.

11

Schools, Lay Teachers, and Graduates

As early as March 12, 1833, Father John Boullier (1828–1936) had thought about establishing a school for girls in Old Mines, and Bishop Joseph Rosati had given him permission to proceed to do so. However, nothing materialized from Boullier's thoughts. At some time later, Father Phillip Borgna, one of Boullier's assistants who had grown to detest living in Perryville, went to live with Boullier in Old Mines in the hope of erecting a school. However, again nothing happened. Finally, by May 9, 1837, Father Peter J. Doutreluinge, the associate of Father John Brands (1836–1839), began a school. He had a log cabin made for the school, and, at that time, was in the process of erecting a second log cabin for more students, because by June 16, 1837, he reported that the school was doing well. The school was for both boys and girls. A Mr. Doherty was the teacher. No one knows how long this school was in operation, where it was located, or the number of students attending it. Doutreluinge grew unpopular in Old Mines because he preached in English to French-speaking parishioners! He left the parish in 1839.

LAMARQUE SCHOOL

With money from Marie-Louise Lamarque, Father James Fox (1852–1868) built what is now known as the Lamarque School (its other names being Tin Can University and Teen Town) in 1857. It was located to the north (right) of the front doors of St. Joachim Church. It seems to have been open to both Catholic children and others. The one-room school was built in the Greek Revival style in an attempt to capture in wood what the Greeks had built in stone. The rectangular building featured three windows on either side, a window at each end, and two doors near the end on one side. It also had a chimney for a wood stove, which heated the one-room school in the winter. Maude Flynn and Helen DeClue taught in the Lamarque School, but records are incomplete as to other teachers and the number of students who attended it.

Schools, Lay Teachers, and Graduates

At some time between 1923 and August 1924, the pastor of St. Joachim Parish—Father John P. Daly (1916–1928)—had the Lamarque School moved to a location behind the church. This move was to facilitate its use in conjunction with the convent/school he built and opened in 1924. The location was prepared with a cellar and foundation upon which the Lamarque School was placed. To accommodate it to its new location and to insulate its wooden exterior, pressed galvanized metal siding was wrapped around it. Corner trim boards, beam, and any trim wood that stuck out past the wood siding was pulled off to make the walls smooth for the attachment of the metal siding. The two doors on the side were turned into windows, and two windows—one on the end and one on the other side—were turned into doors. In 1937, the Lamarque school was named Tin Can University by the nuns who taught in it. The building continued to be used for various grades (usually the eighth grade) of the school until the late 1950s, when it became a multi-purpose room for rummage sales, youth dances, and other functions.

By the 1960s it was used only occasionally, as it continued to sit in the middle of what had become the asphalt parking lot behind the church. Father Bernard A. Suellentrop (1962—1970) had a foundation built for it and had it moved to the west side of the school that had been built by Father Edward Bruemmer (1948–1954). In its new location close to the school, it was used as a Boy Scout Hall, a mini-gym, a storage room, an occasional bingo hall, etc. From 1993 to 1994, Kent Bone, Brian Bequette, and Matthew Pratt restored the Lamarque School. They removed the metal siding and discovered where the original doors and windows had been located. They found the corner trim boards and beam and all trim that had been removed in the 1920s to have been used to turn doors into windows and to fill in other openings. Outlines of where trim had been on the building was determined by the old paint still on the outer walls. Other original woodwork that had been removed when the pressed metal siding was attached was found on the building and used to restore it to the way it looked in 1857, when it was built. The cost of the restoration was paid by La Brigade a Renault, which sponsors two rendezvous in Old Mines every year.

CONVENT/SCHOOL

Because of the growing number of students, Father John P. Daly, pastor from 1916–1928, decided to build a convent/school—referred to as the Old Convent—before August 1924. The convent/school, located behind and to the right (north) of the church, was a two-story building with living quarters on the top floor for the Incarnate Word nuns he got to teach in the school, and three classrooms, a chapel, and a parlor on the first floor. Grades 1 & 2, 3 & 4, and 5 & 6 were held in the three classrooms on the first floor; grades 7 & 8 were held in the Lamarque School. In the winter, eighth-grade boys were responsible for feeding the fire in the wood stove in the Lamarque School. The original convent/school building did not have porches on the front (south side).

Those were added later, and, after that, the top one was enclosed to provide more living space for the nuns who came to teach in the school. The building was blessed on September 10, 1924. See chapter 12 on Convents and Nuns for more information on the convent/school.

On the first day of school in September 1924, one hundred nine students were registered. By the beginning of 1925, one-hundred fifty students were attending classes in the three classrooms in the convent/school and in the Lamarque School. By 1934, there were twenty-five eighth-grade graduates, the largest number since the school had been opened. In September 1934, 213 students were registered for school; that number was the largest in the then-history of the school.

NEW SCHOOL: FIRST FLOOR

By the early 1940s, it was clear that more room was needed for students. Father Vincent L. Naes (1941–1948) had done the planning for a new school, but he was transferred before the building could begin. Father Edward A. Bruemmer (1948–1954) took over where Naes had left off with revised plans. Groundbreaking for the new school took place on July 3, 1949, for the basement/cafeteria and first floor of the building. On October 19, 1949, Dorothy Daugherty and Margaret DeClue began the Hot Lunch Program for the school; the former was the cook, and the latter was the dietician. On November 13, 1949, the corner stone was laid. Bishop Charles H. Helmsing, Auxiliary Bishop of the Archdiocese of St. Louis, blessed the stone. An address was given by the Superintendent for Catholic Schools of the Archdiocese of St. Louis, Father James E. Hoflich, and Father Bernard A. Suellentrop, who was Breummer's associate pastor, served as the Master of Ceremonies. The school cost $108,662.75. A.F. and Arthur Stauder were the architects, and A.H. Cheatham was the contractor.

In the basement was the boys' bathroom, the furnace/utility room, the kitchen, the cafeteria/multi-use space, and a stage with wings on either side for storage of costumes and props; there was also a door to the outside backstage. On the first floor was the girls' bathroom, a closet from which school supplies could be sold to students, an office, a library, and five classrooms. There was also a back door that exited to a small porch with steps down to the outside. Even though this new building was open, the three classrooms in the convent/school continued to be used at various times and in various ways.

The school opened on September 6, 1950. There were 396 elementary students and thirty-six Freshmen in high school. On May 15, 1952, forty-five eighth-grade students graduated, and twenty-two high school students had finished their Sophomore year. On May 14, 1953, forty-four eighth grade students graduated, and nine students finished their Junior year of high school. On May 25, 1955, St. Joachim High School graduated its first class of five members: Gregory Bequette, Paul Bourisaw, Mary Loreda Boyer, Benedict Hanson, and Mary Ann Roderique. Those five students were honored with the presence of Helmsing, who was assisted by Fathers Joseph G. Helfrick and Alphonse H. Hoormann.

NEW SCHOOL: SECOND FLOOR

Because of the large number of students attending St. Joachim School, work began on the second story on March 26, 1954. Again, the architects were A.F. and Arthur Stauder, but the contractors were Mueller and Becker. The addition of the second floor cost $65,198.69, with an additional six thousand dollars paid for the coal-fired boiler heating system installed by Henry C. Scott. On September 9, 1954, there were 460 elementary school students and 104 high school students. On September 11, 1954, the second floor was opened; on October 7, 1954, Helmsing, who had blessed the corner stone in 1949, returned to bless the second floor of St. Joachim High School, which contained a home economics center, a laboratory, three classrooms, a typing room, and a small counselling room. The first Junior-Senior banquet for St. Joachim High School took place on April 21, 1955, and the next day the first Junior-Senior prom was held in the basement/cafeteria/auditorium.

On May 25, 1956, eighteen seniors were graduated from St. Joachim High School. Father Thomas Flynn was the speaker for the graduation ceremony. The eighteen graduates included: Johnny Bequette, Cyrilla Ann Boyer, Mary Theresa Charboneau, Anthony DeClue, Thomas Davis, Robert Hall, Cecil Heifner, David Jackson, Charles Pashia, Ruth Politte, Shelba Portell, William Portell, Mary Elizabeth Sansoucie, Sherman Schmidt, Natalie Villmer, Dorothy Wall, Norman Wilson, and Jane Young.

Enrollment continued to grow. When the school year began on September 7, 1956, there were a total of 540 students in the school, and the next year's opening day, September 6, 1957, stands as the all-time total number of students in St. Joachim School: 640. As already noted in the chapter on St. Joachim Catholic Church, Father Alphonsus H. Hoormann (1955–1962) began a debt-reduction campaign on the funds borrowed to build the two-story school on March 11, 1957. The goal was forty thousand dollars. By April 5, 1957, $49,700 had been realized.

On March 20, 1968, the National Honor Society was begun in St. Joachim High School. Known as the St. Louis IX Chapter, six members from the Junior and Senior class were inducted: Mark Boyer, Sheila Boyer, Regina Daugherty, Jerry DeClue, Phillis Koch, and Mary Ann Politte.

St. Joachim Elementary School and High School continued through the remainder of the 1950s and 1960s. However, the number of students continued to decline as parents decided to send their children to high schools in the area that were able to provide more opportunities or because they could not afford the cost of tuition. After the high school graduation of 1972 of fifteen students, Father Richard Suren (1970–1975), the pastor of the parish, closed the high school. With the lower number of students, the fewer nuns available to teach in the high school, the cost of paying lay teachers, and the cost of tuition, Suren, in conjunction with the Superintendent of Catholic Schools of the Archdiocese of St. Louis, decided that the best course of action was to close the high school and focus assets on elementary school students. The total number of a high school graduating class was never more than twenty-six which occurred in 1966.

After the high school closed, enrollment in the elementary grades dropped steadily in the years following, even though the entire two floors of St. Joachim School were dedicated to elementary students. A kindergarten program was added in 1977, and a pre-school program and daycare in the early 1990s. The kindergarten was among the first in Catholic Schools in the Archdiocese of St. Louis with Joyce (Daugherty) Politte as the first teacher. While she and the principal, Sister Rosemary Politte, designed a curriculum, fathers of future students built tables, and mothers shopped yard sales for educational supplies. The kindergarten opened with twenty-five students.

By the early 1990s, both parents were often working and in need of adequate childcare. During Linda Markway's term as principal, Kathy (Kitty Politte) Portell began a daycare in the new convent building which moved in the mid-1990s to two vacant classrooms in the school; one room was used for activity and the other was used for sleep. Jackie O'Hanlon succeeded Portell in the daycare; she taught prayers to the children, read stories to them, and sang songs to them. The daycare continued to operate until 2013, when it could no longer remain open financially. At the same time as the daycare was begun, a preschool for three- and four-year-old children was opened.

In the late 1970s, Sister Rosemary Politte, an Incarnate Word nun, native Old Miner, and then-principal, under the guidance of the St. Louis Archdiocesan Education Office, participated in the first self-study to evaluate the educational program and to plan for the future of St. Joachim School. The self-study involved a visit from a team of administrators and teachers from other Catholic schools who gave direction to the plans. As a result of the successful study, the North Central Accrediting Association granted accreditation to St. Joachim School, which has remained to the present.

Due to decreasing enrollment, around 1985, classes were combined; it was an idea reminiscent of the one-room school houses earlier in the same century. Teachers became proficient in managing that model while students excelled. That model continues to the present.

Also around 1985, Apple computers became a part of the educational process in the classrooms. The internet came to Old Mines in the early 2000s.

Until 1980, the Incarnate Word Sisters continued to send at least one nun to serve as principal of St. Joachim School. In 1980, Linda Markway was hired as the first lay principal of the school. Joyce Politte succeeded her in 1985, continuing until 2013. From 2013 to 2019, Carmen Litton was principal; she was followed by Matt Farr (2019–2021). Litton took over as principal again for the 2021–2022 school year.

Schools, Lay Teachers, and Graduates

Likewise, after 1995, when the last Incarnate Word nun-teacher left St. Joachim School, lay teachers have staffed it. Many of those teachers were former students, such as Carmen (Coleman) Litton, Gayle (Paul) Boyer, Peg (Bone) Portell, Trish (Bone) Boyer, Donald Boyer, Ronald Boyer, Joyce (Daugherty) Politte, Claudia (Boyer) Harper, Regina (Daugherty) Pinson, and Cathy (Daugherty) Blasé.

St. Joachim School staff has consistently participated in workshops and classes to keep St. Joachim on the forefront of educational innovations but not to the exclusion of maintaining solid core curriculum and Catholic identity. In the mid-1990s, Whole Language was brought to the classrooms. Students were supposed to learn to read by immersing themselves in the story without phonics and through experiences, like cooking. St. Joachim faculty tried the Whole Language curriculum but did not get rid of phonics.

Then there was emphasis on Critical Thinking Skills, Differentiated Instruction, Integration of Technology, and more into the classroom. Classrooms exchanged chalk boards for white boards. Now each classroom has a Smart Board connected to the internet, and each student has a Chromebook. Students have fewer textbooks and rely on the instruction from technology. For twenty plus years, teachers have taken on the role of facilitators of education. They have also had to become psychologists, safety coordinators for intruders and safe touch, nurses, and more. The demands on a teacher today are overwhelming, but at St. Joachim teaching remains a ministry, not just a job. Ronald Boyer wired the school for internet connections and completed the necessary electrical writing for smart boards in classrooms, electrical repair, and lighting. He also installed a new sound system in the school cafeteria/auditorium.

In 2021, all rooms of St. Joachim School on all floors are used. In the basement is still found the kitchen, the cafeteria (a multi-use room), the stage, the boiler and storage room, the boys' restroom, and a handicapped restroom. On the first floor are found classrooms, an advisory board room, a secretary's office, the principal's office, and the girls' restroom. The second floor contains classrooms, a music room, the computer room, an art room, the library, and storage rooms. All classrooms have window air conditioners.

Because the school was not handicapped accessible, in 1982, Father Robert Johnston had a ramp built from the parking lot to the cafeteria/auditorium by removing a small part of the basement wall. Funds for the ramp came from a walk-a-thon for the poor sponsored by the St. Vincent de Paul Society. Half of the three thousand dollars raised by eighty parishioners went to the cost of creating the ramp, and one half went to the poor. The dedication of the ramp took place on November 1, 1982, after an All Saints Day Mass for the elderly. Rose Pratt, retired rectory housekeeper, cut the ribbon stretched across the ramp over which all present then walked into the cafeteria for coffee and doughnuts.

St. Joachim Elementary School continues despite all odds. In 1995, enrollment was about one hundred ten students. The enrollment at the time of the writing of this book was eighty students, which was a rise after a fall in the previous years to around 60 students. A strong Parish School of Religion program has become a viable and accepted alternative for students attending public schools. All students are required to participate in sacramental preparation programs for first Penance, first Eucharist, and Confirmation. Even though the Rite of Christian Initiation of Adults is not a part of the school, there continues to be an increase in the number of adults seeking baptism or full reception into the Catholic Church, and some of them are the parents of students in the school. Some students in the school are not Catholics but children of parents who value the education provided. Many of those adults seeking full communion with the Church were baptized, but they were never catechized.

LAY TEACHERS

In addition to Incarnate Word Nuns teaching in the schools, there have been, and there continue to be, lay teachers. Below is a list in alphabetical order of those who taught in both elementary school and high school.

Before 1970: Sandra Bartlett, Blanche Bourbon, Cyrilla Boyer, Loreda Boyer, Phyllis Boyer, Agnes (Thebeau) Courtway, Thomas Davis, Thomas Paul, Ruth (Polite) Pinson, Catherine (Thebeau) Politte, Dorothy Politte, Angela Portell, Rose Ann (Coleman) Richards, JoAnne Thebeau.

1970–1990: Brenda Bone, Debbie (Stillwell) Boyer, Gayle (Paul Woodrow) Boyer, Kathleen Boyer, Patricia (Bone) Boyer, Ronald Boyer, Cecilia Davis, Mrs. Eisman, Marita Freymuth, Claudia Harper, Pamela Harris, Karen Huffman, Vicki (Koch) Johnston, Carmen Litton, Regina (Daugherty) Pinson, Carolyn (Thebeau) Politte, Joyce (Daugherty) Politte, Anne Portell, Margaret (Peg Bone) Portell, Mrs. Turk.

1990–1995: Brenda Bone, Kathleen Boyer, Bonnie Loeffler, Linda Markway, Joyce Politte, Denise Schaeffer, Harriet Smith.

1995–2013: Kathleen Boyer, Cathy (Daugherty) Blasé, Brenda Bone, Pam Boyer, Angie Coleman, Connie Coleman, Joni Coleman, Catherine Dickey, Michell Harmon, Vickie (Bone) Haynes, Krista Heddy, Helen Hochstatter, Misty Horton, Abby Johnston, Debra Koch, April Manning, Maria McCauley, Kelly Nolan, Jarah Politte, Mary Ann (Politte) Pratt, Monica (Politte) Pratt, Joyce (Daugherty) Politte, Yvonne Rill, Mickey Self, Jennifer Swift, Laura Villmer, Debra Wilkinson, Maria Yap.

2013–2019: Megan Arnold, Dana (Litton) Boyd, Bailey Coleman, Steve Davis, Carmen Litton, Breanna Juliette, Virginia Peterson, Margaret (Peg Bone) Portell, Rachel Pratt, Melissa Tindall.

2019–2021: Megan Arnold, Pam Boyer, Steve Davis, Bill Farr, Matthew Farr, Tiffany Gallagher, Breanna Juliette, Debra Koch, Megan Randolph, Melissa Tindall, Meaghen Trent.

Schools, Lay Teachers, and Graduates

OLD MINES COMMUNITY AND EDUCATION TRUST

In 1986, with the vision of Thomas Paul, the Friends and Alumni of St. Joachim was begun to help support the school. The first organizational meeting was held on January 23, 1986, with Father Robert Johnston (1981–1987), Father John Bolderson (1984–1987), Sister Margaret McCormick, Natalie Villmer, Brenda Bone, Charlotte Bone, Steve and Joyce Politte, Theresa Missey, Joanne Hahn, Doris Bequette, Gayle (Paul) Boyer, Gil Anderson, Claudia Harper, Carolyn Politte, and Thomas and Edna Paul. The primary goal of the founding of the Old Mines Community and Education Trust (OMCET) was to create a financial foundation to support the tradition of Catholic education over and above normal school income (tuition, parish subsidy, archdiocesan subsidy). The first elected officers were Thomas Paul, president; Joanne Hahn, vice-president; Charlotte Bone, secretary; Brenda Bone, treasurer; and Joyce Politte, Theresa Missey, and Mary Ann Pratt, members.

OMCET's constitution and by-laws were developed and approved, its not-for-profit corporate status for the State of Missouri was attained, and its U.S. Internal Revenue Service tax-exempt status was achieved. Thus, in 1996, OMCET was incorporated as the Old Mines Community and Education Trust (OMCET) as a 501(c)(3) charitable organization, Missouri Charter N00053941. The OMCET is governed by a board of seven members with a financial advisor. The original funds during the first few years were raised through small donations, primarily using a phone-a-thon. Those donations were invested in interest-bearing mutual funds and certificates of deposit chosen by a financial committee approved by the board of directors; the interest was used to sponsor scholarships for students to attend St. Joachim School and as support for the school through teacher assistance when purchasing items to be used in the classroom. Over the years, fundraisers designed to contribute more to the OMCET have been held, such as a yearly phone-a-thon and solicitations at alumni reunions and gatherings. Other support for the school came from the Archdiocese of St. Louis from its Annual Catholic Appeal in the amount of $120,000 with another $80,000 from its Emergency Fund.

The bylaws of OMCET require a public meeting to report activity, status, and future plans. This annual meeting is held on the Saturday afternoon of the St. Joachim Parish Fall Festival, usually in September.

The OMCET board also oversees the Tony and Irene Koch Memorial Scholarship fund, which provides monetary grants toward tuition, academic fees, or technology required for successful students. Over the course of the years and with wise financial investments, more than $155,000 have been used to support Catholic education in St. Joachim School, Old Mines, through scholarships, grants, and building funds as recommended by the school administration.

All of those monies help to keep the seventy-year building repaired, modified to meet government standards, and renovated to serve students' needs. The funds help pay teachers a living wage and provide health insurance. They help pay gas bills and electric bills, and they helped to save the school when it encountered a $60,000 shortfall in 2018–2019.

At the time of the writing of this book, tuition assistance, teacher support, and emergency needs continue as the primary purpose of OMCET. In the year 2000, $12,638 were given to the school for remodeling and electrically rewiring the building; the Knights of Columbus remodeled and replaced the windows in the school. After that, single-unit air conditions were added to each classroom. In 2012, OMCET remodeled the women's restroom with a donation of $6,825, and in 2013, remodeled the men's restroom with a donation of $4,000. In 2014, OMCET provided $6,680 for the removal of asbestos, and in 2016, renovated a computer room that had been created in 1994 in a room on the second floor of the school with a donation of $5,000. Thus, to date, $35,143 have been given for school repairs and renovation, and $34,955 have been given for tuition assistance and teacher/classroom needs.

Realizing that most St. Joachim Elementary School graduates could not afford the tuition to attend a Catholic high school, in 2007, OMCET began to assist eighth-grade graduates who desire to attend St. Pius X High School by providing a yearly cash supplement based on successful completion of the first half of the academic school year. Since 2007, $13,250 have been awarded in tuition assistance.

Because of the increasing complexity of investing, the OMCET board most recently decided to place the financial holdings in the care of a commercial brokerage agency: Edward Jones Company in Potosi, Missouri. At the time of the writing of this book, Jeff Boyer is president, James Johnston is secretary/treasurer, and David Pratt, Kathy Coleman, Tom Haynes, and Daniel Boyer are board members.

St. Joachim Elementary School remains open today due to OMCET support, sponsored events, like the Dinner-Auction, Golf Tournament, Fall Festival, and Dough Drive, and grants from the Archdiocese of St. Louis (Annual Catholic Appeal in the amount of $120,000 with another $80,000 from its Emergency Fund), Today and Tomorrow Grants, The Roman Catholic Foundation Grants, and tuition. Modern technology presents the greatest burden on this small, Catholic school because of the cost of keeping current with it.

ST. JOACHIM BOARD OF EDUCATION (EDUCATION COMMITTEE)

St. Joachim Board of Education began during the principalship of Sister Rosemary Politte (1977–1985). It served as an advisory board to the principal in matters of policy development and finance. The members of the board establish the philosophy and goals of the educational program, implement the policies of the Archdiocese of St. Louis, formulate and evaluate the implementation of policies, review and approve the educational budget submitted to the Parish Finance Committee, recommend employment of principals, review the recommendations of the administration in hiring teachers, and develop long-range planning and community relations dealing with the educational program. Past board presidents include Thomas Paul, Dennis Boyer, Ed Coleman, Al Sampson, Richard Davis, Benjamin Dewaal, and Kim Boyer. The current president is Leslie (Hopkins) Cox, the secretary is Kim Boyer, and the members of the board include: Chris Horton, Kelly Harris, Carmen Litton (principal 2021–2022), Matthew Farr (current principal), and Father Anthony Datillo (pastor).

ST. JOACHIM HOME AND SCHOOL ASSOCIATION

During Father Bernard Suellentrop's pastorate (1962–1970), what was known as the Parent Teacher Association became St. Joachim Home and School Association. The purpose was to develop a deeper appreciation for the aim and ideals of Catholic education, develop a closer relationship between parents and teachers, and assist the school to provide adequate facilities for physical, social, and moral development of students.

Today, the members of St. Joachim Home and School Association are parents, who provide a communication connection between the home and the school. The Home and School Association provides parent education in the areas of safety, health, educational trends, and more. The association assists parents as co-educators of their children by providing opportunity to discuss and explore aspects of child development essential to the better formation of the whole child. The association is responsible for much of the fundraising that includes the annual auction. Begun in the late 1990s, the funds from the auction provide for operational costs of the school. Cafeteria lights, copiers, paper, tile for the floors, technology equipment, and more have been funded through the work of the Home and School Association. Past presidents include Rachel Pratt and Laura Villmer. The current president is Kaitlin Govero. Two yearly meetings are held.

SECRETARIES AND STAFF

Kathy (Thebeau) Coleman was the first paid secretary after the closing of the high school in 1972. She was hired by Sister Rosemary Politte. From 1978 to 1990, she typed documents, prepared records, made liturgy booklets, copied teachers' masters on a mimeograph machine, served as school nurse, supervised lunch duty, answered the phone, and performed other duties as requested by the principal. Phyllis (Kamper) Pashia, Mary Ann (Politte) Pratt, Maria Yap, Connie (Politte) Coleman, Laura (Missey) Villmer, and Dana (Litton) Boyd have successively served as professional and efficient school secretaries. In recent years, the school secretary position became an administrative assistant to the principal.

Among school staff, there are always a few people who are outstanding in what they do. The first of these was Monica Pratt. When her daughter began school in 1992, Pratt became a volunteer librarian, after which she became the librarian and health teacher. In 1995, she became the P.E. teacher and CYC coach for volleyball. On alternate days in 1995, she added computer teacher to her titles. In 1999, she became the cook, famous for her pizza. Her creative talents were revealed when she planned Catholic Schools Week activities, Field Days, Parent and Grandparent Days, Faculty Treats, and Special Meals on request.

The second of these is Mary (Lynch) Boyer, who began volunteering in 1999 and continues to do so to the present day. She has worked in the cafeteria, as a classroom aide, an auction solicitor of items, a librarian, a book fair worker, and a general assistant to teachers and other staff. She has also worked at Vacation Bible School for years.

The third of these is Joyce (Daugherty) Politte. After graduating from St. Joachim High School in 1966, she attended college and earned a teaching degree in 1970. She wanted to make a difference in education, and she chose St. Joachim School as the place to make that difference. She taught in the high school until it closed in 1972. Then, in 1977, she moved to being the first kindergarten teacher in St. Joachim School. In 1985, she became the second lay principal of the school, a position she held until 2013. She continues to serve as the Director of Religious Education and works with those in the RCIA program. For fifty years of teaching, leadership, and music ministry in St. Joachim Parish—and before that in St. Joseph Parish, Tiff, Missouri— she considers herself blessed to have a part of many births, baptisms, first communions, confirmations, weddings, funerals, graduations, and anniversaries. She has watched pastors, Incarnate Word nuns, teachers, friends, and students come and go. She has walked with, laughed with, and cried with many. She has been nominated and received awards. However, her most memorable moments are those when students return and say, "You made a difference in my life," or when she sees those whom she has instructed in the Catholic faith living their faith and contributing to the growth of St. Joachim Parish.

KITCHEN STAFF

Closely aligned with the school's operation is the kitchen staff, who prepare meals for students five days a week. The school hot lunch program began on October 19, 1949, with Dorothy Daugherty as the cook and dietician Pat DeClue as her helper. Among those in need of mentioning among school cooks is Helen Thebeau, who began work in the school cafeteria in 1950 and worked there for thirty-two years, retiring around 1982. Helen (Mercille) Thebeau, born in 1917 and died April 13, 2004, was the wife of Neil Thebeau, the maintenance man for St. Joachim Church, School, Convent, and Rectory for over thirty years. Many people remember Helen's freshly-made hot rolls sending tempting aromas from the basement kitchen to the first and second floors of the school. For one Fall Festival, she used five hundred pounds of flour to make hot rolls! Helen was assisted by other cooks from time to time. Among them, in alphabetical order, are Agatha Bequette, Rosie Bequette, Louise Bourisaw, Lucy Boyer, Mary

(Lynch) Boyer, Helen Brewer, Rose Brewer, Joyce Campbell, Larry and Janet Gillespie, Mary Govero, Blanche Heifner, Vicki Johnson, Donna Malloy, Nancy Politte, Monica Pratt, Loretta Thebeau, Karen Veach, and Jeanette Wright.

EIGHTH-GRADE GRADUATES OF ST. JOACHIM SCHOOL

1928: John Agnes, Bernard Coleman, Donald Mercille, Leona Mercille, Loretta Paul, James Politte, James Lester Politte.

1929: Marie Koch, Vincent Paul, Lulu Politte, Mary Rose Politte, Bertha Portell.

1930: Louise Bequette, Mary Louise Bourisaw, Julian Boyer, Leo Koch, Agatha Sansoucie, Edgar Sansoucie, Lloyd Thebeau, Minnie Torrence.

1931: Fabian DeClue, Fred Politte, Gus Z. Portell, Robert Politte, Fabian Thebeau, Nelson Thebeau.

1932: Thomas Bequette, Francis Bone, Jesse Bone, Fabian Boyer, Cynthia Coleman, Gertrude Coleman, Lucille Koch, Sylvia Mercille, Kathleen Pashia, Henry Robart.

1933: Leigh Bequette, Rita Bequette, Jesse L. Boyer, Lena Boyer, Aloysius Coleman, Lucille DeClue, Monica Juliette, Rachael Long, Helen Mercille, Florence Politte, Robena Pratt.

1934: Alberta Bequette, Aurelia Bequette, Aloysius Bourisaw, Ivan F. Bourisaw, Edward Boyer, Lucille Boyer, Valerine Boyer, Albert Coleman, Bernard Coleman, Bernice Coleman, Clyde Coleman, Mary Coleman, Cynthia DeClue, Mildred DeClue, Jimmie DeGonia, Mabel Juliette, Edna Koch, Timothy Pashia, Edwin W. Politte, James Politte, Donald Portell, Edward Sansoucie, Mary Thebeau, Nicholas Thebeau.

1935: Henrietta Bourisaw, Harold Boyer, Ethel Boyer, Dorothy Coleman, Dorothy Osia, Lucy Alma Pashia, Mary Sylvia Thebeau, Lucille Warden.

1936: Dolores Bequette, Harry Bequette, Vianna Bequette, Hannah Bourisaw, Bernard Boyer, Margaret Boyer, Richard Boyer, Donald Coleman, Lawrence Coleman, Lennie Coleman, Margaret Coleman, Ellen DeClue, Nazarine Juliette, Bernard Koch, Stephen Mercille, Veronica Pashia, Ruth Politte, Raymond Portell, David Burnham Pratt, Delia Pratt, Bertha Robart, Orpha Ruby, James Sansoucie, John Augustus Thebeau, Marie Villmer, James Warden.

1937: Harold Bourisaw, Virgil Bone, Catherine Boyer, Jennie Boyer, Thomas A. Boyer, Mary Lee Coleman, Leon Coleman, Margaret Mary Coleman, Mary Sylvia Coleman, Paul Coleman, William Ananstie Coleman, Anne Lucille DeClue, Vergie DeGonia, Lawrence Flynn, John J. Juliette, Margaret Portell, Clarence

Joseph Pratt, Louise Marie Thebeau, Evelyn Pratt, Evelyn Osia, Anna Louise Portell, Dorothy Ross, Bernard Thebeau.

1938: Dorothy Mary Bourisaw, Paul Hanson, Mary Ann Huskey, Monica Koch, Raphael Joseph Mercille, Rachel Mary Mercille, Zita C. Pashia, Rachel Politte, Walter Politte, Verna Portell, Margaret Elizabeth Robart, Elmer Sansoucie, Cecil Schmidt, Jr., Hilda Thebeau, Vincent Thebeau, Theresa Warden.

1939: Cecilia Marie Battreal, Thelma Bequette, Kathleen Bone, Frieda Marie Boyer, Verna Marie Boyer, Bernard Courtois, Francis DeClue, William David DeClue, Georgia Flynn, Rachel Teresa Huskey, Alma Osia, Carl Joseph Osia, Loretta M. Pashia, Daly Politte, Glennon Roderique, Marcella Roderique, Donald Schmidt, Cecilia Thebeau.

1940: James H. Bourisaw, Joseph Coleman, Thaddeus Coleman, Julia Hanson, Winifred M. Huskey, Matthew Koch, Mary Alice Lalumondiere, Nancy Long, Russell Osia, Charles Donald Pashia, Cecelia Portell, Thomas Portell, Joseph Lynn Robart, Lucille Mary Robart, Dorris Thebeau.

1941: Michael Allen, Paul Bourisaw, Edward Bone, Jr., Bernard James Boyer, Thomas Coleman, Helen Marie Daly, Dorothy Juliette, Ruth Osia, John S. Politte, Catherine Sansoucie, John Warden, Everette Williams, Marcella Thebeau, Angela Thebeau, Nora Portell.

1942: Thelma Boyer, John Daly, Mary Catherine Johnston, Delores Koch, Clifford Osia, George Portell, Lois Roderique.

1943: Rose Mary Bequette, Catherine Rose Bourisaw, John Boyer, Fabian Joseph DeClue, John Anthony Huskey, Francis Juliette, Eugenia Knott, Glennon Osia, Frank Thebeau, Glennon Thebeau, Paul Bequette.

1944: Loretta Battreal, Celestine Bequette, Burnham Boyer, Ronald Boyer, Edna DeClue, Thelma DeClue, Leonard Flynn, Edward Folk, Virginia Osia, Virginia Polhemus, Donald Roderique, Virgil Sampson, Floyd Thebeau, Cornelius Young.

1945: Regina Bequette, Glennon Bourisaw, Anna Lee Boyer, Arthur Boyer, James J. Boyer, Anna Rose Coleman, Leonard Hanson, James Higginbotham, George Huskey, Norma Faye Politte, Richard Politte, Joseph J. Portell, Paul Portell, Charles H. Pratt, Cynthia Robart, Lucy Robart, Maxine Sampson, Harold Sansoucie, Wilfred Thebeau, Maxine Villmer.

1946: Gerald Bequette, Barbara Boyer, Norma Jean Boyer, Orville Boyer, Joseph Coleman, Cornelius Daly, Mary Lee Doyen, Ralph Doyen, Viola Juliette, Adrian Pashia, Leroy Portell, Adrian Robart, Jessie Mae Ross, Mary Lou Schmidt, Roussan Thebeau, Charles Ward, Clyde Warden, Francis Young.

1947: Opal Barton, Bernita Boyer, Godfrey Boyer, Theresa A. Boyer, Vincent Folk, Robert Higginbotham, Aurelia Juliette, Joan Koch, Maxine Koch, Marjorie

SCHOOLS, LAY TEACHERS, AND GRADUATES

LaChance, Catherine Osia, Rose Marie Pratt, Eugene Politte, Everette Portell, Chester Reando, Marion Reando, Betty Recar, Ann Robart, Edna Robart, JoAnn Schmidt.

1948: Martha Aubuchon, Burgess Barton, John Boyer, William Gene Boyer, Theresa Boyer, Norma Jean Boyer, Mary Lee DeGonia, Suzanne Higginbotham, Morris Long, Ina Mae Politte, Betty Portell, Charlene Robart, Paul Sampson, Eddie Thebeau, Thomas Villmer, Bernadette Young.

1949: Jean Bequette, Patricia Bequette, Regina Bequette, Dorothy Bourisaw, Paul Bourisaw, Benita Boyer, Juanita Boyer, Leo Boyer, Jr., Paul Boyer, Virginia Boyer, James Hanson, Betty Ann Juliette, Geraldine Koch, John Osia, Paul Politte, Donald Reando, Charlene Roderique, Geraldine Thebeau, Jerry Thebeau.

1950: Christine Bequette, Doris Ann Bequette, Donald Boyer, Dolores Boyer, Glennon Boyer, Odelia Boyer, Gene M. Coleman, Maurice Daly, Mrs. Herbert A. Diercks, Marcella Heifner, Noah Juliette, Patsy Politte, Doris Ann Pratt, Magdalen Ross, Richard Schmidt, Bernard Thebeau, Charles Thebeau, Glenda Wall, Alvin Warden, Anthony Young.

1951: JoAnn Aubuchon, Gregory Bequette, Paschal Bequette, Frankie Bourisaw, Rita Bequette, Adrian Boyer, Cynthia Boyer, Cyrilla Boyer, Joseph Boyer, Loreda Boyer, Gerald Coleman, Pat DeClue, Catherine DeGonia, Betty Eckhoff, Shirley Eckhoff, Clayton Govero, Randell Hall, Benedict Hanson, Jane Huskey, Thomas Juliette, Veronica Osia, Monica Pashia, Rose Pashia, James Pinson, Mary C. Polhemus, Hazel Politte, Ruth Ann Politte, Corrine Portell, Mary Ann Roderique, James Thebeau, Rosalie Thebeau.

1952: Carl Barton, Donald Bates, Cecilia Bequette, John F. Bequette, Leona Bequette, Dennis Boyer, Kathleen Boyer, Norma Boyer, Rebecca Boyer, Ruth Ann Boyer, Veronica Boyer, Theresa Charboneau, Imelda Coleman, Joan Coleman, Tom Davis, Anthony DeClue, Mary Lou Dougherty, Maxine Govero, Cecil Heifner, Bernard Hopkins, Christine Hopkins, David Jackson, Joseph Knoblouch, Leroy Minx, Mary Knott, Kenneth Politte, Robert Politte, William Portell, Nancy Pratt, Wilma Robart, Leroy Rolens, Joan Sampson, Patrick Sampson, Mary E. Sansoucie, Sherman Schmidt, Regina Thebeau, Russell Thebeau, Ursula Thebeau, Natalie Villmer, Dorothy Wall, Norman Wilson, Jane Young.

1953: Ellen Bates, William Bone, Jackie Bourbon, Glennon Bourisaw, Emma Boyer, Jerry Lee Boyer, Leroy Boyer, Martha Boyer, Mary Ester Boyer, Mary Pat Boyer, Wilma Boyer, Cabrinie Coleman, Joyce Ann Coleman, Delores Davis, JoAnn DeGonia, Leroy Huskey, Glennon Juliette, Lavern Maness, Raymond Moss, Larry Pashia, Hilda Politte, James H. Politte, Joan Politte, June Politte, James Portell, Mary Rose Portell, Veronica Pratt, Ruth Ann Reando, James Ross, Sally Rolens, Janet Rundel, Judy Schmidt, Agnes Thebeau, Narvel Thebeau, Rita Thebeau.

1954: John Agnew, Jr., Jean Aubuchon, Bernadette Bequette, Kenneth Bone, Virginia Bone, Judy Bourisaw, Charlotte Boyer, Joan Boyer, Joseph Boyer, Kenneth Boyer, Vincent Boyer, David Coleman, William J. Coleman, Viola Courtway, Patricia Davis, Marilyn DeGonia, Larry Farrell, Charles L. Hill, Rita Kincaid, Jerry Merseal, John Miller, Kenneth Miller, Bernice Osia, Bernadette Pashia, Marjorie Pashia, Paul Pashia, Virginia Pinson, Rosalie Polhemus, Judy Politte, Margaret Politte, Mary Angela Pratt, Leo Pratt, Sylvester Pratt, Vincent Pratt, Alice Price, Norma Jean Rundel, Earl Sansoucie, Nancy Sansoucie, Lloyd Thebeau, Jr., Joseph G. Thebeau, Mildred Thebeau, Rita Jane Thebeau, Glennon Villmer, Mary Lou Villmer, Robert Villmer, Joyce Wall.

1955: Leo Battreal, Jr., Danny Benton, Richard Bequette, Clifford Boyer, Eddie Boyer, Peggy Sue Boyer, Stanley Boyer, Thomas Boyer, Catherine Coleman, Charolette Coleman, Roger Coleman, Ruth Ann Coleman, Agnes Courtway, Carol Mae DeGonia, Louis Golden, Philip Govero, Paul Huskey, Rose Lalumondiere, Kenneth Osia, Thaddeus Pashia, Thomas Paul, Patsy Politte, Wilma Politte, Bonnie Jean Portell Jerry Pratt, John Price, Ray Roderique, Alberta Ross, Robert Rundel, Catherine Sansoucie, Mary Lee Sansoucie, Janet Schmidt, Gloria Thebeau, George Ann Wall, Barbara Wickersham, Jerry Wickersham, Magdalyn Young.

1956: William Agnew, Elaine Aubuchon, Ann Battreal, Dorris Battreal, John Bequette, Stephen Bequette, Robert Bone, Thomas L. Bone, Annette Boyer, James Boyer, Joan Boyer, Joyce Boyer, Margaret Boyer, Odelia Boyer, Paul Boyer, Loretta Charboneau, Carol Mae Coleman, David Coleman, Mary Jane Coleman, Rita Ann Coleman, Ruth Ann Coleman, Suzanne Daugherty, Bernard DeClue, Dorothy DeClue, Geraldine DeGonia, Virginia Hill, Thomas Kincaid, Ruth Ann Missey, Lavern O'Shea, Kenneth Pace, Catherine Pashia, Cecelia Pashia, Francis Pashia, Patsy Pashia, Francis Politte, Joseph Politte, Kenneth Politte, Thomas Portell, Virginia Portell, John Pratt, Carelyn Pratt, JoAnn Pratt, Ronald Pratt, Ruth Rundel, Joyce Sampson, Ronald Thebeau.

1957: Ruth Ann Battreal, William Bone, Leroy Boyer, Veronica Boyer, Cabrini Coleman, Eugene DeClue, Joanne DeGonia, Joan Politte, Janet Rundell, Judith Schmidt, Patsy Thebeau.

1958: Regina Ayers, Jackie Battreal, Margaret Mary Bone, Nancy Bone, John Francis Boyer, Michael Boyer, Nancy Boyer, Sheila Ann Boyer, Ursula Coleman, Michael DeClue, Rose Mary DeClue, Hattie Hammond, Harry Hopkins, Lindell Jackson, James Jones, Ruth Ann Kincaid, David Lalumondiere, Kenneth Merseal, Catherine Politte, Kenneth Politte, Mary Lee Politte, Margaret Ann Pratt, Sandra Pratt, James Robart, Patricia Sansoucie, Catherine Thebeau, Charles Thebeau, Russell Thebeau, Rebecca Wall.

Schools, Lay Teachers, and Graduates

1959: Eileen Aubuchon, John Battreal, Patricia Battreal, Rita Battreal, George Boyer, Janet Carol Boyer, Magdalene Boyer, Patricia Boyer, Patrick Paul Boyer, Carley Coleman, Judy C. Coleman, Judy M. Coleman, Margaret Karen Coleman, Wayne Coleman, Edith Hammond, Ronald Hill, Barbara Jackson, Nancy Juliette, Helen Lalumondiere, Terry Mercille, Brenda Missey, Mary Catherine Pashia, Mary Martina Polhemus, Ronald J. Politte, Ronald Lee Politte, Sue Portell, Sylvia Portell, Vincent Portell, Ronald Pruitt, Louise Ruby, Margaret Mary Pratt, Rita Robart, Virginia Singer, Donald Thebeau, James D. Thebeau, Judy Thebeau, John Veach, Margaret Mary Wall, Virginia Wickerham.

1960: Carolyn Battreal, Richard Battreal, Janet Bone, Joyce Boyer, Judy Boyer, Kenneth Boyer, Larry J. Boyer, Nettie Boyer, James Adrian Boyer, Diane Coleman, Elizabeth Coleman, Imelda Coleman, John Z. Coleman, Laverne Coleman, Paul Coleman, Richard Coleman, Janet Courtway, Paulette Courtway, Mary Ann Govero, Paul Govero, Sharon Maxwell, James Melton, Everette Merseal, Michael Nephew, Charlene Pashia, John Pinson, Robert Pinson, Gloria Politte, Richard Politte, Charles Portell, Elizabeth Portell, Geraldine Portell, Mary Lou Price, Charles Robart, Janice Sampson, Mildra Sampson, Larry Sanders, Steve Sansoucie, Alva Veach, Mary Jane Yates, John G. Young.

1961: Linda Battreal, Philip Bequette, Charlotte Boyer, Joyce Boyer, Judy Boyer, Judy M. Boyer, Marvin Boyer, Paul Boyer, Shirley Boyer, Raymond Coleman, Francine Crippen, Nancy DeGonia, Elaine Goff, Lawrence Govero, Carol Hinch, Stephen Hinch, Carol Kincaid, Harold Koch, Patsy Malloy, Rebecca Martin, Carolyn Pashia, Paschal Pashia, Dorothy Politte, James Politte, Carol Portell, Ronald Pratt, Paul Pruitt, John Robart, Dennis Ross, Paul Ross, Elaine Sansoucie, Richard Sansoucie, Rose Singer, Judy Veach, Richard Villmer.

1962: Philip Aubuchon, Catherine Battreal, Patsy Belt, Linda Blair, Joey Bone, Judy Bone, Rita Bourisaw, Roy Bourisaw, Donald Boyer, Edward Boyer, Shirley Boyer, Diane Coleman, Ramona Coleman, Ruby Coleman, Joyce Daugherty, Donald DeClue, Ronald DeClue, David DeGonia, Mary Frances Govero, Roger Hammond, John Kite, Joseph Lalumondiere, Charles Martin, John Minx, Jr., Judy Missey, Marsha Missey, Rose Missey, Betty Pashia, Karen Pinson, Janet Politte, John Politte, Stephen Politte, Catherine Portell, Benny Price, Gloria Price, Mike Robart, Clarence Ross, Lindell Sampson, Gary Sansoucie, Anita Thebeau, Antionette Thebeau, Bernard Thebeau, Bobby Thebeau, Carolyn Thebeau, Paul Adrian Thebeau, Paul Anthony Thebeau, Sharon Thebeau, Judy Thurmond, Marilyn Veach.

1963: Brenda Aubuchon, Glenda Aubuchon, Philip Aubuchon, Billy Battreal, Mary Bequette, James Bone, Eddie Boyer, Richard Boyer, Robert Boyer, Carol Coleman, Joseph Daugherty Jr., James Johnston, Richard Juliette, Glennon Kincaid,

Barbara Koch, Patricia Missey, Donald Pinson, Wayne Pratt, Sharon Sansoucie, James Thebeau.

1964: JoAnn Bone, Marilyn Bone, John Boyer, Mark Boyer, Michael Coleman, Jerry DeClue, Robert Finch, Wayne Koch, James Pashia, Mary Ann Politte, Geraldine Sampson, Kenny Sansoucie, Catherine Singer, George Wall.

1965: Judy Battreal, Mark Bequette, Barbara Bone, Geraldine Boyer, P. Gregory Boyer, Sheila Boyer, Regina Daugherty, LaDonna Kite, Phyllis Koch, Roger Missey, Vernon Portell, Dale Pratt, Louis Pratt, Brenda Pruitt, Paul Recar.

1966: Gaul Aubuchon, Chris Bequette, Paul Bone, Kenny Bourisaw, Dennis Boyer, Joseph Boyer, Richard Boyer, Shirley Boyer, Rita Brown, Elaine Coleman, Philip Coleman, Billy Crippen, Catherine Daugherty, Theresa Daugherty, Jerry Juliette, David Kite, Nancy Koch Donna Pashia, Janice Pashia, Jean Politte, William Portell, Freda Pratt, Larry Sansoucie, Beverly Thebeau.

1967: Donna Battreal, Larry Battreal, Elain Bone, Gary Bone, Jennifer Boyer, Rita Boyer, Debbie Brown, Patricia Coleman, Margaret Daugherty, Beverly Kincaid, Theresa Pashia, Monica Politte, Elizabeth Portell, Debbie Pratt, Karen Robart, Anthony Ward.

1968: Dennis Aubuchon, Linda Barton, David Bone, Danny Boyer, Diane Boyer, Mary Jo Boyer, Mary Jane Coleman, Gary Koch, Mike Maness, James McMahon, James Pashia, Joe Portell, Terry Price, Barbra Robart, Marilyn Thebeau.

1969: William Boyer, Marcia Brown, Stephanie Coleman, Connie Daugherty, Frances Juliette, Denise Koch, Janice Maness, Marcia Maness, Barbara McMahon, Joseph Pashia, Joe Politte, Kathy Politte, Rosemary Robart.

1970: Paulette Bequette, Phyllis Bone, Donald Boyer, Karen Boyer, Ronald Boyer, Andy Daugherty, Bernadette Daugherty, Robert Johnston, Jackie McMahon, Marilyn Oshia, Judy Pashia, Philip Pashia, Barbara Price, Dennis Politte, Randy Portell, Julie Thebeau, Larry Ward.

1971: Christina Barton, Patricia Bone, David Boyer, Mark Boyer, Barry Brown, Anthony Coleman, Tim Daugherty, Sheila DeClue, Kenny Gaylord, Sharon Govero, Diane Johnston, Denise Koch, Bernard Maness, Roger McMahon, Anne Pratt, Harry Robart, Billy Sampson, Sandy Thebeau.

1972: James Battreal, Kevin Bone, Michael Bone, Mary Frances Boyer, Randall Boyer, Terry Coleman, Janice Crippen, Jane Daugherty, Thomas Daugherty, Judy Hochstatter, Kathleen Juliette, Carmen Koch, Michael Koch, George Lowe, Bryan Maness, Linda McMahan, Geraldine Pashia, David Politte, Claudia Portell, Richard Pratt, Donna Pruitt, Bernard Robart, Charles Singer, Helen Wall.

1973: Margaret Aubuchon, Philip Aubuchon, Kenny Barton, Kimberly Bone, Margaret Bone, Michael Bone, Randy Bone, Sharon Boyer, Wayne Boyer, James

Schools, Lay Teachers, and Graduates

Brown, Christy Coleman, Martin Coleman, Russell Coleman, Sandra Coleman, Kimberly Courtaway, Patricia Daugherty, Rebecca Daugherty, Morgan DeClue, Gary DeGonia, Patricia Gaylord, Cheryl Hochstatter, Roger Johnston, Michael Juliette, John Koch, Lynn McMahan, Richard Merseal, Rhonda Pinson, Timothy Pinson, Patricia Pinson, Paul Politte, Richard K. Politte, Judith Portell, Kenny Portell, Frank Thebeau, Joseph Thebeau, Neil Thebeau, Jr., Judy Wall.

1974: Glenda Battreal, Linda Battreal, Kimberly Benson, Lisa Bone, Rhonda Bone, Judy Boyer, Kathy Boyer, Michelle Brown, Tony Coleman, Kinberly Courtaway, Patricia Daugherty, Linda DeClue, Donald Johnston, Walter Jolly, William Juliette, Randy Kincaid, Paul Koch, Andrew Maness, Julia McMahan, Mike Mercille, Dennis Portell, Jerry Portell, Timothy Portell, Eddie Robart, Lisa Robart, Theresa Robart, Lisa Sampson, Robert Thebeau, Timothy Thebeau, Ginger Thurmond, Donna Ward.

1975: Angela Aubuchon, Michael Aubuchon, Donald Battreal, Nanette Benson, Timothy Bone, Vicki Bone, Christine Boyer, Clyde J. Boyer, Jeffrey Coleman, Timothy Coleman Tina Courtaway, Karen DeClue, Curtiss Govero, Robert Juliette, Yvonne Kincaid, Janice Koch, David Maness, Joseph Pashia, Patricia Pinson, Robert Portell, Jacqueline Thebeau, Jamie Thebeau, John Thebeau, Kevin Thebeau, Marcia Thebeau, John Wilson.

1976: Crystal Benson, Cheryl Bourisaw, Marcia Boyer, Mary Kay Boyer, Annette Brown, Phillis Coleman, Anthony Daugherty, Christa DeGonia, Joe DeGonia, Albert Dorlac, John Johnson, Marsha Juliette, Julie Maness, Rhonda Politte, Sandra Politte, Andrew Portell, Philip Portell, Mary Kay Pratt, Angela Robart, Colleen Thebeau, Katherine Thebeau, Gary Thebeau, Raymond Ward.

1977: Mary Bone, Timothy Bone, Donna Bourisaw, Janice Boyer, Martin Boyer, Melissa Boyer, Raymond Boyer, Kathryn Coleman, Patricia Coleman, Scott Coleman, Greg DeClue, Lisa DeGonia, Tracy Hanger, Lawrence Juliette, Howard Kincaid, Randy Kincaid, Monica McMahan, Dwight Pashia, Carma Pinson, Paula Politte, Ann Ward.

1978: Tammy Battreal, Tina Benson, Deneen Bequette, Eddie Bone, Vincent Boyer, Anthony Brown, Darryl DeClue, Karla DeClue, Delores Dorlac, Betty Gaylord, Nancy Johnston, Steve Jolly, Timothy Merseal, Jerome McMahan, Glen Osia, Gloria Pinson, Lynn Politte, Eugene Steif, Thomas Wilson.

1979: Philip Aubuchon, Joey Lee Barton, John Benson, Yvonne Bequette, Kelly Bone, Kraig Bone, Margaret Brown, Marty Boyer, Christie Govero, Debbie Karsch, Steve Maness, Chris Pashia, James Pashia, Dorothy Pratt, James Rhinehart, Tammy Sternard, Lisa Walton, Lucy Ward.

1980: Kathy Allen, Gina Bone, Mary Bourisaw, Shawn Coleman, Lisa Gregory, Ritchie Hanger, Linda Osia, Debbie Pinson, Laura Politte, Eddie J. Politte, Belinda Portell, Brenda Portell, Phillip Pratt, Diane Slayton, Mary Slayton, Joey Walton.

1981: Kathy Barton, Ronnie Bourbon, Susie Bourisaw, Brian Brown, Stacey Coleman, Jamie DeClue, Rhonda Ford, Maria Hays, Bennie Hays, Norvel Johnson, Elaine Lowe, Robert Malloy, Angela Pinson, Bradley Pinson, Tina Portell, Peter Thebeau, Brenda Thebeau, Jodie Jurntine, David Veach, Chris Ward.

1982: Greg Daugherty, Barbara Lawson, Angie Malloy, Doug Mercille, Raymond Osia, Dawn Politte, Dion Politte, Brian Politte, Sheila Santhuff, Tammy Thebeau, Robert Ward.

1983: Kelly Bourbon, Cindy Boyer, Kevin Boyer, Michelle Coleman, Lonnie Goff, Jeff Govero, Marty Govero, Michelle Hanson, Dale Hays, Melisa Kite, Sharon Lawson, Robert Mercille, Richard Pashea, Laura Pinson, Angie Politte, Stephanie Politte, Denise Portell, Stacey Sansoucie.

1984: Michael Bequette, Michelle Boyer, Paul Coleman, Kimberly Coleman, Dawn Daugherty, David Finley, Barry Hanger, Melissa Johnston, Doug Karsch, Connie Politte, Madonna Portell, Stevie Riddle, Alva Veach.

1985: Leann Adams, Darryl Bequette, Wendy Bone, Randall Boyer, Tony Bridges, Anthony Coleman, Lisa Coleman, Theresa Coleman, Cindy Govero, Marquette Govero, Julian Hanson, Brian Johnston, Keith Kamper, Elliot Kite, James Missey, John Pace, Connie Pashea, Maria Pashia, Khara Paul, Nanette Politte, Sandy Smith, Jason Turntine, Billy Veach, Dianna Veach.

1986: Shannon Benson, Ryan Bone, Daniel Bourbon, Donald Boyer, Melissa Coleman, Billy DeClue, Deanna Gaylord, Tyler Juliette, Frances Miley, Karrie Miller, Laura Osia, Jennifer Paul, Cindy Politte, Aaron Portell, Jamie Sansoucie, Michaela Skiles, Brian Skiles, Melissa Smith, James Tallo, Linda Thebeau, Robert Veach.

1987: Daniel Bone, Carol Bourisaw, Angie Boyer, Renee Boyer, Scott Boyer, JoAnn Bridges, Pamela Coleman, Ronald Haarmann, Scott McGlothlin, Geromy Miller, Lisa Politte, Victoria Pratt, Lindel Sampson.

1988: Brian Belt, Chris Boyer, Jeffrey Boyer, John Coleman, Ralph Degonia, Vicki Govero, Renee Haarmann, Leslie Hopkins, Jay Miller, Dale Missey, Jeffrey Pinson, Patrick Politte, Krista Portell, Carissa Sansoucie.

1989: Scott Blair, Melissa Boyer, Michael Boyer, Dennis Brown, Karrie Brown, Eric Coleman, Kenneth Coleman, Nichole Johnston, Bradley Juliette, Lori Karsch, Jennifer Kincaid, Cindy Missey, Chris Pashia, Mark Pashia, Brian Pinson, Brian Politte, Curtis Politte, James Politte, Karen Politte, Cathy Pratt, Erin Pratt, Jennifer Pratt, Chad Skiles, Nichola Skiles, Donald Smith.

Schools, Lay Teachers, and Graduates

1990: Jerry Adams, Chad Aubuchon, Joseph Bone, Benjamin Boyer, Bradley Coleman, Lori Hopkins, Kelly Juliette, Michelle McGlothlin, Tammy Malloy, Andrew Politte, Stanley Portell, William Portell, Matthew Riddle, Cory Sansoucie.

1991: Christopher Belt, Jason Bone, Laura Bone, Brandon Boyer, Nathan Boyer, Ronnie Boyer, Christopher Govero, Connie Mercille, Paul Pratt, Ryan Sampson, Kerie Sansoucie, Robert Veach.

1992: Kyle Bone, Jennifer Campbell, Laura Missey, Marcella Malloy, Jason O'Hanlon, Erica Paul, Clinton Portell, Anna Sansoucie, Donald Trokey.

1993: Joshua Aubushon, Angela Coleman, Scotti Jo Courtaway, Jennifer Juliette, Matthew Miley, Jennifer O'Hanlon, Joshua Portell, Jason Thebeau, Keith Thebeau.

1994: Keith Bone, Larissa Boyer, Nathan Boyer, Sophia Coleman, Timothy Johnston, Kevin Mercille, Audra Missey, Nicholas Portell, Matheaw Pratt, Erin Weissgerber.

1995: Susan Boyer, Rachel Coleman, Abbey Jarvis, Benjamin Juliette, Melissa Miley, Rachel Missey, Jodi O'Hanlon, Shannon Politte, Danna Pratt.

1996: Amy Boyer, Emmylu Boyer, Billie Joan Coleman, Zachary Coleman, Rachael Craig, Zachary Politte, Jason Portell, Angela Pratt.

1997: Melissa Boyer, Sara Boyer.

1998: Adam Politte, Anna Politte, Jodi Pratt.

1999: April Duing-Davis, Sarah Nickelson, Amanda Pashia, Austin Pratt, Paul Ricketts.

2000: Andrea Coleman, Samantha Lawson, Nichole Peppers, Jeremy O'Hanlon.

2001: Marcus Bequette, Cassandra Coleman, Krista Litton, Corey Murphy, Jordan Politte, Sarah Pratt, Edie Sansoucie.

2002: Megan Cain, Joseph Daugherty, Kyla Nichols, Jacyln Pratt.

2003: No Graduates.

2004: Derek Bremerkamp, Andrew Daugherty, Katherine Nickelson, Joe Thebeau.

2005: Molly Bollefer, Daniel Boyer, William Boyer, Sarah Duing-Davis, Justin Murphy, Jerry Portell.

2006: Mariah Boyer, Brody Elsey, Christopher Henson, Christopher Koch, Krista Murphy, Katie Thurmond.

2007: Dustin Bremerkamp, Dustin Coleman, Tanner Hanger, Maggie McCauley, Megan Thebeau, Andrew Thurmond, Andrea Wills, Michael Yates.

2008: Anthony Bowles, Hannah Brown, Nick Shadrick, Emily Short, Jeffrey Yates.

2009: Adam Boyer, Blake Gibson, Conner Missey, Collin Osia, Jacob Reese, Marisa Thurmond.

2010: Kenneth Duing-Davis, Abby Koch, Emily Sanders, Ethan Short.

2011: No Graduates.

2012: No Graduates.

2013: Lucien Bequette, Kyle Osia.

2014: No Graduates.

2015: No Graduates.

2016: Mackenzie Coleman-Portell, Benjamin DeWaal, Nathaniel Hahn.

2017: Matthew Aubushon, Isaac DeWaal, Hanna Villmer.

2018: Maxmillian Politte.

2019: Dane Dickinson.

2020: No Graduates.

2021: Lanae Dickinson, Valarie Govero, Emily Hahn, Clara Villmer.

HIGH SCHOOL GRADUATES OF ST. JOACHIM SCHOOL

1955: Gregory Bequette, Paul Bourisaw, Mary Loreda Boyer, Benedict Hanson, Mary Ann Roderique.

1956: John Francis Bequette, Cyrilla Boyer, Kathleen Boyer, Mary Theresa Charboneau, Thomas Davis, Anthony DeClue, Robert Hall, Cecil James Heifner, David Jackson, Charles Glennon Pashia, Ruth Politte, Shelba Portell, William Portell, Patricia Robart, Mary Elizabeth Sansoucie, Sherman Schmidt, Irene Natalie Villmer, Dorothy Elaine Wall, Norman Wilson, Jane Catherine Young.

1957: Ruth Frances Battreal, William Edward Bone, Charles Leroy Boyer, Cyrilla Ann Boyer, Veronica Marie Boyer, Cabrini F. Coleman, Eugene Kenneth DeClue, Doris JoAnn DeGonia, Joan M. Politte, Janet M. Rundell, Patricia Ann Thebeau.

1958: Mary B. Bequette, Kenneth F. Bone, Virginia Ann Bone, Verna Marie Bourisaw, Vincent Boyer, William J. Coleman, Marilyn Sue DeGonia, Philip Govero, Charles Lee Hill, Kenneth Miller, Lawrence J. Pashia, Paul T. Pashia, Judith E. Politte, Margaret Mary Politte, Mary Angela Pratt, Sylvester Pratt, Nancy Ann Sansoucie, Joyce C. Wall.

1959: Ann Mildred Battreal, Richard Bequette, Joseph Clifford Boyer, Charlotte Ann Coleman, Mary Joan Coleman, Carol Mae DeGonia, Rose Ann Lalumondiere, Thomas G. Paul, Patricia Ann Politte, Jerry P. Pratt, Raymond D. Roderique,

Rose Mary Lee Sansoucie, Janet Dolores Schmidt, Agnes Ann Thebeau, George Ann Wall, Mary Magdalen Young.

1960: Elaine Mary Aubuchon, Doris Elizabeth Battreal, Stephen F. Bequette, Robert Francis Bone, Thomas Lynn Bone, Roy David Boyer, Loretta Ann Charboneau, Carol Mae Coleman, Rita Ann Coleman, Ruth Ann Coleman, Suzanne Daugherty, Dorothy DeClue, Geraldine Faye DeGonia, James Dale Fenwick, Virginia Ann Hill, Laverne Annie Oshea, Catherine Marie Pashia, Cecelia Lorraine Pashia, Francis G. Pashia, Thaddeus J. Pashia, Joseph M. Politte, Virginia Ann Portell, Ronald J. Pratt, Ruth Ann Rundell, Joyce Ann Sampson, Ronald Joseph Thebeau.

1961: Margaret C. Aubuchon, Donald J. Bequette, Donna M. Boyer, Geraldine M. Boyer, Shirley Ann Boyer, Billie Sue Courtois, Richard Charles Govero, Doris Ann Osia, Rose Ann Pinson, Thomas W. Politte, Donald Lynn Portell, Grace Marie Thebeau, Charles W. Veach, Vernon Paul Warden.

1962: Margaret M. Bone, Nancy Carol Bone, John F. Boyer, Nancy Ann Boyer, Sheila Ann Boyer, Mary Etta Coleman, Mary Ursula Coleman, Michael Wayne DeClue, William Francis Heifner, Ruth Ann Kincaid, David E. Lalumondiere, Kenneth E. Merseal, John B. Pashia, Catherine Y. Politte, Mary Lee Politte, Margaret Ann Pratt, Saundra Ann Pratt, Patricia Sansoucie, Raymond Stroup, Rebecca J. Wall.

1963: Mary Eileen Aubuchon, Homer J. Battreal, Patricia Battreal, Jackie Battreal, Donald Boyer, Janet Carol Boyer, Magdalen Boyer, Carley Coleman, Judy Coleman, Ronald George Hill, Alice Ann Juliette, John Knoblauch, Helen Lalumondiere, Terry Mercille, Brenda Joyce Missey, James Dale Robart, Louise E. Ruby, Mary Agnes Thebeau, Margaret Wall.

1964: Carolyn Marie Battreal, Janet Bone, Joyce Boyer, John Z. Coleman, Richard J. Coleman, Paulette Courtway, Rose Marie Daugherty, Michael Nephew, Mary Catherine Pashia, Gloria Politte, Elizabeth Portell, Charles Robert, Mary Jane Yates, John Gregory Young.

1965: Philip Bequette, Paul Boyer, Judy Boyer, Raymond Coleman, Richard Courtois, Nancy DeGonia, Elaine Goff, Carol Kincaid, Harold Koch, Rebecca Martin, Everette Merseal, Carolyn Ann Pashea, Charlene Pashia, Mary Lou Price, Dennis Ross, John Stephen Sansoucie, Richard Sansoucie, Rose Marie Singer, Michael Thebeau, Lenore Ann Thebeau, Richard Lynn Villmer.

1966: Catherine Battreal, Linda Blair, Jesse J. Bone, Judy Bone, Charlotte Boyer, Diane Coleman, Raymona Coleman, Joyce Daugherty, Lawrence Govero, John Kite, Joseph Lalumondiere, Charles Martin, Marsha Fae Missey, Elizabeth Jane Pashia, James Politte, Stephen Politte, Catherine Portell, Ronald Pratt, Gloria Price, Louis Price, Mary Ann Price, John Robart, Michael Robart, Lindell Sampson, Bernard Thebeau, Carolyn Thebeau, Sharon Thebeau, Paul Thebeau.

1967: Brenda Aubuchon, Glenda Aubuchon, Philip Aubuchon, William Joseph Battreal, Mary Bequette, James Bone, Edward Boyer, Richard Boyer, Robert Joseph Boyer, Carol Coleman, Joseph Daugherty, James Johnston, Richard Juliette, Glennon Kincaid, Barbara Koch, Patricia Missey, Roger D. Missey Donald Pinson, Wayne Pratt, Rose Sharon Schmidt, James Thebeau.

1968: JoAnn Boner, Marilyn Bone, Mark G. Boyer, John E. Boyer, Michael Coleman, Jerry DeClue, Robert Finch, Wayne Koch, James Pashia, Mary Ann Politte, Geraldine Sampson, Kenneth Sansoucie, Catherine Singer, George Wall.

1969: Judy Battreal, Mark Bequette, Barbara Bone, Geraldine Boyer, Paul Gregory Boyer, Sheila Boyer, Regina Daugherty, LaDonna Kite, Phyllis Koch, Roger Missey, Vernon Portell, Dale Pratt, Louis Pratt, Brenda Pruitt, Paul Recar, Arthur Rolens, Robert Ross, Wilma Ross, Dorothy Ruby, Norma Jean Thebeau, Sharon Wall.

1970: Gail Aubuchon, Martin Chris Bequette, Paul Bone, Kenneth Ray Bourisaw, Dennis Boyer, Joseph Boyer, Richard Boyer, Shirley Boyer, Rita Ann Brown, Elaine Coleman, Philip Coleman, William Edward Crippen, Catherine Daugherty, Theresa Daugherty, Jerry Juliette, David Kite, Nancy Koch, James Merx, Donna Pashia, Janice Pashia, Beverly Jean Politte, Joan Marie Politte, William Portell, Freda Pratt, George Larry Sansoucie, Beverly Thebeau.

1971: Donna Battreal, Larry Battreal, Rita Benedick, Gary Bone, Mary Elaine Bone, Rita Elena Bone, Jennifer Boyer, Rita Carol Boyer, Debbie Brown, Patricia Coleman, Margaret Daugherty, Beverly Kincaid, Theresa Pashia, Monica Politte, Elizabeth Portell, Debbie Pratt, Karen Robart, Anthony Ward.

What followers are the final high school classes of 1972, the year the high school was closed.

1972 Freshmen: Brenda Battreal, Patricia Bone, David Boyer, William Boyer, Barry Brown, Anthony Coleman, Michael Coleman, Timothy Daugherty, Sheila DeClue, Kenny Gaylord, Sharon Govero, Diane Johnston, Elaine Juliette, Stephen Kite, Denise Koch, Roger McMahan, Bernard Maness, Ann Pratt, Marie Price, Harry Robart, William Sampson, Sandra Thebeau.

1972 Sophomores: Paulette Bequette, Phyllis Bone, Ronald Bone, Donald Boyer, Ronald Boyer, Karen Caldwell, Andrew Daugherty, Bernadette Daugherty, Robert Johnston, Debra Kite, Jackie McMahan, Judith Pashia, Philip Pashia, Dennis Politte, Randolph Portell, Barbara Price, Deana Price, Laura Rolens, Julie Thebeau, Lawrence Ward.

1972 Juniors: Willy Boyer, Marcia Brown, David Coleman, Stephanie Coleman, Connie Daugherty, Deborah Flynn, Frances Juliette, Janice Maness, Marsha

Maness, Barbara McMahan, Joseph Politte, Kathy Politte, Rosemary Robart, Joseph Pashia, Mary Jo Pashia.

1972 Seniors: Dennis Aubuchon, Linda Barton, David Bone, Daniel Boyer, Diane Boyer, Mary Jo Boyer, Mary Jane Coleman, Gary Koch, Michael Maness, James McMahon, James Pashia, Carl Joseph Portell, Terry Price, Barbara Robart, Marilyn Thebeau.

OTHER SCHOOL-RELATED ENDEAVORS

While the following are not directly related to St. Joachim School, each does have an educational component. Because of that, they are presented here.

Children's Liturgy of the Word

Realizing that there was a need to catechize young children while their parents were attending Sunday Mass, the Children's Liturgy of the Word was begun during the pastorship of Father Theodore Pieper (1987–2013). A number of dedicated volunteers have led children to love, know, and serve God during the 10 a.m. Sunday Mass, as well as increasing the number of adults attending Mass. Catechists include Lorri Hedrick, Andy and Donna Laramore, Angie Mitchell, Sarah Mosier, Debbie Phipps, and Robin Portell.

Parish School of Religion

For many years, St. Joachim Parish has had a Confraternity of Christian Doctrine (CCD) or Parish School of Religion (PSR) program for students who did not attend St. Joachim School. In 1950, it was taught by the Rural Parish Workers of Christ the King and then by volunteer trained parishioners. According to the PSR mission statement, with the help of Jesus Christ, the master teacher, and the power of the Holy Spirit, St. Joachim PSR assists and supports parents in faith formation, spiritual development, and the transformation of their children into full, active, and participating Catholics and missionary disciples. At the time of the writing of this book, enrollment consists of fifty students with a volunteer staff of catechists, who have a passion for passing on their faith.

Catechists participate in online classes provided by the Archdiocese of St. Louis and paid for by the parish through Dayton University. In addition to an approved curriculum, students are formed through Sunday Scripture texts, prayer, sacraments, Masses, Devotions, and a monthly Children's Mass. Parents are required to attend the Masses, Devotions, Sacraments, and Parent Meetings. In addition, parents of children preparing for the sacraments of Baptism, Penance, Eucharist, and Confirmation are required to attend a meeting focused on catechesis on the sacrament. PSR teachers receive a stipend for their work.

PSR Coordinators include Cyrilla Boyer (14 years), Sister Mary Ann Seeker (late 1980s), Deacon Steve Politte (1993–1998), Loretta Kelly (1998–2001), and Joyce Politte (2001–2021).

PSR Teachers, in alphabetical order, include: Alma Allen, Cyrilla Boyer, Kelly Brueggen, Sarah Gibson, Janet Gravatt, Lorri Hedrick, Susan Heuer, Stephen Johnson, Mary Maxwell, Angie Mitchell, Debbie Phipps, Regina Pinson, Joyce Politte, Steve Politte, Rose Ann (Coleman) Richards, Emily Sanders, Vickie Thurmond.

Rite of Christian Initiation of Adults

Both St. Joachim Parish, Old Mines, and St. Joseph Parish, Tiff, began the Rite of Christian Initiation of Adults (RCIA) under the direction of associate pastor Father Robert Rosebrough (1977–1984). He began with a team of volunteer catechists. While members have changed over the years, the team of catechists continues to be responsible for evangelization, catechesis, and formation of adults in Catholicism. Both parishes bring their adults to the St. Louis Cathedral every year for the Rite of Election. On average, between three and five catechumens and candidates are in preparation for Baptism or full initiation each year.

Joyce Politte has served as the RCIA Coordinator for twenty-five years. Team catechists over the years, in alphabetical order, have included: Father Anthony Dattilo, Catherine Dickey, Stephen Johnson, Linda Lewis, Monica Pashia, David Politte, Joyce Politte, Steve Politte, and Mary Ann Pratt.

For Further Reading: *History of St. Joachim Parish: 1822–1972; 1723–1973*, Mark G. Boyer.

12

Convents and Nuns

As early as March 1833, Father John Boullier had tried to get Sisters of Loretto from Ste. Genevieve to come to St. Joachim Parish in Old Mines. Bishop Joseph Rosati had given Boullier permission to bring Sisters of Loretto to Old Mines to begin a school for girls. As far as anyone knows, the nuns never made it to Old Mines. And that seems to be the way it was for almost the next one hundred years.

CONVENT/SCHOOL

At some time before August 1924, Father John P. Daly, pastor of St. Joachim Parish (1916–1928), entered into negotiations with the Sisters of Charity of the Incarnate Word who had a motherhouse in Normandy, Missouri, a city in St. Louis County. The Incarnate Word Sisters agreed to send a few nuns to Old Mines if Daly had a convent and school built to house them. Thus, before August 1924, Daly had a two-story white clapboard structure erected with a kitchen, dining room, community room, several dormitory living quarters, two bathrooms, and the superior's office and bedroom on the top floor and three classrooms, a chapel, and a parlor on the bottom floor. The structure was blessed on September 10, 1924. The building measured forty feet by fifty feet. Because much of the labor to build the convent/school was donated—the basement was hand dug and all concrete was hand mixed—it cost $4,400.

Missouri Highway 21, that runs along the eastern boundary of the church property, had been built and paved in 1922; before that a dirt or gravel road existed in its place. Daly went to DeSoto to meet the sisters at the train station in his Model T Ford. Accompanying him was a delegation of parishioners in automobiles. As they got closer to Old Mines, after meeting the sisters and loading their luggage, parishioners in cars and on foot were led by the men of the St. Joseph Society in full regalia and mounted on horses and brought to the convent/school. After serving dinner to the sisters, nuns and parishioners went to the church to recite the rosary and celebrate Benediction of the Blessed Sacrament. Then, the sisters moved into their new home.

In the lists of Incarnate Word Sisters that follow, a name in parentheses, like (Mary), indicates a former name or a part of a name that was changed by the nun sometime before she died. A name in brackets, like [Sister Mary Grace] indicates a discrepancy in various lists obtained from the Archives of the Sisters of Charity of the Incarnate Word in San Antonio, Texas, and parish sources. Some of the discrepancy is caused by the repeated use of the first name Mary or in most cases merely M. On some lists only "Sister Mary" is identified, but it could be Sister Mary of the Assumption, Sister Mary Grace, or Sister Mary of Nazareth, etc. After cross-referencing three lists, any discrepancy—meaning a name is not found on two of the three lists—is placed in brackets. Furthermore, even though nuns did not begin to use their last or family names until the late 1960s, family names are provided for all sisters when they are known in order to remove some of the ambiguity of simply listing Sister Mary.

The first four nuns for the 1924–1925 school year were Mother (M.) Ernest O'Leary, and Sisters Catherine (of Bologna) Ryan, (Mary) Gonzaga Bourke, and Mary Anne Fogarty. In those days, when making their vows, nuns got a name that was different from their baptismal name, and last names were never used. One of the group of sisters was named the mother of the group, indicating that she was the superior of the small community and, usually, the principal of the school. Each of the four nuns had a classroom: there were three on the first floor of the convent/school, and there was one in the Lamarque School.

When signing their names, the sisters wrote C.C.V.I. after their name. Those four letters form the abbreviation in Latin for *Congregatio Caritatis a Verbo Incarnato*, translated into English as: Congregation of Charity of the Incarnate Word.

With the presence of the first four Incarnate Word nuns, students were taught how to greet an Incarnate Word Sister. Upon seeing the nun, the student said: Praised be the Incarnate Word! Good morning (afternoon, or evening), sister. And the nun replied: Forever. Amen. Good morning (afternoon, or evening), John (Mary, etc.).

The Incarnate Word Motherhouse continued to send four or five nuns for the next ten years after 1924. When an extra sister was sent to Old Mines, her primary duty was to clean, cook, and take care of laundry for the other nuns, while also teaching a single class or doing something else for the small community. In later years, Thelma A. Boyer and Mary Ann Crippen, to name two housekeepers, would take over the duties of cleaning, cooking, and laundry.

Thus, the 1925–1926 and the 1926–1927 school year brought Mother (M.) Ernest O'Leary and Sisters Catherine (of Bologna) Ryan, Mary Anne Fogarty, and (M.) Cecile Watters to Old Mines. For the 1927–1928 school year, Mother (M.) Ita Gorry, and Sisters Mary Anne Fogarty, (M.) Cecil Watters, and Mary Joseph Maher conducted classes in Old Mines. The 1928–1929 and the 1929–1930 school year saw sisters come to Old Mines who had not been there before: Mother (M.) Evangelista O'Brien, and

Sisters (M.) Gregory Rihm, (M.) Norbert Allen, and Agnes Dominic Skehan. For the 1929–1930 school year, Sister Peter Joseph Kaullen also came.

For the 1930–1931 school year, five Incarnate Word Sisters arrived in Old Mines: Mother Mary of the Cross O'Brien and Sisters Mary Faith Byrne, (M.) Bonifacia Hoffmann, (M.) Albeus Hartigan, and Asteria Mees. Five nuns came for the 1931–1932 school year: Mother (M.) Alphonsus Delaney and Sisters (M.) Albeus Hartigan, (M.) Asteria Mees, John Michael Dallmeier, and Therese Allen. Another five came for the 1932–1933 school year: Mother (M.) Alphonsus Delaney and Sisters (M.) Albeus Hartigan, (M.) Canisia Brzezinka, (M.) Adelaide Wiedemann, and (M.) Patricia O'Connor. And five more for the 1933–1934 school year: Mother (M.) Alphonsus Delaney and Sisters (M.) Albeus Hartigan, (M.) Patricia O'Connor, (M.) Asteria Mees, and (M.) Tarcisius Hardey.

Beginning in the 1934–1935 school year, five or seven Incarnate Word nuns came to Old Mines: Mother (M.) Alphonsus Delaney and Sisters (M.) Brendan O'Connell, (M.) Asteria Mees, (M.) Patricia O'Connor, Mary Gonzaga Hogan, [Josephine Brosnan, and Joseph Marie Savage]. The 1935–1936 list of sisters includes: Mother (M.) Alphonsus Delaney and Sisters Catherine (of Bologna) Ryan, Joseph Marie Savage, Dolores Marie Murphy, (M. Huberta) Eleutheria Roach, [(M.) Asteria Mees, and Charles William Dircks]. The 1936–1937 school year was staffed by Mother (M.) Alphonsus Delaney and Sisters Patricia O'Connor, Joseph Marie Savage, (M. Huberta) Eleutheria Roach, (M.) Asteria Mees, [and Thomas Aquinas Lynch]; that was the last of six years under Mother Alphonsus Delaney as superior.

Only four or six nuns came for the 1937–1938 school year: Mother Rose Teresa McCann and Sisters (M.) Asteria Mees, (Lawrence Justinian) Kathleen Kelliher, Joseph Marie Savage, [(M. Huberta) Eleutheria Roach, and Hilary Brennan]. However, four or five sisters returned for the 1938–1939 school year: Mother Rose Theresa McCann and Sisters (M.) Asteria Mees, Joseph Marie Savage, (M.) Attracta Allen, [Redempta, and (M.) Gregory Rihm]. But only five sisters staffed the 1939–1940 school year: Mother Rose Teresa McCann and Sisters Charles William Dirckx, (M.) Ambrosia Hartigan, (M.) Nazaria Jablonski, and Joseph Marie Savage.

For the 1940–1941 school year, Mother (M.) Bonifacia Hoffmann and Sisters Charles William Dirckx, (M.) Nazaria Jablonski, (M.) Raymond Borgmeyer, (M.) Regina La Voie, and [Anna Theresa Bignell] came to Old Mines. Five or Seven Incarnate Word nuns came for the 1941–1942 school year: Mother (M.) Bonificia Hoffman, (M.) Nazaria Jablonski, (M.) Magdalen Connelly, (M.) (Alpheus) Christine Murphy, Stephen Marie Glennon, [Celine O'Leary, and Mary of Good Counsel]. Five or six Incarnate Word nuns were sent to Old Mines for the 1942–1943 school year: Mother (M.) Bonificia Hoffmann and Sisters (M.) Henrietta Oliver, Patricius Conlan, (M.) Nazaria Jablonski, (M.) (Alpheus) Christine Murphy, [and Kenneth O'Connor]. Five were sent for the 1943–1944 school year: Mother Francis Gabriel Roderick and Sisters

(M.) Henrietta Oliver, (M.) Nazaria Jablonski, (M.) Fidelis Corcoran, and (M.) Odelia Keaveney.

Five or six sisters returned for the 1944–1945 school year: Mother Francis Gabriel Roderick and Sisters (M.) Henrietta Oliver, (M.) Ruperta Meyer, Mary Julia Delaney, Joseph Alphonsus Dedericks, [and Joseph Marie]. With the growing number of students in St. Joachim School, more Incarnate Word sisters came to Old Mines for the 1945–1946 school year: Mother Francis Gabriel Roderick and Sisters (M.) Henrietta Oliver, (M.) Flaviana Bussmann, Francis Regis Hoffmeyer, Joseph Alphonsus Dedericks, [Concordia, Evangelista, and Evangeline]. For the 1946–1947 school year, the following nuns came to Old Mines: Mother Francis Gabriel Roderick and Sisters Ramunda Van der Laak, Francis Regis Hoffmeyer, (M.) Theresa Allen, Joseph Alphonsus Dedericks, [(M.) Michael, (M. Fintan) Margaret McCormack, and (Evangelista) Rosemary Politte].

More Incarnate Word sisters were sent to Old Mines for the 1947–1948 school year: Mother Francis Gabriel Roderick and Sisters Theresa Allen, Mary Michael Kennelly, (M.) Coleman Calame, (Peter Celestine) Elizabeth King, Anne Catherine Shaw, [Michael, Simplicia, and Thomas Aquinas Lynch]. Mother Francis Gabriel Roderick returned for the sixth and last time for the 1948–1949 school year with Sisters Mary Gonzaga Hogan, Thomas Aquinas Lynch, Ann Bernard Allred, (Mary Francis) Patricia O'Donnell, and (M.) Veronica Wojcik. For the next three school years—1949–1950, 1950–1951, and 1951–1952—Mother (Lawrence Justinian) Kathleen Kelliher served as superior of the Sisters for the 1949–1950 school year: Mary of the Sacred Heart Masek, (M.) Henrietta Oliver, Mary Michael Kennelly, (M.) Lioba Barczewski, Bridget Anne Spellman, and Mary (Baptist) Catherine Tiffin; for 1950–1951: Sisters Henrietta Oliver, (M.) Lioba Barczewski, Jeanne de Matel Hogan, Bridget Anne Spellman, Mary (Baptist) Catherine Tiffin, and (M. Damien) Patricia Daley; and for 1951–1952: Sisters Flaviana Bussman, Bridget Ann Spellman, (M. Alpheus) Christine Murphy, Jeanne de Matel Hogan, (M.) Henrietta Oliver, Rodriguez Gilmore, and (Mary of the Assumption) Frances Vetter.

With the opening of the first floor of the new school in 1950 and the second floor with a high school in 1954 (see chapter 11 on Schools, Lay Teachers, and Graduates), more Incarnate Word nuns came from their Normandy Motherhouse to teach the many students who had enrolled in St. Joachim Elementary and High School. As the number of sisters coming to Old Mines grew, the need for more living space also grew. In the early 1950's a two-story porch was built all across the front of the convent/school. The lower level served as open porch; the upper level was enclosed to provide another bedroom for the sisters on the second floor of the convent/school.

For the 1952–1953 school year, there came Mother Mary Brenden O'Connell with Sisters Jeanne de Matel Hogan, Henrietta Oliver, [(M.) Huberta], (M.) Flaviana Bussmann, James Joseph McBeath, (M.) Odilia Keaveney, (Peter Celestine) Elizabeth King, Mary Grace Pomora, (M.) Leonilla Battenton, [Cresentia, (M. Huberta)

Eleutheria Roach], and Mary Imelda Moriarty. For the 1953–1954 school year, there came Mother (M.) Ambrosia Hartigan with Sisters Jeanne de Matel Hogan, (M.) Flaviana Bussmann, Julietta DeClue, Mary Imelda Moriarty, Mary Grace Pomora, (M. David) Nadine Luebbert, and (M. Leonard) Martha Ellen Maguire. Mother (M.) Ambrosia Hartigan returned as superior for the 1954–1955 school year with Sisters James Joseph McBeath, (M.) Julietta DeClue, (M.) Flaviana Bussmann, (M. Domitius) Teresa Ann O'Connor, (Mary Jude) Geraldine (Geri) Eveler, (M. Leonard) Martha Ellen Maguire, and (M. Gwendolyn) Joan Grothoff. For the 1955–1956 school year, Mother (M.) Ambrosia Hartigan brought Sisters James Joseph McBeath, (M. Domitius) Teresa Ann O'Connor, (M. Gwendolyn) Joan Grothoff, Francis Gabriel Roderick, Mary (of Nazareth) Catherine Buckley, George Marie Workman, and (Francis Clare) Mary Louise Mueller to Old Mines.

Mother (M.) Brendan O'Connell came to Old Mines as superior for the 1956–1957 school year with Sisters Bridget Anne Spellman, (M. Liboria) Ellen Broderick, (M.) Laura Magowan, Francis Gabriel Roderick, James Joseph McBeath, Mary (of Nazareth) Catherine Buckley, and (Francis Clare) Mary Louise Mueller. Mother (M.) Brendan O'Connell returned for the 1957–1958 school year with Sisters Francis Gabriel Roderick, James Joseph McBeath, (M.) Reparata Donnelly, Mary (of Nazareth) Catherine Buckley, (M. Liboria) Ellen Broderick, (M. Finton) Margaret McCormick, (M.) Laura Magowan, and (Francis Clare) Mary Louise Mueller.

There is a lot of discrepancy in lists for the 1958–1959 school year. The nuns accompanying Mother (M.) Brendan O'Connell for the 1958–1959 school year included Sisters Mary Josephine Marischen, (M.) Martina Gruna, James Joseph McBeath, (M.) Reparata Donnelly, (M.) Angela Hipwell, (M. Finton) Margaret McCormick, (M. Alfred) Eileen Friel, (M. Ligouri) Mary Ann Kendrick, (M. Wendelinus) Patricia Ann Kelley, Mary Achille Bugnitz, and (M.) Mabel Kelly. **OR** the nuns accompanying Mother (M.) Ambrosia Hartigan for the 1958–1959 school year included Sisters Mary Achille Bugnitz, Mary Grace Pomora, (M. Leonard) Martha Ellen Maguire, (M. Finton) Margaret McCormick, (M. Wendelinus) Patricia Ann Kelley, (M. Liguori) Mary Ann Kendrick, (M.) Mabel Kelley, (M.) Rosita Hyland, and (M. Rose) Carol Bird.

The discrepancy in the lists for the 1958–1959 school year is mirrored in the 1959–1960 school year. However, there are fewer inconsistencies as can be seen below. Mother (M.) Ambrosia Hartigan served as superior and principal, and she was accompanied by Sisters Mary Achille Bugnitz, Mary Grace Pomora, (M. Leonard) Martha Ellen Maguire, (M. Fintan) Margaret McCormick, (M.) Rosita Hyland, (M. Ligouri) Mary Ann Kendrick, (M. Wendelinus) Patricia Ann Kelley, (M.) Mabel Kelly [(M.) Cronin Smullen, and (Rose) Carol Bird].

Mother M. Ambrosia Hartigan returned for the 1960–1961 school year with the following Sisters who staffed St. Joachim School: (Mary Leonard) Martha Ellen Maguire, (M.) Josetta Eveler, Mary Achille Bugnitz, (M.) Cronan Smullen, (M.) Rodriguez Gilmore, (M.) Rosita Hyland, and (M. Liguori) Mary Ann Kendrick. For the

1961–1962 school year, Mother (M.) Ambrosia Hartigan was accompanied by Sisters Cronan Smullen, Mary Achille Bugnitz, (Mary Wilbert) Rita Boul, Mary Grace Pomora, Mary Bernadette Burke, [Mary Vera], (M.) Josetta Eveler, (M.) Rosita Hyland, [(M. Alpheus] Christine Murphy], and Mary (Baptist) Catherine Tiffin.

Under the leadership of Mother (M.) Ambrosia Hartigan, Sisters Louis Katherine Schuler, Cronan Smullen, (M. Domitius) Teresa Ann O'Connor, (Mary Patrick) Alice Marie Leahy, (M.) Josetta Eveler, (M.) Rosita Hyland, and (M.) Yvonne DeGonia staffed the schools for the 1962–1963 school year. For the 1963–1964 school year, Mother (M.) Ambrosia Hartigan was principal and superior with Sisters M. Achille Bugnitz, (M. Evangelista) Rosemary Politte, (Mary Patrick) Alice Marie Leahy, Mary Grace Pomora, (M.) Loraine Bourisaw, (M.) Rosita Hyland, and (M. Evarista) Anne Therese Glynn staffing the schools. Classes for the 1964–1965 school year were taught by Mother (M.) Ambrosia Hartigan, who was superior and principal, and Sisters (M. Evangelista) Rosemary Politte, [Mary (Immaculate) of the Assumption] Frances Vetter, (M. Felicitas) Norene Morrissey, Mary Grace Pomora, (M. Louis) Katherine Schuler, (M. Ignatius) Helen Ann Collier, (M. Evarista) Anne Therese Glynn, and Carolyn Higgins.

Classes for the 1965–1966 school year were taught by Mother Stephen Marie and Sisters (Mary of the Assumption) Frances Vetter, Thomas Aquinas Lynch, (Ita Patrice) Patricia Kennedy, (Albina) Mary Sheila Foley, (Damien) Patricia Daly, (Mary Leonard) Martha Ellen Maguire, (Joseph Sarto) Margaret Lucille Bonnot, (M.) Rosita Hyland, and Novice Marie Rene Bequette. For the next three school years—1966–1967, 1967–1968, 1968–1969—Sister (M.) Rosita Hyland served as superior; the title mother was dropped. Thus, the 1966–1967 school year was staffed by Sisters Rosita Hyland, (Ita Patrice) Patricia Kennedy, (M. Damien) Patricia Daly, (M. Gwendolyn) Joan Grothoff, Thomas Aquinas Lynch, (M.) Lucille Bonnot, James Joseph McBeath, Alice Marie Holden, and (M.) Margaret Snyder. The 1967–1968 school year was staffed by Sisters Rosita Hyland, James Joseph McBeath, (Rose) Carol Bird, (Catherine Marie) Evelyn Lambert, (M. Gwendolyn) Joan Grothoff, (M. Damien) Patricia Daly, Thomas Aquinas Lynch, Mary Martha Maguire, Julietta DeClue, and Mary Conception O'Kelly.

Once the new school was opened in 1950 and the high school in 1954, the classrooms on the first floor of the convent/school were used for various purposes throughout the years including as classrooms. The classroom opposite the chapel on the first floor became the typing room for the high school at one time. The two classrooms to the rear were used for the clinic before the Daughters of Charity moved it to the George Wallace building. One classroom was used as a workroom for the sisters before that. Once the chapel was moved to the new convent, opened in 1967, that room was used as an art studio.

The basement of the convent/school held a coal furnace for heating, a laundry room, and storage for the trunks in which the nuns packed their belongings. During the Great Depression (August 1929–March 1933) and at times during the recession

(1937–1938) that followed it, the nuns served lunch in the basement to the students attending school. Before the new school was built, the basement of the convent/school was used to prepare meals for the annual parish July 4 Picnic, which later became the Fall Festival. Before the second floor of the new school was added, the basement of the convent/school was also used to teach home economics. The old convent/school was razed by Donald Portell during the pastorship of Father Richard Suren (1970–1975); it was still standing in 1973, but was gone when Suren was reassigned in 1975. By then, it had become a serious fire hazard, was in need of lots of repair, and was no longer used.

NEW CONVENT

In the latter part of the 1960s, during the pastorate of Father Bernard A. Suellentrop, it became obvious that a new convent was needed for the Incarnate Word nuns to live in. Not only was the convent/school, built before 1924, too small for the number of sisters coming to teach in St. Joachim School, but its facilities were out of date. Groundbreaking was done in 1966 to the east of the convent/school and north of the church, while a capital campaign was in progress and a building committee had been formed. A two-story brick structure was built by Arthur Boyer and Howard Aubuchon Contractors of Old Mines at the cost of thirty-five thousand dollars. On December 10, 1967, the New Convent was dedicated. After a thanksgiving service was held in St. Joachim Church during which Suellentrop recounted the history of the Incarnate Word Sisters in Old Mines since 1924, Associate Pastor Father Anthony J. Jansen celebrated Benediction. Then, the Incarnate Word Sisters, Suellentrop, and Jansen with Monsignor Vincent Naes, a former pastor of the parish invited to bless the new building, led a procession of others in attendance from the church to the front of the New Convent for the dedication services during a very light rain.

As parishioners stood on the sidewalk in front of the New Convent, standing on the second-floor balcony over the front door of the new building, Naes blessed it. He presented Scripture texts, a lesson for the Feast of St. Joachim, and reflections on his time as pastor of the parish, while Suellentrop served as master of ceremonies, assisted by Jansen. After the blessing, Naes presented Sister Rosita a cross to be used in the chapel. Following the presentation, all present were invited to tour the new building and share refreshments in the new dining room.

On the first floor, the New Convent featured a parlor, an office, a chapel, a community room, a utility/laundry room, a back door, stairs leading to the second floor, a kitchen, and a dining room with a sliding glass door opening onto a patio. On the second floor, there were ten private bedrooms, each with a sink, closet, and single bed. There was also a community bathroom and showers and a door opening to the balcony.

For the 1968–1969 school year, ten Incarnate Word Sisters taught classes in St. Joachim Elementary School and High School: Sisters Rosita Hyland (superior and principal), Mary Conception O'Kelly, (Declan) Sara Brennan, Mary Martha Maguire, Ambrosia Hartigan, Julietta DeClue, Thomas Aquinas Lynch, (Damien) Patricia Daly, Jeanne de Matel Hogan, and (Catherine) Evelyn Lambert. However, for the 1969–1970 school year, only nine sisters came to Old Mines: Sisters Laura Magowan (superior), Kathleen O'Driscoll, Thomas Aquinas Lynch, Mary Martha Maguire, Ambrosia Hartigan, Jeanne de Matel Hogan, (Catherine) Evelyn Lambert, Loraine Bourisaw, and James Joseph McBeath.

Nine nuns staffed the schools for the 1970–1971 school year: Sisters Laura Magowan (superior), Kathleen O'Driscoll, Thomas Aquinas Lynch, Mary Martha Maguire, Ambrosia Hartigan, Mary Achille Bugnitz, Loraine Bourisaw, Jeanne de Matel Hogan, and Margaret Anne Bosch. The Incarnate Word Sisters had only seven nuns to send to Old Mines for the 1971–1972 school year: Sisters Odilia Keaveney (superior and principal who died in February 1972), Laura Magowan (superior and principal after Keaveney's death), Mary Ellen O'Connor, Ambrosia Hartigan, Mary Agnes O'Leary, Mary Achille Bugnitz, and Patricia O'Connor.

With the closing of the high school in 1972, due to decreased enrollment, decreased available Incarnate Word faculty, the cost of lay faculty, and other extenuating circumstances, Father Richard H. Suren, pastor of St. Joachim Parish, officially closed St. Joachim High School with the graduation of the high school class of 1972. This action further decreased the number of nuns coming to St. Joachim Elementary School. Also at this time, the superior of the small community of Incarnate Word Sisters was not necessarily the principal of the school. Before the high school was closed, the superior, the principal of the high school, and the principal of the elementary school were two or three different sisters.

Thus, the 1972–1973 school year brought only five nuns to St. Joachim Elementary School: Sisters Mary Ellen O'Connor (superior and principal), Sophia Oviedo, Mary Achille Bugnitz, Ritamary Corso, and Mary Agnes O'Leary. Sister Mary Ellen O'Connor returned as superior and principal for the 1973–1974 school with Sisters Celine O'Leary, Mary Achille Bugnitz, Ritamary Corso, and Mary Agnes O'Leary. Likewise, Mary Ellen O'Connor returned as superior and principal for the 1974–1975 school year with Sisters Celine O'Leary, Mary Achille Bugnitz, Ritamary Corso, (Peter Celestine) Elizabeth King, Rose Therese McCann, Mary Agnes O'Leary, and Mary Rose Winkle.

Mary Ellen O'Connor served as principal and superior for the last time for the 1975–1976 school year with Sisters Mary Agnes O'Leary, (Frances Marie) Patricia Freeman, (Peter Celestine) Elizabeth King, Rose Therese McCann, and Celine O'Leary. For the 1976–1977 school year, Sister (Frances Marie) Patricia Freeman served as superior and principal with Sisters Mary Ellen O'Connor, Rose Therese McCann, Margaret McElligott, and Mary Agnes O'Leary. The staff of Incarnate Word nuns for the 1977–1978 school year included Sisters Anne Maloney (principal and superior), Rose Therese McCann, Margaret McElligott, Mary Agnes O'Leary, and (Evangelista) Rosemary Politte. The last time that five Incarnate Word Sisters were assigned to St. Joachim School, Old Mines, was the 1978–1979 school year. They were Sisters Margaret McElligott, Mary Magdalen Cross, Mary Agnes O'Leary, (Evangelista) Rosemary Politte, and Sheila Teresa Ruane.

Beginning with the 1979–1980 school year, the Incarnate Word Sisters had only four nuns to send to Old Mines, and two of them—Sisters Loraine Bourisaw and (Evangelista) Rosemary Politte—were native Old Miners. Accompanying them were Sisters Mary Agnes O'Leary and Mary Magdalen Cross. The same four nuns returned for the 1980–1981 school year. By the 1981–1982 school year, there were only three Sisters: Mary Magdalen Cross, (Frances) Anne Moloney, and (Evangelista) Rosemary Politte. While there were only two nuns for the 1982–1983 school year—Sisters (Frances) Anne Moloney and (Evangelists) Rosemary Politte—four came for the 1983–1984 school year: Sisters Julietta DeClue, (Fintan) Margaret McCormack, (Frances) Ann Moloney, and (Evangelista) Rosemary Politte. Sisters (Fintan) Margaret McCormack, (Frances) Anne Moloney, and (Evangelista) Rosemary Politte came for the 1984–1985 school year.

For the next three school years—1985–1986, 1986–1987, and 1987–1988—the same two Incarnate Word Sisters came to teach in St. Joachim Elementary School. They were Sisters (Fintan) Margaret McCormack and (Frances) Anne Maloney. For the 1988–1989 school year, five nuns came to teach in the school: Sisters (Mary Wilbert) Rita Boul, Yvonne DeGonia, (Fintan) Margaret McCormack, (Frances) Anne Moloney, and Mary Ann Seeker. And for the 1989–1990 school year, four nuns came: Sisters Loraine Bourisaw, Yvonne DeGonia, (Frances) Anne Moloney, and Mary Ann Seeker. Three sisters came for the 1990–1991 school year: Sisters Loraine Bourisaw, Yvonne DeGonia, and Mary Ann Seeker. Only two nuns were present for the 1991–1992 school year, and both of them were native Old Miners: Sisters Loraine Bourisaw and Yvonne DeGonia. For the 1992–1993, 1993–1994, and 1994–1995 school years, only Sister Yvonne DeGonia taught in St. Joachim School. She was the last Incarnate Word Sister to be sent to Old Mines since 1924. As of 1990, the first lay principal, Linda Markway, had been hired for the school. When Markway left in 1995, Joyce (Daugherty) Politte was hired until she retired in 2013. See chapter 11 on Schools, Lay Techers, and Graduates for more about principals and lay teachers.

At the time of the writing of this book, only five of the Incarnate Word Sisters who taught in St. Joachim Schools remain alive: They are, in alphabetical order: Sisters (M. Rose) Carol Bird, (M.) Josetta Eveler, (M. Alfred) Eileen Friel, (M.) Rosita Hyland, and (M.) Laura Magowan.

NEW CONVENT OTHER USES, INCARNATE WORD CENTER

With the last of the Incarnate Word Sisters gone from Old Mines, the new convent underwent many different uses. In the early 1990s, the bottom floor was updated and brought up to code to be used for a daycare; it was moved to the school in the mid-1990s. In the mid-1990s, it was the home of the Head Start Program and Community 2000, which sponsored a clinic with a visiting Washington University psychologist and other health care workers. The chapel was used for eucharistic adoration. After that came to an end, it was turned into two apartments for rent, while daily Mass was held in a chapel made on the top floor by Father Theodore Pieper. Then, it sat empty for a few years.

After Pieper retired and Father Anthony Dattilo became pastor in 2013, every parish building was in disarray and needed immediate attention and repair. More on the repair of buildings can be found in chapter 7 on St. Joachim Catholic Church and Pastors. After he held a parish meeting in the school cafeteria to discuss building repair issues, Dattilo also sought input from the attendees as to what to do with the most neglected building: the new convent. Some people thought it should be razed, but it still had good structure. What it needed was for someone to have a vision of how to use it. Carmen Litton, school principal from 2013 to 2019, suggested that her husband, Johnnie Litton, and school custodian, Ray Thebeau, be permitted to remodel and update it to be used as a community room with kitchen, restrooms, and two offices on the bottom floor at little cost to the parish.

Litton and Thebeau designed plans, removed walls, and proceeded to renovate the kitchen and replace kitchen appliances. Ronald Boyer, with some assistance from his son, Adam, rewired all the electrical outlets, and installed lights and smoke detectors. Ed Coleman and Jim Skiles served as the carpenters. When the renovation work on the first floor was finished, the parish had a large meeting room, which could be used for meals cooked in the kitchen, a waiting room for clients for the rural clinic (see chapter 17 on Health Care for more information), an exam room, a medical supplies room, and an office for the coordinator of the clinic. The building was named the Incarnate Word Center.

With the success of turning the first floor of the new convent into the Incarnate Word Center, and with the urging of Mary Ann (Politte) Pratt, full-time parish secretary, and Vicki (Pratt) Thurmond, part-time parish secretary, in 2017, Johnnie Litton, Ray Thebeau, and John Veach began renovating the top floor for use as parish offices, a religious education office, a break room, file (records) rooms, and a multi-purpose small meeting room, which can be used by those participating in the Rite of Christian Initiation of Adults (RCIA) and children's liturgy. While the labor and supplies were donated, Litton and Thebeau removed all the carpet and plumbing (each of the ten rooms in the convent had its own sink and there was a community restroom), and installed sheetrock where needed; the new floor was paid by the parish. After a ramp was built from the sidewalk to the door over the balcony of the first-floor entrance, the parish offices were moved out of the rectory to the Incarnate Word Center in 2017. A new roof was donated by JV Contracting (Tyler Juliette), which also put new roofs on the church, the school, and the garage. Ronald Boyer and Adam Boyer electrically rewired the offices, installed fiber optics, and did other electrical repair work.

When walking into the Incarnate Word Center today, a person would not recognize what had once been the new convent. The repurposing of the building saved it from destruction. Not only does it meet the need for parish office space and file room space, but it meets the need for the rural clinic and provides a large meeting area, which can easily also be used for small parish dinners cooked in the renovated kitchen. Parishioners can rent and use the meeting area and kitchen for birthday parties, anniversary celebrations, or reunion dinners. Naming it the Incarnate Word Center pays homage to the over 135 Sisters of Charity of the Incarnate Word who taught in St. Joachim Schools from 1924 to 1995. In 2024, St. Joachim Parish will mark the one hundredth anniversary of the Incarnate Word Sisters coming to Old Mines.

For Further Reading: *History of St. Joachim Parish: 1822–1972; 1723–1973*, Mark G. Boyer, *Historical Program-Pageant Book: 250th Anniversary, Old Mines, Missouri*, Natalie Villmer.

13

Parish Societies and Committees

PARISH SOCIETIES

1800s

Rosary and Scapular

Father John Brands pastor of St. Joachim Parish, 1836–1939, formed the Holy Rosary Society on September 8, 1836. The Rosary Society lasted until 1840. Father John Cotter, pastor from 1841 to 1851, began a Society of the Scapular in 1842; it lasted until 1844. Members and the date of their induction are as follows: Terese Robert, Mary Marsh (May 5, 1842), Margaret Murphy, Mary Biet (May 15, 1842), Mary Boildire (June 21, 1842), (no first name) Daugherty, Mary Anne Daugherty (August 15, 1842), Marie Boyer (August 22, 1842), Madame Detchemendy (August 26, 1842), Margaret ([possibly a slave of] Mad. Lamarque) (August 28, 1842), Ann (no second name) Ditts (September 18, 1842), Mary Olympia Boyer (November 1, 1842), Ellen Kincaid (December 8, 1843), and Adele Becquette (January 21, 1844). Cotter may have also begun a Society of the Blue Scapular with Stephanie Bouchard, Sophie Bouchard, and Mary Coleman listed as members.

Father James Fox (1852–1868) began the Society of the Scapular of Mount Carmel on July 16, 1856, but there are no extant records of who joined the society. He began the Confraternity of the Red Scapular in 1866 with Sarah Johnston listed as joining on January 14, 1866, and Clementine Boyer on January 21, 1866. There was a Sacred Heart Union in 1881, during the pastorate of Father P.F. Cooney (December 3–11, 1881) and 1892, during the pastorate of Father E.T. Gallaher (1887–1893) with over one hundred active members.

Parish Societies and Committees

St. Joseph Society

In 1883, there was a revival of the Rosary Society during the pastorate of Father Nazareno Orfei (Nazaveno Ovfei) (1883–1885). Orfei began the Society of St. Joseph for male parishioners on August 5, 1883, and the Society of the Children of Mary for young ladies at the same time. On July 29, 1883, he spoke to the St. Joachim parishioners about the subject. On the following Sunday, August 5, 1883, he urged the men to form the St. Joseph Society. Seventeen men joined the Society of St. Joseph that same day, but one week later, August 12, 1883, the number had arisen to twenty-six; after Orfei explained the purpose of the society, membership went up to sixty.

Because Coadjutor Bishop of the Archdiocese of St. Louis Patrick J. Ryan was coming to St. Joachim Parish to administer the sacrament of Confirmation to about four hundred people, the members of the St. Joseph Society went as a body to meet him at the rail station in DeSoto and accompany him to the rectory. The next day, August 19, 1883, all sixty of the members of the St. Joseph Society processed from the sacristy through the iron gate of the church yard (removed sometime in the latter half of the twentieth century) and to the rectory, where they formed an honor guard four men deep. After Ryan blessed them, they processed to the church and formed an honor guard for him there. On August 20, 1883, they wanted to accompany Ryan to the DeSoto train station in a similar way as they had met him, but he declined.

The first meeting of the society was held on September 2, 1883. Officers were elected: W.F. Bolduc was chosen president; F.L. Bequette, vice-president; P.S. Coleman, secretary; John Z. Coleman, treasurer; Acan Thebeau, master of ceremonies; James Dean, first assistant; John Ross, second assistant; Charles Sullivan, third assistant; James Ackerson, bearer of the banner; and Loomis Boyer, bearer of the U.S. flag. At that first meeting, the names of the original seventeen members were recorded: P.S. Coleman, John Z. Coleman, Acan Thebeau, Francis L. Bequette, Zenon Portell, Willis Bolduc, Francis Thebeau, Edward Boyer, J.C. Coleman, Joseph Bequette, William Sullivan, Adrian Coleman, James Dean, Alexis Coleman, John E. Coleman, Francis S. Bourisaw, and Paschal Duclos. The Society of St. Joseph continued in existence until 1955. Members paid dues, which were used to help defray doctors' bills, funeral expenses, and to have Masses said for members.

Typical monthly meetings began with a call to order and prayer by the president. Roll call followed, and fees were collected. New business could be brought to the floor. Then, the meeting was closed by the president with a prayer.

J.Z. Coleman served as secretary of the St. Joseph Society from 1888 to 1915. Officers elected on August 22, 1915, included: Melvin Politte, president; Clarence Pashia, secretary; Paschal DeClue, treasurer; and Joseph Reando, grand marshal. Clarence W. Pashia served as secretary from August 1915 to October 1930. Elections on October 5, 1930, declared Wilfred Pashia, president; Charles Pashia, vice-president; Andrew Coleman, secretary; and James Bourisaw, treasurer. The last elections were held in

1954: John Agnew, president; Edgar Bequette, vice-president and secretary; and Charles Coleman, treasurer. There are no records after 1955.

At some point between 1916 and 1922, the archbishop of St. Louis, John J. Glennon, came to Old Mines in a horse-drawn wagon to celebrate the Sacrament of Confirmation. Behind the wagons marched the members of the St. Joseph Society in full regalia, while on either side of the dirt road stood St. Joachim Church parishioners.

In August 1924, during the pastorate of Father John P. Daly (1916–1928), the members of the St. Joseph Society met Daly and the first Incarnate Word Sisters coming to Old Mines. Daly and a delegation of parishioners in cars—Highway 21 was paved in 1922—had met the sisters at the train station in DeSoto. As the procession got closer to St. Joachim Church, they were met by the men of the St. Joseph Society; they were dressed in full regalia, mounted on horses, and they led the nuns to the new convent/school Daly had just constructed.

The Children of Mary, also begun August 5, 1883, was a society for young ladies. Their duties were to care for the altar, purchase vestments with their dues, and sponsor bingo games, May-Crowning ceremonies, and Sunday-a-Month Communion Services. In 1884, a society for the married women was begun; it was called the Sacred Heart of Mary Sodality.

1900s

St. Ann(e) Sodality

In 1922, Daly began the St. Ann(e) Sodality—spelled Ann and Anne—for the women of the parish. The first prefect of the St. Ann Sodality was Mrs. Mickey Politte, and the first secretary was Susan Pashia. The members of the St. Ann Sodality—named to honor the wife of St. Joachim and the mother of the Blessed Virgin Mary—cared for the altar, cleaned the church, bought church supplies, sponsored bingo games, and fostered other activities.

In 1929, the prefect was Mrs. Daly Politte, the secretary was Mrs. William Pashia, and the director was Father John F. Walsh. In 1971, the president was Ann Pashia, the vice-president was Regina Brown, the secretary was Charlene Campbell, and the treasurer was Margaret Kite.

In the last ten years of the previous millennium, the members of the St. Ann Sodality took a break, but it was restarted in 2000 with a few members: Rose Ann Coleman, Rita Kamper, Brenda Skiles, and Joan Karsch. By 2002, the sodality had twenty members, whose first project for the new millennium was to raise funds to replace the carillon, commonly referred to as the bells. The sodality was assisted by Ronald Boyer, who provided the information about carillons and explained that the one that had been in operation since 1964 was no longer repairable. By 2003, the St. Ann Sodality raised funds to replace the carillon with a new electronic semiconductor

Parish Societies and Committees

digital system costing $8,100. All new cable from the sacristy to the four new speakers in the bell tower was installed. The system was dedicated on July 26, 2003, the Memorial of Sts. Joachim and Ann. At some point before 2019, an electrical power surge destroyed that system. However, the St. Ann Sodality went to work again and raised $9,000 to purchase the Verdin Sonata Digital Carillon, a carillon computer system. The amplifier was replaced along with the main processor and the speakers in the bell tower. That system continues to ring bells at the time of the writing of this book.

Since the sodality was restarted, the members have fulfilled their mission—to help the parish in any way needed—in a variety of ways. In 2005, the members assumed responsibility for the cost and preparation of the dinner accompanying the school auction fundraiser. In 2006, the sodality began Mardi Gras, paying all the costs associated with this annual event on the Tuesday before Ash Wednesday. Every July 26, the Memorial of Sts. Joachim and Ann, members provide a meal for the parish. In August, members sponsor a shower to fill a wooden cedar chest with household items raffled at the annual Fall Festival. In November, the sodality holds its annual Christmas Bazaar in the Knights of Columbus Hall. They prepare eight to ten baskets to raffle. All the proceeds go to the school or the church. They also donate five hundred dollars to the St. Vincent de Paul Society and another five hundred dollars to the Rural Parish Workers to assist with their Christmas baskets. They provide another five hundred dollars for the Fall Festival raffle.

The St. Ann Sodality paid for the supplies used by Benedict Thebeau to build the rock platform holding the display sign for the church on Highway 21 and make repairs to statues in the cemetery. In 2009, the members purchased a new Nativity set for the church. Among other accomplishments since 2000, the members of the St. Ann Sodality have paid for the cost of new carpet in the church sanctuary, new cabinets in the rectory kitchen, blinds for school windows, Weekly Readers for the school, a wall map for the school, carpet in the school office, flooring for the Knights of Columbus kitchen, a flag pole in cemetery 2, and tables for the Incarnate Word Center meeting area, along with funds to help pay the cost of renovation of the convent. They help with funeral dinners at the Knights of Columbus Hall, and they pay the cost for flowers used in the church.

The members raise funds by sponsoring a Basket Bingo in April and a Turkey Bingo the Sunday before Thanksgiving, each with a soup and sandwich meal. Annually, they sponsor a quilt raffle, a cup auction, and two bake sales.

St. Ann Sodality members, according to Rita Kamper, current president, are focused on sponsoring events that bring people together. That is the way they assist the parish in any way needed. Other officers include Jane Lawson, vice-president; Jackie O'Hanlon, secretary; and Opal Johnston, treasurer. In 2022, the St. Ann Sodality celebrates its one hundredth anniversary.

St. Vincent de Paul Society

The St. Joachim Conference of the St. Vincent de Paul Society was established on January 15, 1950, during the pastorate of Father Edward A. Bruemmer (1948–1954). The mission of the society is to furnish food, clothing, rent, and help with electric bills for those in need. The original officers for the society were: Pat DeClue, president; Clarence Pashia, vice-president; Wilfred Pashia, secretary; and P.C. Daly, treasurer. In 1971, the officers were: Edwin W. Politte, president; Edward N. Coleman, vice-president; and Morris Daly, treasurer. Officers at the time of the writing of this book, 2021, are: Fran(cis) Pashia, president; Natalie Villmer, vice-president; Laura Buskin, secretary; and Mary Norbut, treasurer. Pashia has served as president for the past fifteen years. Those who form a consultative board are Joseph and Geraldine Politte, Carolyn (Thebeau) Politte, Monsignor James Hanson, and Kenny DeGonia.

The St. Vincent de Paul Society helps those in need, serving on an average of seventy-five people every month. After someone in the parish seeks help, two of the members of the society go to his or her home to investigate and determine what needs to be done. Sometimes a family needs help with paying the rent; if the members investigating determine that the society should help with the rent, then they notify the other members of the society through phone calls, and rent is paid directly to the person to whom the rent is due. The same procedure follows for those seeking help with the payment of electric bills, help with broken water lines, and other home repairs. The Society of St. Vincent de Paul pays only a portion of a bill; those being helped are given three months to make and implement a plan to keep the same issue from arising again.

Monthly meetings are held in the Incarnate Word Center in order to take care of the business of the society. Funding for its work comes through monthly collection envelopes (five to six hundred dollars a month) given to parishioners and returned with individual donations. Immaculata Parish in St. Louis sends a donation every two months (seven hundred dollars). And the society accepts other donations from individuals or groups, such as the proceeds from a walk-a-thon.

Members of the St. Vincent de Paul Society consider their work very rewarding. They have joy when seeing electricity turned on, repairs made, or another problem solved. Their joy is enhanced by the verbal and written thank-you notes they receive from those they have assisted in their time of need.

Prayer Blanket Ministry

Monica (Politte) Pratt began the Prayer Blanket Ministry in 2008, after the death of her son in December 2007. After experiencing the consolation that a prayer blanket can give, Pratt spoke to Susan Davis about the possibility of making prayer blankets for others. Rachel (Miller) Politte and Georgia (Miller) Veach also got involved in making the blankets, which are more accurately described as small quilts.

The original idea for the ministry was to give them away to the sick, the grieving, those suffering in any way, those in nursing homes, and those who might request one—men, women, and children. The women making the blankets pray as they are preparing them. Then, periodically, the pastor of the parish blesses them. Around seventy-five to eighty blankets are given away each year. Since the ministry was begun, an estimated five hundred or more prayer blankets have been distributed.

The small tacked quilts, called prayer blankets, are currently made by Politte and Veach and stored in the Incarnate Word Center. The fabric out of which the blankets are made is donated by parishioners and others. The batting is donated by the St. Ann Sodality. The prayer blanket ministry attempts to wrap in prayer those who receive a blanket, to let them know that no matter what is occurring in their lives that they are not alone; they are being remembered in prayer by others. If they receive comfort from the blanket, then the ladies involved in this ministry consider what they set out to do accomplished.

Youth Group

St. Joachim Parish has had a long record of youth organizations, diverse and lasting for a few years. Most youth organizations preserved no records. In 1972, the Youth Club had president Joseph Politte, vice-president Julie Thebeau, secretary Diane Johnston, and treasurer Paulette Bequette. The club sponsored skating trips, hay rides, dances, and other social events throughout the year for parish youth.

In 1974, another youth group was born out of a Catholic Youth retreat organized by Natalie Villmer, a Rural Parish Worker, and Father James Moll, then associate pastor of St. Joachim Parish. The retreat was held at Camp Mater Dei in Hillsboro, Missouri. It set the foundation for an active and involved youth organization.

The retreat was followed by a weekly prayer meeting in the home of Joey and Barb Bone. The prayer meetings consisted of Bible readings, spontaneous prayer, sharing reflections, and singing. As the youth group grew from five to twenty in membership, additional married couples in the Old Mines area agreed to host members in their homes for prayer and fellowship.

Youth-centered retreats continued to be held approximately twice a year at many different places in the area, including Camp Penuel at Lake Killarney in Arcadia Valley, a Boy Scout ranch in Valles Mines, and Rock Haven in House Springs. Days of recollection and other activities were also held in conjunction with other youth organizations in the surrounding area. Many members of the youth group attended and became involved with archdiocesan-offered retreat experiences, such as Teenagers Encounter Christ (TEC) and SEARCH weekends. Youth retreats continued through

1988, when the retreats were being led and directed by those who had attended the retreats in the 1970s.

A social aspect grew out of the prayer groups. Activities such as Teen Nights, Dances in St. Michael House, skating parties, and service-oriented projects emerged. A newsletter was established and circulated within Washington and Jefferson counties to keep area youth informed. Originally named *Teen Post* from 1975 to 1976, the name was changed to *Miner Reflections* in 1977. As circulation grew, expenses increased. Sponsorships were acquired from many local businesses at the cost of $5 in exchange for advertising in the newsletter. In order to solicit the support of local businesses, the letter stated: "Advertise through the youth of today, for the youth of today are the people of tomorrow." At its highest level of circulation, *Miner Reflections* average five hundred mailed copies. It was organized, written, and edited by members of the youth group. In its five- to seven-page edition, it covered past and upcoming events, activities, student recognitions from high schools, word games, sponsorships, and other items of interest to the youth of the area. The last issue of *Miner Reflections* was mailed in 1979.

The youth group hosted a Dinner and Variety Show once a year from 1976 through 1980 in the St. Joachim School auditorium. Ready or Not was presented in 1976, Ready or Not: Part 2 in 1977, Ready or Not: Part 3 in 1978, Ding-a-Ling Diner in 1978, Those Were the Days in 1979, and The Time Tunnel in 1980. The dinners accompanying the shows were prepared and served by members of the youth group with supervision of parishioners with expertise in food preparation. The shows were planned, written, and directed by members of the youth group. Each show consisted of singing, dancing, comedy skits, and storytelling. For an entry fee, members of the community ate dinner and saw the show; the proceeds were used to support the newsletter, future group activities, and make a donation to St. Joachim Parish.

After the first Ready or Not performance, Catherine Politte praised the youth for being sincere and dedicated, spreading the love of God and neighbor. She reminded the audience that the youth were the future of Old Mines. She thanked Joey and Barb Bone and Dick and Gloria Sansoucie, Bill and Laney Portell, Tom and Edna Paul, and Natalie Villmer for supporting the youth. Many of the youth who were involved with the early prayer groups and activities continue to serve in active leadership roles in St. Joachim Parish today. Emily Sanders is in the process of reconstituting the youth group on the second Sunday of the month in St. Michael House. On the third Sunday of the month, youth attend Sunday Mass together. A group of them attend the pro-life march in Washington, D.C., every year and the Steubenville Youth Conference in Springfield, Missouri. Under youth leaders Barb Bequette and Anita Hahn, bake sales are organized to fund these activities.

Parish Societies and Committees

PARISH COMMITTEES

Parish Council

The goal of the parish council is to minister to the members of the parish and help them grow in faith and service to one another and the wider community of faith. Reuben Lawson is the current president; Carolyn Politte, vice-president; Mary Catherine Norbut and Dianne Riddle, members. Meetings are held on the first Tuesday of each month in the Incarnate Word Center under the guidance of the pastor. Members are currently working on celebrating the 200th anniversary of the parish and the parish fall festival. Last year, members worked on guidelines for the cemeteries.

Finance Council

The finance council assists with setting parish financial goals and allocating money for various parish projects. Robert Hahn and John Veach serve as officers, and Mark Veach and Sue Jackson are members. The council meets three times a year in the Incarnate Word Center.

Maintenance Committee

The maintenance committee is responsible for maintaining all the buildings and grounds of the parish, including the cemeteries. John Veach serves as president, and members include Mark Veach, Steve Sansoucie, Bill Portell, and Kenny Thebeau. Grass cutters are Benny Merseal, Gary Boyer, Lynn Boyer, Johnny Litton, Kenny Degonia (and friend Harold), and Mike Coleman. The members of the committee meet twice a year in the Incarnate Word Center. The members of the maintenance committee save the parish thousands of dollars a year.

Fall Festival Committee

Chris and Tracy Farrell serve as co-presidents of the annual fall festival committee. Almost every other family in the parish works during the September fall festival. It is a major event for the parish, bringing parishioners together for a common goal. Funds from the festival help support the parish and the school. Originally, it was begun when Father Janson (1961–1969) was the associate pastor to enhance funding for the school to provide sports equipment and other extras needed in the school.

Liturgy Committee

The non-meeting liturgy committee consists of Joyce Politte, president, and all musicians. Organists and piano players are Joyce Politte and Tiny Courtaway. Guitar players and singers include Jeff Boyer, Donald Boyer, Joey Politte, Ronald Boyer, and Adam Boyer. Also, Vickie Johnston plays the piano, David Pratt plays the harmonica, Kenny Portell plays the guitar, David Politte, Krista Coleman, and Kenny Portell cantor. Natalie Villmer serves as cantor and leads the funeral choir.

Church Decorating Committee

Ronald Boyer leads the church decorating committee. He is assisted by Adam Boyer, Vicky Johnston, Rita Kamper, and Kathy Coleman. They decorate the church throughout the year, but especially at Easter and Christmas.

Other Activities

Natalie Villmer leads a Bible Study group; for many years, this was held in parishioners' homes, but now it takes lace in the Incarnate Word Center. Life Chain, a prayerful witness to the pro-life message, takes place the second Sunday of October on the Knights of Columbus campus in conjunction with the Cadet Baptist Church; parishioners stand along Highway 21 and 47 displaying pro-life posters and witnessing to all who drive by. On the Octave of Easter, Divine Mercy Sunday, the parish sponsors a holy hour. The rosary is recited daily before the 8 a.m. Mass. And Perpetual Help Devotions are held on Tuesday.

For Further Reading: *History of St. Joachim Parish: 1822–1972; 1723–1973*, Mark G. Boyer.

14

Rural Parish Workers of Christ the King

BEGINNINGS

LaDonna Hermann, a graduate of Maryville College, and Alice Widmer, a graduate of Webster College, founded the Rural Parish Workers of Christ the King in Cottleville, Missouri, in 1942. They had heard Monsignor Leo J. Steck of the Catholic Rural Life Conference of St. Louis speak on the lack of priests in the rural areas of the Archdiocese of St. Louis and had given birth to the idea of offering themselves to a program of spiritual and corporal works of mercy to spread the message of the gospel through religious instruction and service to the neighbor while working closely with the pastor of a parish.

Father William Pezold had a home available on parish grounds—two 12' x 12' rooms and one 6' x 6' bathroom—for those two lay women, who, after kneeling before the altar in St. Joseph Church, Cottleville, dedicated themselves by vow to God and service to his people. Their work centered on the spiritual and temporal welfare of their neighbor as demonstrated in conducting vacation Bible schools, teaching skills—knitting, crocheting, quilting, and sewing—making adoption connections, preparing first communicants, giving instructions to converts, opening a library of spiritual books, providing counseling, and other such works. During their seven-year stay in Cottleville, Hermann and Widmer, a convert to Catholicism, helped found Immaculate Heart of Mary Parish in New Mele, Missouri.

In 1949, the Archbishop of St. Louis, Joseph E. Ritter, asked them to move the center of their operation to Old Mines. The pastor of St. Joachim Parish, Father Edward Bruemmer, welcomed them on January 12, 1949. He and his associate pastor, Father Bernard Suellentrop, were not able to meet all the needs of the people living in Old Mines. In 1949, World War II had ended only four years before, leaving 65 percent or more of the men of the parish unemployed. Furthermore, many parishioners had not attended church in years, and many of their children had not been baptized or confirmed. Children attending public schools needed religious instruction. While a new school was in the planning process, contact needed to be made with families who lived in small communities off the main road. Bruemmer told the two women, "Come as soon as you can."

ESTABLISHMENT IN FERTILE

They did. The next week Suellentrop took them on a tour of the parish, indicating where they might be able to rent rooms and property they might want to consider purchasing. Several similar trips followed that one. Finally, in February 1949, they arrived in the village of Fertile—located eight miles from St. Joachim Church—and spotted an old brick two-story house built by Zachary Filmore Higginbotham, who married Ann Hawkins in 1874. They had two children: Preston, who married May, and Stella, who married Howard Brown, in a double wedding ceremony in the brick home, whose ownership passed to Preston and May Higginbotham and, after them, to John Thompson in DeSoto, Missouri; the house had been built in 1876 with bricks made from clay on the property.

Hermann and Widmer purchased the house and thirteen acres of land for six thousand dollars on July 30, 1949. Then, they borrowed twenty-five thousand dollars to repair, restore, and enlarge the house and construct a building for a garage and carpenter shop. On September 2, 1949, they took their possessions to Fertile and moved into the home that would become the Rural Parish Workers of Christ the King Center. While the repair and renovation work were going on, Hermann and Widmer lived in the kitchen; they slept on cots and cooked their meals over an outdoor brick fire pit until all the scrubbing and cleaning and remodeling were completed. To supplement their diet, they made frequent trips to the Golden Pheasant Restaurant one mile south of the Center on Highway 21.

At a previous time in history, Fertile was a thriving mining town with a town hall, a blacksmith shop, a tavern, a large mercantile store with a post office, a lead furnace, and numerous barns. The store, named the Z.F. Higginbotham and Sons Mercantile Store, featuring General Lead and Barytes Ore, Farming, and Livestock, operated until 1930. The blacksmith shop had a Woodman Hall over it which was used for Woodman Organization Meetings, Methodist Sunday School, dances, pie suppers, and other community gatherings. Around forty log or frame houses were the homes of families working the strip mines for lead, which came to an end around 1900, and tiff, which continued into the 1920s, and working the farm. Some of the houses lined the road, while others were scattered in the hills.

The Higginbothams farmed hundreds of acres, which they owned, even including what is now Washington State Park. From their vast land holdings, they produced maple syrup from their maple grove. Also, they had vegetable gardens, hay fields, and grew tobacco, corn, sugar cane, wheat, oats, and hay. The lead and tiff they mined by hand were hauled in wagons to Blackwell, four miles away, for shipment on the railroad.

Robert Ray Higginbotham, son of Preston and May, had learned to fly at Curtiss Aeronautical School in St. Louis, where he became friends with Charles Lindberg and Harlan A. Gurney. On some weekends Higginbotham, Lindberg, and Gurney would travel on motorcycles from St. Louis to Fertile to enjoy home cooking and the area. In the 1920s, they invested in a small plane, which they flew to Fertile, landing in a pasture. On many afternoons they entertained villagers with rides and stories of their flying exploits. During St. Joachim Church festivals, they often did stunt flying over the parish grounds. On one occasion Lindberg made a forced landing in a field north of the old Baptist Church in Old Mines. Later, Lindberg would make what has become known as his solo flight across the Atlantic Ocean.

While the days were filled with work on the Higginbotham house and the building of the cinder block house/garage into which Hermann and Widmer moved, the two Rural Parish Workers got acquainted with St. Joachim parishioners. Some members of the parish came to help with the work. Suellentrop enlisted some young men to build a trough to carry the plaster they removed from the rooms located upstairs in the Center. Others removed weeds, while still others pulled out the old water pump to prepare for a new one. A new driveway was installed. The St. Ann Sodality ladies sponsored a food shower, and a family loaned a heating stove with the required coal.

When not working on the Center, Hermann and Widmer brought people to church, gave religious instructions to over ninety children, enrolled students in the parish school that was under construction, and prepared over thirty youngsters for First Communion. They also transported a number of people to area hospitals. As Christmas 1949 drew near, St. Joachim Church Carolers arrived with Suellentrop to grace the Parish Workers with Christmas Carols.

On January 9, 1950, Hermann and Widmer moved from the cinder block house/garage into the completely renovated Center. They day before they had accepted a shipment of food from an anonymous donor; on moving day they began to distribute it to those who came to their front door in need. After establishing a food pantry, they received countless donations to be distributed to the unemployed. The Daughters of Charity of St. Vincent de Paul sent clothing to be distributed to those in need.

While ladies of the parish assisted at the monthly well-baby clinic in the basement of St. Joachim Rectory, the Workers transported pregnant women and children to see doctors and nurses staffing the clinic. At other times they took women and children to the pre-natal clinic in Potosi. Meanwhile, in June and July of 1950, volunteers from Incarnate Word Academy in St. Louis established a library of 525 books in the Center. Also, during the summer, the Workers began to host summer-session volunteers; among the first of those were Christine Bequette and Doris Ann Bequette, who would later join the Rural Parish Workers. At an open house Hermann and Widmer welcomed one thousand people to the Center.

In subsequent years, the ministry of the Rural Parish Workers expanded. Their contacts with parishioners brought an increase in enrollment in St. Joachim School. Those attending public high school were given religious instructions, while vacation Bible schools of religion, crafts, games, and songs were attended by over one hundred children, who were taught by Workers and volunteers. Home visitation, sacramental preparation, medical and legal care assistance, and work for social justice and education continued.

In 1954, the Rural Parish Workers were instrumental in getting the Old Mines Diagnostic and Referral Clinic established with Doctors L.G. Cassidy and George Carroll of DePaul Hospital in St. Louis. The clinic was located on the first floor of the convent/school, where the doctors saw patients bi-monthly. After a number of years, the clinic was moved to the former George Wallace Store, owned by the Daughters of Charity, located on Old Mines Creek. It operated there until it closed in the 1960s; in 1972 it burned and was razed. See chapter 17 on Health Care for more information on clinics.

NEW MEMBERS

After three years of volunteer service and training, Mary Margaret Siegfried made vows as a Rural Parish Worker on the Feast of Christ the King in 1955. Now, there were three Rural Parish Workers. Siegfried remained a RPW for the rest of her life, teaching in the PSR in the parishes of St. Joachim, Old Mines, and St. Stephen, Richwoods, and the Vacation Bible School held in both parishes. Besides serving as the RPWCK treasurer, Siegfried, who came from Holy Rosary Parish, St. Louis, sorted and filled orders for clothing for families, worked in rummage sales, and did clerical work with the Old Mines Diagnostic Clinic and the St. Michael Dispensary in addition to participation in general activities. She died in April 2005.

Also, in 1955, Irene Natalie Villmer of St. Joachim Parish, made first promises as a RPW. In 1957, Villmer made her final vows as a Rural Parish Worker of Christ the King on the Feast of Christ the King. Now, there were four RPWs. Villmer had been interested in the RPWs since she was a Sophomore in high school. At age sixteen, she volunteered and went to live with the Workers. After graduating from St. Joachim High School in 1956 and making final vows in 1957, Villmer worked in the annual Vacation Bible Schools, participated in Christmas caroling, formed and directed a St. Joachim Parish choir, conducted adult Bible studies, and engaged in all other RPW general and annual activities. In 1989, Villmer was elected General Directress of the RPWs, and she continues to serve in that capacity at the time of the writing of this book.

With more Workers and an increase in donations, work was begun on an addition to the cinder block garage building. Called the St. Joseph Room, it was used for dances, quilt-making, and a clothing depot. Later in 1955, sixteen acres of property across the road from the Center was purchased from Eugene Gibson by James Michael Keller, an eye specialist from St. Louis, for the Workers' activities. The farm house on the property, once the home for the overseer of the Higginbotham estate, was named St. Michael House; it was repaired and painted. Dances, sewing classes, cooking classes, and more activities began to take place in it.

ST. MICHAEL HOUSE

After completing the payment on the loan Hermann and Widmer had incurred in renovating the Center, they burned the mortgage and made plans for another loan to build a new St. Michael House in 1966. They were assisted in that venture by their former pastor, Bruemmer, who had raised thirty-five thousand dollars from parishes in St. Louis which were donated to the RPWs. The steel building featured a large event room, several meeting rooms, and kitchen facilities designed by Ladue Architects and Engineers. It was dedicated on August 28, 1966, by Auxiliary Bishop Glennon P. Flavin of St. Louis as a Christian activity center. While Hermann and Widmer held a ribbon across the front doors, Flavin cut it with a pair of scissors. In September of 1966, the Archbishop of St. Louis, Joseph Cardinal Ritter, visited the new St. Michael House, which became the scene for boys' nights, ladies' days, recreation for young and old, dances, clothing giveaways, spiritual search days, annual Easter, Halloween, and Epiphany celebrations, dances, health programs, vacation Bible schools, days of recollection, auctions, food pantry days, the Christmas Food and Gift Program, and other events. Once a month a potluck dinner with Bingo games is offered from January to May. Volunteers organize, decorate, and prepare food. Until recently, those who attended those events, also went on trips to area shrines, such as Our Lady of the Snows, Immaculate Conception, and the Cathedral Basilica in St. Louis, along with state parks and historic sites.

Adjacent to St. Michael House is a storage building, which houses the used clothing and items distributed monthly in the food pantry and used for the bi-annual rummage sale, which serves as a fundraiser. Several tractor trailers on the grounds serve as storage containers for the furniture sold in the sales. In the storage building is located the studio, in which Hermann gave ceramic lessons for several years.

After completing the building of St. Michael House, Lavina Roberts Widmer, the mother of Alice Widmer, decided to build a small home across from the Center. Her son, Arthur J. Widmer, an architect and an engineer, designed and built a five-room brick cottage in which Lavina lived until her death. The cottage contained a main bedroom, a guest bedroom, a sitting or living room, a kitchen, and a bathroom. Upon

Widmer's death, the cottage was named Widmer House and became a residence and/or guest house for the Rural Parish Workers.

Until COVID-19 arrived in 2020, VBS was held for sixty to eighty children in St. Michael House. Before VBS moved to St. Michael House, VBS was held outdoors in several locations: near St. Joachim Church, Bottom Diggins, Sour Hill, Cadet, Tiff, and Richwoods. Under the direction of a RPW, tables, benches, water, and a portable toilet were brought to the chosen site for the two weeks of VBS. Attendees could also enjoy the Green Cathedral, an open area in the woods with trails branching off from the open green space partially outlined by a flowing creek on the RPW property.

MORE MEMBERS

Mary Ann DeMoor came to the RPWs from St. Louis in 1966. She earned a nursing degree from Mineral Area College and spent a year practicing at Jefferson County Memorial Hospital. Then, for sixteen years as a RPW she practiced home nursing, while taking care of the beef cattle and participating in other projects on the RPW property. In 1980, DeMoor heard the call to serve the elderly in nursing homes and left the Rural Parish Workers. DeMoor died in Florissant, Missouri, in 2019.

While DeMoor was serving a year as an apprentice, Diana Corvaglia (Schnitzius) was doing the same; after three years with the RPWs playing the guitar for Mass and participating in other RPW works, she decided to answer a call to marriage. She moved to New Orleans, where she met her husband, became a nurse, and gave birth to two children. They now live in Texas.

After receiving a bequest from Monsignor George Hildner, the Workers bought property in 1968 that had a frame building on it—the old Maplewood School. The school had been built around 1905 from lumber from the 1904 World's Fair in St. Louis. Valle Higginbotham, daughter of Preston and Stella Higginbotham, taught in the Maplewood School. In that building in March 1971, the Workers opened St. Michael Dispensary in Fertile in cooperation with St. Mary Health Center in St. Louis and the Twenty-Fifth Surgical Hospital United States Army Reserve. See chapter 17 on Health Care for more information.

On the Solemnity of Christ the King, November 21, 1971, Dorothy Irene Keller and her twin sister, Doris Ileen Keller, from Cedar Rapids, Iowa, made their final promises as Rural Parish Workers; they had come in 1966. After seventeen years of home visitations, gardening, and teaching in parish school of religion programs in St. Stephen, Richwoods, and St. Joachim, Old Mines, the Kellers left the RPW and joined the Glenmary Lay Missionaries in Appalachia. They retired to South Carolina, where Dorothy died in 2020.

In 1975, Doris Ann Bequette, a former member of St. Joachim Parish, returned to Old Mines after pursuing a business administration career, working for Cupples Company in St. Louis before moving to California to work for AAA and a modeling agency. As a high school student, she had volunteered with the RPWs; she even spent time with the Incarnate Word Sisters in San Antonio, Texas. Ultimately, she made final promises as a Rural Parish Worker in 1975. Before she died in 2020, she was engaged in extensive organic gardening of vegetables, fruits, and herbs; she also worked with the food- and clothing-giveaway programs for over one hundred families per month, ran the food pantry for families, the Christmas program, organized the Old Mines part of the Priestly Formation Program for the seminary in St. Louis, visited families with needs, and assisted in regular activities of the RPWs.

Marilyn Oshia and Sue Dittmaier spent two years, 1976–1977, with the RPWs after making temporary promises, and then they decided to pursue different paths. Oshia, from St. Joachim Parish, became a nurse (RN) and moved to Nevada. Dittmaier, from North St. Louis County, played guitar, helped with RPW activities, and gardened. She joined the Pallotines in Florissant. Later, she married and moved to several places in the U.S.

SECULAR INSTITUTE OF THE ARCHDIOCESE OF ST. LOUIS

After joining the Rural Parish Works on June 26, 1992, in celebration of their fiftieth anniversary, the Archbishop of St. Louis, John L. May, verbally declared the Rural Parish Workers of Christ the King to be a Secular Institute of the Archdiocese of St. Louis. On August 18, 1992, Edward J. O'Donnell, Auxiliary Bishop of St. Louis, confirmed in writing what May had said a few weeks before. On August 24, 1992, the five Rural Parish Workers of Christ King—Alice L. Widmer, LaDonna Hermann, Mary M. Siegfried, Natalie Villmer, and Doris Ann Bequette—cosigned a letter thanking May for making them a Secular Institute of the Archdiocese of St. Louis.

In 1995, Mary Catherine Saffa joined the RPWs. She had served as the organizer and director of Seedbearers, groups of young people who, with their youth leaders and parents, volunteered to spent a week working on homes needing repair in St. Joachim Parish. During the day, they painted and restored wood; they repaired and renovated homes. During the evenings, these youth from Catholic parishes in St. Charles County, prayed, ate, and slept in St. Michael House. While a RPW, Saffa worked with St. Joachim Church choir, vacation Bible schools, and other young people. However, in the fall of 2001, Saffa heard the call to a different lifestyle in the church and left the RPWs.

In January 1998, Mary Virginia Petersen and Neva Calvert came to Fertile as RPW apprentices. Petersen became active instructing women in Bible studies and preparing teachers for the parish school of religion program in St. Stephen Parish, Richwoods, Missouri. However, in the fall of 2001, she heard the call to leave the RPWs for a different lifestyle. After retiring from teaching, she worked with the elderly in St. Louis, where she died in 2020.

Calvert stayed. She had experience in refrigeration and counseling people with addictions. After completing a Master's degree in Clinical Psychology, she got involved in civic affairs. She made final vows as a RPW in 2005. She transports people to support groups and engages in counseling. She along with Villmer are the Rural Parish Workers of Christ the King in 2021.

In 1999, the RPWs purchased a metal building at the junction of Highway 21 and CC, which had been built to serve as a smoke house for processing meat. The venture did not succeed. However, the RPWs bought the building and thirteen acres of property at a bargain price on the Washington County Courthouse steps. At first, it was leased to K-14 as a preschool building, then used as a day care. It now houses the Fertile Farms Thrift Shop, run by volunteers. Funds from the sale of items in the shop are used to assist families needing help paying electric bills. Also, free clothing and household items are given to those who are unable to afford them.

On the Solemnity of Christ the King in 2003, Monica Pashia made a vow as a RPW oblate. As a retired nurse (RN) from St. Joachim Parish, she lived in her home until she moved to a nursing home. While active, she served as a school nurse for the K-14 school, visited the elderly, served as a parish organist, sang in the parish choir, assisted with the Rite of Christian Initiation of Adults program, and served on several community service boards. As an oblate, she participated in RPW activities and prayer. She lives in Potosi Manor, Potosi, where she prays for the RPWs, their benefactors, and all they serve.

During the year, some RPWs taught in the weekly elementary school Parish School of Religion program in St. Stephen Parish, Richwoods, on Sunday; high school was taught on a weekday. In the 1990s, a RPW trained the youth in St. Joachim Parish to present a religion program for grade-school students for a week in the summer for a few years along with a preparation for Confirmation program. Religious programs were offered in St. Michael House for adults. Under the leadership of a RPW, youth participated in the Christmas caroling program to the elderly and homebound.

The Rural Parish Workers have developed a working relationship with other agencies in Washington County. Through the instrumentality of the Community Partnership, which grew out of a program begun by Sister Connie Probst in the 1980s, monthly meetings draw together representatives for agencies, schools, and churches to share information about services cooperating with one another in helping area families with basic needs for food, clothing, housing, medicine, and utilities.

DEATHS

Widmer died February 7, 1998, and was the first to be buried in the plot of land in Cemetery 3 of St. Joachim Parish that had been given to the Rural Parish Workers by Suellentrop, when he was pastor of the parish. Siegfried, who died in 2005; Hermann, who died in 2014; and Bequette, who died in 2020, are buried there.

While alive, Widmer ran the RPW Self-Help Program, which offered employment and training opportunities to individuals who worked around the Center doing landscaping, building, cleaning, secretarial work, finance work, organizing, machinery upkeep, cooking, etc. She served as General Directress from 1942 to 1971.

One of Widmer's special works was to repay all those who had invested in the Washington County Development Company, which built a metal facility along Highway 21 in between Brown Hollow Road and Brown's Store. While the building never became the factory the investors and Widmer hoped it would be, it did become the location of a thriving vinyl fence business.

While alive, Hermann, co-foundress with Widmer, lived the life of a RPW by transporting others to numberless places, teaching elementary and high school students in Parish School of Religion programs, painting thousands of note cards, hundreds of Easter eggs, and candles, and crafting ceramics that she made and fired in the kiln in the RPW studio. She served as General Directress from 1971–1989.

Over the years, there have been five young women, who have volunteered a year or two of service by participating in the activities of the RPWs. Darleen Winchester from New Orleans, Louisiana; Jan Patrias Goettl from Mankato, Minnesota; Patricia Orlet Huermann from Belleville, Illinois; Rebecca Glen from Ballwin, Missouri; and Maxine Connaway from St. Louis, Missouri, have transported people to church, women to Ladies Day, and many to medical appointments, area locations, pick-ups in St. Louis, and VBS. They have taught religion to public school children and VBS children, and they have participated in general RPW activities.

Others came for short periods to volunteer in the RPW Summer Volunteer Program. Young women have taught in the VBS program, visited families, and helped around the Center. In the 1970s, a Youth Prayer Group was formed in St. Joachim Parish with a RPW leading the teens in retreats, organizing a Teen Newsletter, and creating social activities and weekly prayer meetings in homes. RPWs have also supervised Catholic high school students from Ursuline Academy and Rosati-Kain in St. Louis in community service as part of their senior year activities. With the help of a St. Joachim parishioner, RPWs organized the Archdiocesan Seminary programs Core II for theology students in St. Joachim Parish for several years.

In 2017, Villmer approached the Archbishop of St. Louis, Robert Carlson, and mentioned the need for free health care in Old Mines. This resulted in the Rural Parish Mobile Health Clinic and the Rural Parish Dental Clinic. See chapter 17 on Health Care for more information.

FUTURE

Two Rural Parish Workers of Christ the King remain: Natalie Villmer and Neva Calvert. One oblate remains: Monica Pashia. In 2022, they will mark the eightieth anniversary of their founding by Widmer and Hermann. As a Secular Institute of the

Archdiocese of St. Louis, they continue the work begun by their foundresses. They are vowed—poverty, chastity, and obedience—Catholic women, living in rural Missouri, who join in eucharistic celebrations in St. Joachim Church and pray the Liturgy of the Hours. They live according to the Rule of St. Benedict with Christ-centered spirituality, hospitality and service, and, following the gospel mandate, welcoming, serving, and witnessing to their neighbors. Their goal is to restore all things in Christ.

As they live their mission, they assist their neighbors with food, clothing, and housing. They conduct religious, educational, cultural, recreational, and social events in St. Michael House. Assisting with transportation to church, to health providers, and to community activities, they also visit the homebound and bring the Eucharist to them. Those needing medical, dental, and legal aid are assisted by the RPWs. Furniture and household items are provided in emergencies. They are instrumental in development of work programs and participate in civic and religious programs, ever encouraging spiritual development. They foster neighbor-to-neighbor activities and self-help programs for both men and women, while providing spiritual and emotional development activities for teenagers.

In their work, they are assisted by associates, those interested in learning more about their work; by volunteers, who pledge a period of service to their work; by King's Men, a St. Louis group, 1951–2007, who supported their apostolate; by Friends of the RPWs, women who offer financial assistance by sponsoring an annual Fashion Show Luncheon in a St. Louis Hotel; by Rural Shepherds, men and women who supported their work financially through a dinner held in the Knight of Columbus Hall, Hillsboro, Missouri; by other individuals and groups, who support their activities through assistance, gifts, and prayer; and by benefactors, who are remembered in daily prayer. Since 1994, the Annual Catholic Appeal of the Archdiocese of St. Louis has awarded them a substantial grant each year.

Over the course of eighty years, they have had three General Directresses. Widmer guided the RPWs from their founding in 1942 to 1971, when Hermann was elected by the members to serve in that capacity. She resigned as General Directress in 1989, when Villmer was elected to serve; Villmer continues as General Directress today.

The Rural Parish Workers of Christ the King see their future in teaching others how to carry on their mission. Their success with the Rural Parish Mobil Health Clinic and the establishment of Fertile Farms confirms that their future exists in training others, primarily volunteers, to continue the work they have begun in the oldest village in the State of Missouri: Old Mines. They continue to work toward that goal in other areas of their apostolate.

For Further Reading: *History of St. Joachim Parish: 1822–1972; 1723–1973,* Mark G. Boyer; *Historical Program-Pageant Book: 250th Anniversary, Old Mines, Missouri,* Natalie Villmer; *To Restore All Things in Christ,* LaDonna Hermann; "Lucky Lindy" Visits Old Mines, *The Diggin's* 8:1.

15

Vocations

SISTERS OF ST. JOSEPH

The first vocations from St. Joachim Parish were to the Sisters of St. Joseph of Carondelet in St. Louis, Missouri. Sister Mary Antoinette Kincaid, born Marie Kincaid, the daughter of J. and H. Kincaid, was the first to enter the order. She was followed by Sister Mary Febronia Boyer, born Theresa Rosalie Boyer, daughter of Louis and Mary (Jeanne Portais) Boyer. She was born in Old Mines on December 13, 1829, and she was baptized December 15, 1829.

The other Old Miners who joined the Sisters of St. Joseph of Carondelet, in alphabetical order, include:

Sister Mary Herman Boyer, born Edna Frances Boyer, daughter of Willis Boyer and Rosemary (Boyer) Boyer, Tiff, Missouri;

Sister Mary Georgiana Casey, born Louise Casey, daughter of George James Casey and Stephanie (Bouchard) Casey;

Sister Mary Dorothy Casey, born Rose Casey, daughter of George James Casey and Stephanie (Bouchard) Casey and sibling of Sister Mary Georgiana Casey;

Sister Mary Nazarene Dean, born Cornelia Dean, daughter of James Dean and Odelia (Portell) Dean;

Sister Melanie Joseph Portell, born Henrietta Portell, daughter of Gilbert and Pearl (Oyster) Portell;

and Sister Mary Alda Recar, born Maryrose Recar, daughter of Robert Recar and Mary (Catlett) Recar.

INCARNATE WORD SISTERS

Because the Sisters of Charity of the Incarnate Word taught in the schools in St. Joachim Parish from 1924 to 1995, they attracted a number of young women to their convent. Among those vocations, in alphabetical order, are:

Sister Loraine Bourisaw, born Catherine Rose Bourisaw, the daughter of James P. and Frances I (LaChance) Bourisaw;

Sister (Finian) Marie Coleman, born Mary Coleman, the daughter of Timon and Mary Rose (Juliette) Coleman;

Sister Yvonne DeGonia, born Helen Catherine DeGonia, the daughter of Howard W. and Esther (Cook) DeGonia;

Sister Dorothy Mary (Catherine) Politte, born Dorothy Mary Politte, the daughter of Francis (Frank) and Cora (Battreal) Politte;

and Sister (Evangelista) Rosemary Politte, born May Rose Politte, the daughter of Willis S. and Sarah Anne (Semar) Politte.

OTHER NUNS

Other women who joined religious communities from St. Joachim Parish, in alphabetical order, include:

Sister Marie Daugherty, OP, born Margaret Mary Daugherty, the daughter of Thomas and Mary Ellen (DeClue) Daugherty;

Sister Mary Jerome Dean, OSU, born as Mary Nazarena Dean, the daughter of Augustine (Gus) and Sophia (Boyer) Dean;

Sister Nazerene Dean, CSSJ, born Cornelia Dean, the daughter of James and Odeil (Portell) Dean;

Sister Miriam Pace, SMP, born Valerine Boyer, daughter of John L. and Elizabeth (DeClue) Boyer;

Sister M. Bertille Pashia, born Mary Pashia, the daughter of Thomas and Alice (Daugherty) Pashia;

Sister Edward Aloysius Portell, born Viola Rose Portell, daughter of William C. and Mary S. (Politte) Portell.

RURAL PARISH WORKERS

There were two vocations from St. Joachim Parish to the Rural Parish Workers of Christ the King, a secular institute of the Archdiocese of St. Louis, located in Fertile, Missouri:

Irene Natalie Villmer, daughter of Max Joseph and Eileen Marie (Coleman) Villmer, joined the Rural Parish Workers in 1955 and made final vows in 1957;

VOCATIONS

and Doris Ann Bequette, daughter of Roussan and Agatha (Sansoucie) Bequette, joined the Rural Parish Workers in 1973 and made final vows in the 1975.

PERMANENT DEACONS

There have been two permanent deacons from St. Joachim Parish:

Stephen Politte, son of Edwin and Catherine (Boyer) Politte, was ordained in 1989. After serving the parish for eighteen years, he retired in 2007 and lives in Old Mines.

Edward Boyer, son of Edward and Iona (Sansoucie) Boyer, was ordained in 1995. He serves in St. Rose of Lima Parish, DeSoto, Missouri, and occasionally in St. Joachim Parish.

PRIESTS

The first priest from St. Joachim Parish was Father John P. Daly, the son of Patrick and Marie (Fitzpatrick) Daly. He attended Kenrick Seminary in St. Louis and was ordained a priest on April 3, 1954; he celebrated his first Mass in St. Joachim Church on April 4, 1954. Later, he was laicized in January 1968.

The second priest from St. Joachim Parish was Monsignor James E. Hanson, the son of Patrick P. and Nelia M. (Saunders) Hanson. After attending Kenrick Seminary in St. Louis, he was ordained March 18, 1961, and he celebrated his first Mass in St. Joachim Church on March 19, 1961. At the time of the writing of this book, he is retired from active ministry and living in Old Mines. He marked the sixtieth anniversary of his ordination in 2021.

The 250th anniversary celebration of 1973 was just over—but the twin banners remained—when Mark G. Boyer, the son of Jesse Lee and Verna Marie (Boyer) Boyer, became the first transitional deacon to be ordained in St. Joachim Church. On March 8, 1975, the Saturday before the Fourth Sunday of Lent, Bishop Bernard F. Law from the Diocese of Springfield-Cape Girardeau came to St. Joachim Church to ordain Boyer to the diaconate for the Diocese of Springfield-Cape Girardeau. Law was assisted by two deacons: Deacon Brother Jeremy King, OSB, a monk of St. Meinrad Archabbey, St. Meinrad, Indiana, and Deacon Dennis Schaefer from the Diocese of Belleville, Illinois. Priests from both the Archdiocese of St. Louis and the Diocese of Springfield-Cape Girardeau concelebrated the Mass. Richard Wildeman (Diocese of Evansville, Indiana), Vernon Meyer, Jr., and Jerome Martinez (Archdiocese of Santa Fe, New Mexico) were masters of ceremonies. Other friends of Boyer from St. Meinrad School of Theology served as thurifer, cross bearer, and book bearer. Kevin Thebeau, Tim Coleman, and Tim Bone from Old Mines were the altar servers. Dennis Boyer and P. Gregory Boyer, cousins of Boyer from Old Mines, were the lectors.

Music was directed by Steven LeBlanc (Diocese of Lafayette, Louisiana) with Thomas Morrison (Diocese of Charleston, South Carolina) playing the organ, David Martin (Diocese of Evansville, Indiana) playing the guitar, and the choir composed of R. Mark Duchaine (Diocese of Sioux City, Iowa), John Giel (Diocese of Orlando, Florida), Glenn Macip (Diocese of Lafayette, Louisiana), and Henry Tully (Archdiocese of Indianapolis, Indiana). Timothy Berg (Archdiocese of Santa Fe, New Mexico) took photographs.

The banner hanging on the ambo was made by LaDonna Hermann. Because there were no motels in Old Mines, Joey and Barb Bone found guestrooms among the parishioners for all people from out of town. Vestments were made by Jane M. (Boyer) Pashia. The St. Ann Sodality provided a reception for all. Before the meal for the clergy, cooked by Sister Achille Bugnitz, Father Richard Suren provided cocktails; the food was provided by the Knights of Columbus.

The next year on April 24, 1976, Saturday in the Octave of Easter, Law returned to St. Joachim Church to ordain Boyer to the priesthood. Like his diaconate ordination before, this was the first priesthood ordination to take place in the historic church. LaDonna Hermann, directress of the Rural Parish Workers of Christ the King, made three new banners featuring the sacraments flowing from baptism to hang in the church. One banner stated, "Live in the Spirit," and the other declared, "Grow in the Spirit."

Among the concelebrating priests were Father Theodore R. Brug, who had become pastor of St. Joachim Parish in 1975, Fathers Richard H. Suren, Amel A. Shibley, Stephen A. Schneider, Thomas E. Reidy, and Ephrem Carr. The transitional deacons assisting Law were Deacon Kevin J. Bryan (Archdiocese of Louisville, Kentucky) and Deacon Brother Noah Casey (St. Meinrad Archabbey, Indiana). Dennis P. Boyer and P. Gregory Boyer were the lectors. Richard Wildeman (Diocese of Evansville, Indiana), Vernon J. Meyer, Jr. (Archdiocese of Santa Fe, New Mexico), and Deacon Joseph N. Dant (Archdiocese of Indianapolis, Indiana) were the masters of ceremonies. Paul Shikany (Archdiocese of Indianapolis, Indiana) was the sacristan. Deacon David D. Tscherne (Diocese of Toledo, Ohio) was the thurifer; Brother Michael Buttner (Belmont Abbey, North Carolina) was the paschal candle bearer, and Peter A. Libasci (Diocese of Rockville Centre, New York) was the book bearer. Altar servers were Timothy Bone and John Wilson.

Music was again under the direction of Deacon Stephen C. LeBlanc (Diocese of Lafayette, Louisiana), and Deacon Thomas F. Morrison (Diocese of Charleston, South Carolina) played the organ, while Anthony J. Trosley (Diocese of Peoria, Illinois) played the guitar, and Girard M. Sherba (Diocese of Raleigh, North Carolina) played the flute. The choir was composed of Michael E. Nelsen (Diocese of Rockford, Illinois), John C. Giel (Diocese of Orlando, Florida), Roger L. Leveillee (Diocese of Springfield-Cape Girardeau, Missouri), and Deacon Henry F. Tully (Archdiocese of Indianapolis, Indiana). Timothy K. Berg was in charge of photographs again.

After the Mass, Boyer gave his first blessing to family and friends, and a reception followed in the school cafeteria. Later, the clergy and other ministers joined the Incarnate Word nuns in the new convent for tea and snacks.

As had been done the previous year, Joey and Barbara Bone took care of finding housing for all out-of-town ministers and guests. Later that Saturday evening, the Rural Parish Workers sponsored entertainment for all in St. Michael House.

The next day, April 25, 1976, the Second Sunday of Easter and the Feast of St. Mark, Boyer celebrated his First Eucharist of Thanksgiving in the afternoon. Fathers Brug, James M. Moll, Shibley, Bernard A. Suellentrop, who preached, James E. Hanson, and Carr concelebrated. Deacon Paul D. Koetter (Archdiocese of Indianapolis, Indiana) and Deacon David D. Tsherne (Diocese of Toledo, Ohio) served as the assisting deacons. Again, the lectors were Dennis Boyer and P. Gregory Boyer. Wildeman and Meyer were the masters of ceremonies. Shikany was sacristan. Deacon Joseph N. Dant (Archdiocese of Indianapolis, Indiana) was thurifer, and Libasci was book bearer. Thomas Wilson and Glen Osia were the altar servers. LeBlanc again directed the music with the same musicians and choir as the day before.

After the Mass, a reception was held in the school cafeteria. Then, all those from out of town headed home. Students from St. Meinrad School of Theology drove back to southern Indiana for classes the next day. Boyer, too, had to attend a seminar that began the next day. After returning to Old Mines a week later, he visited the homes of his grandparents, aunts and uncles, and the Rural Parish Workers to celebrate home Masses with them and whomever they chose to invite as a thanksgiving for their support throughout the eight years he spent in the seminary.

Boyer retired from active ministry in 2016 to his home in Springfield, Missouri.

For Further Reading: Sister Mary Febronia Boyer, *The Diggin's* 5:4, 6:3, 12:2.

16

Knights of Columbus

BEGINNINGS AND HALL

The Washington County Knights of Columbus Council 5936 was begun March 12, 1967, with seventy-three charter members, during the pastorship of Father Bernard A. Suellentrop. After forming the council, the first thing the members did was to make plans to build their own hall. Located less than a mile south of St. Joachim Church along Highway 21 before its junction with Highway 47, the KC Hall was constructed by John Copenhaver, Marion Politte, Charles Faulkner, Bob Moore, Dick Flanton, Lawrence Boyer, Elwood Barton, Jerry Adams, Jerry Lowe, Vincent Boyer, Cy Williams, Nelson Portell, Elmer Eckhoff, Donald Coleman, C.J. Boyer, Benny Thebeau, and Charles Politte. Local company owners donated the free use of machinery, while many non-KC members donated labor. The lower of what would later become a two-story hall was dedicated on February 22, 1969.

As early as 1965, Gilbert Long had spoken to Suellentrop about the possibility of starting a Knights of Columbus (KC) chapter. Suellentrop sanctioned the idea. While someone submitted the necessary paperwork, others began necessary building work. The charter papers had to be submitted three different times to correct the spelling of some of the names of the charter members! The first organizational meeting was held in St. Joachim School auditorium/cafeteria to which thirty-seven men attended. At that meeting Charles Pratt was chosen as the first Grand Knight. After the initial meeting in 1965, consecutive meetings were held in the Union Hall until it burned, then in Kate's Tavern (owned by Vincent Thebeau) in Racola until it burned. Paul Boyer and Bill Polhemus convinced Mickey Allen to sell the property where the current hall and campus are located.

The dedication ceremony, attended by approximately 125 people, began with the raising of the American Flag, which was donated by and presented to the council by

Mr. & Mrs. Francis J. Robart in honor of their son, Henry Robart, a Veteran of Foreign Wars and a charter member of the council. While Bill Polhemus, Grand Knight, held a crucifix to be hung on the wall in the hall, Suellentrop blessed it.

Then, Mass was celebrated in the hall by Suellentrop and concelebrated by the associate pastor, Father Edward J. Schramm. Commentator for the Mass was Jim DeGonia, and Master of Ceremonies was James Karsch. When the Sunday afternoon Mass was finished, a number of speakers followed: Polhemus; Charles Pratt, first Grand Knight of the council; Dan Lenhardt, district deputy; Gilbert Long, past district deputy; Suellentrop, chaplain; Schramm, co-chaplain; Robert Karsnia, state deputy; and Harry F. Chapman, a Potosi accountant and the featured speaker for the dedication services. After Chapman's presentation, a late afternoon luncheon was served to all in attendance.

As a fraternal organization, the Knights of Columbus was started to help the Old Mines community and St. Joachim Church. Because it is known as the Washington County Knights of Columbus, it was also founded to assist Catholic parishes in Washington County through the gift of members' time, talent, and treasure.

In 1971, a top floor was added to the building; in 1994, the top floor was expanded and restrooms were added to accommodate large crowds attending bingo, dances, dinners, funeral luncheons, shooting matches, and the annual toy drive for children. The top floor cost the Knights of Columbus $30,000, a loan which they were able to repay in three years.

In 2012–2013, the Washington County Knights of Columbus filed papers to establish themselves as a legal corporation, called the Blue Knights Home Corporation. This action was taken to protect individual Knights from law suits. The corporation owns all property and buildings and protects them from being taken should a law suit be filed against an individual Knight of Columbus.

PROGRAMS

One integral program developed over the past decade is the Knights as Neighbors Program under the leadership of Bill Portell and Jim Johnston. This program was designed to assist families in Old Mines and member Knights with utility bills, adopting families at Christmastime, and bringing food to families in emergencies. Begun in 2015, it came to an end in 2018, when Knights decided that was it no longer needed because there were many other organizations and groups doing the same thing. Instead of running their own programs, the KCs decided to help fund those of other organizations and groups to support their efforts in Potosi and Richwoods.

The Knights of Columbus provide financial support to the parish and the school by making donations and hosting several fundraisers throughout the year. They provide the use of the hall for community meetings, blood drives, clothing giveaways, and sponsor private fundraisers, and support other parishes, such as St. Stephen,

Richwoods. Their hall also serves as a precinct polling place for elections. Private groups can rent the hall for special occasions. The organization is assisted by the Ladies Auxiliary, wives of knights, who work jointly with members of the council.

The Knights have assisted St. Joachim School with upgrading the electrical wiring and lighting, renovating restrooms, laying new flooring, and providing a new cook stove and refrigerator for the kitchen. They helped put the new roofs on the school, church, rectory, garage, and Incarnate Word Center either with donated labor or individual monetary donations.

Every year they sponsor a car show with thirty to forty entrants (125 in 2021) and with awards presented for various categories. The proceeds for that event, directed by Wendy Golf, go to the Make-a-Wish Foundation.

The Washington County Knights of Columbus chapter joined with other chapters throughout the State of Missouri in sponsoring a wing for Cardinal Glennon Hospital in St. Louis. Every year they continue that support with their annual Tootsie Roll Drive; half of the proceeds from that drive go to continued support of the hospital wing and half support charities in the Old Mines area.

The KCs sponsor a seminarian every year, and they sponsor fifteen to twenty young people to attend the annual March for Life rally in Washington, D.C.

OTHER FACTS

In 2014, Catholic Knights from St. James Parish, Potosi, decided to form their own chapter of the Knights of Columbus. It is known as the St. James Council 15935.

In 2017, the Washington County Knights of Columbus celebrated its fiftieth anniversary. It was acknowledged with a luncheon at the KC Hall, a speech given by the state council representative, and a speech given by the first grand knight, Charles Pratt.

When the Washington County chapter began, the first forty Knights got their first degree from the Festus chapter. Now, there are 221 members in addition to a number of volunteer booster members, who assist at dinners, fish fries, shooting matches, and other events. The first fourth-degree members included Foster (Lou) Coleman, Bernard Politte, Charles Pratt, and Karl Koch. They received their fourth degree on February 13, 1972.

GRAND KNIGHTS

Grand Knights since the founding of Washington County Knights of Columbus Council 5936 include: Charles Pratt (1967–1969), William (Bill) Polhemus (1969–1970), Wilfred Thebeau (1970–1971), Bernard Politte (1971–1973), James Karsch (1973–1974), John Price (1974–1976), Steve Sansoucie (1976–1977), Donald (Sonny) Boyer (1977–1978), James DeGonia (1978–1980);

James Politte (1980–1982), David Politte (1982–1984, 1987–1989), James Johnston (1984–1986, 1989–1990), Donald Bourbon (1990–1993), Steve Boyer (1993–1996), Alex Yarbrough (1996–1997), Tom Villmer (1997–1998), Tom DeGonia (1998–2000);

Norman Wilson (2000–2002, 2009–2010), Randy Mull (2002–2007), Joe Adams (2007–2008), Larry Allen (2008–2009), Rick Hendricks (2010–2012), Kenny Thebeau (2012–2013), Al Gravitt (2013–2014), Benny Hanson (2014; 6 months), Gary Hollingsworth (2015–2016), and Danny Kincaid (2016–present).

LADIES AUXILIARY

The Ladies Auxiliary of Council 5936 has fifty-nine members, who assist the KCs with organizing fundraisers, like chicken, fish, and barbecue dinners, dances, shooting matches, funeral dinners, etc. They assist the annual Tootsie Roll Drive of which some funds support Special Olympics and handicapped organizations. The Ladies have purchased children's literature for the church. During Catholic Schools Week, they give educators, administrators, secretarial staff, and Parish School of Religion staff gifts of appreciation. Members of the auxiliary also support the needy with monetary gifts, support during the car show, and host a Trunk or Treat event, in which candy and treats are distributed from car trunks. The Ladies Auxiliary sponsors an annual family Christmas party for KC members, crafts, games, a bounce house, and a visit with Santa Clause.

At the time of the writing of this book, Tanya Kincaid is president of the Ladies Auxiliary.

For Further Reading: *History of St. Joachim Parish: 1822–1972; 1723–1973*, Mark G. Boyer; *Historical Program-Pageant Book: 250th Anniversary, Old Mines, Missouri*, Natalie Villmer.

17

Health Care

MEDICINE CHEST AND HOME VISITATION

In the earliest days of Old Mines village, health care consisted of home remedies and over-the-counter drugs kept in a medicine chest or on a sideboard. Band-aids, mercurochrome—an external first-aid antiseptic used to prevent skin infection in minor cuts, scrapes, and bruises—and Merthiolate—a mercury-containing substance that was used as a germ killer and preservative in many different products, including vaccines—and aspirin could be found in most medicine cabinets along with Vick's VapoRub, a mentholated salve rubbed on a person's chest to ease both the cough and stuffed nasal passages associated with a head cold.

For more serious issues, one of the doctors in the Old Mines area could be asked to visit a sick person in the late 1800s. Archibald Taylor, M.D., lived in Old Mines and practiced medicine until 1884, when he was stricken with paralysis. Doctor Samuel Thurman, who lived in Blackwell, was a familiar figure wearing a stove pipe hat while riding his horse to visit someone who needed medical care. He and his family moved to Potosi in 1905, and he practiced medicine until 1931. Thurman's son, Doctor Joseph Lynn Thurman, practiced with his father from 1918 to 1931, and after that alone until September 1, 1974. Thurman estimated that he delivered around five thousand babies during his years in Potosi. Also from Potosi, Doctor George F. Cresswell could be called to make a house call or one could visit his office. Creswell practiced medicine from 1896–1970.

Beginning in 1948, Mae Burford, RN, Director of the Washington County Health Department, was found giving inoculations in her office or in schools. The big issue during her term as health director was polio. She gave many shots to children both in and out of school to protect them from polio along with boosters and, finally, vaccine on sugar cubes. After serving as health director for forty years, Burford retired in 1988 and died in 1999.

OLD MINES DIAGNOSTIC AND REFERRAL CLINIC

The Daughters of Charity of St. Vincent de Paul came to Old Mines in 1951 and began the Old Mines Diagnostic and Referral Clinic. Staffed by the St. Louis Catholic Physicians Guild, the clinic operated out of the first floor of the convent/school building, using some of the former classrooms. Nursing staff and, when needed, hospital service, was provided from DePaul, St. Mary, St. John, and St. Anthony hospitals in St. Louis. The Daughters of Charity facilitated a clinic which provided equipment, drugs, and treatment on a regular basis under the direction of a Daughter of Charity named Sister Ann.

In 1962, the Daughters purchased the one-hundred-year-old home and adjoining property of what had been the George Wallace Store and post office. The clinic was moved to the store, where it continued to operate until the late 1960s, when it was discontinued due to lack of continuity of care by physicians, the distance involved, and the lack of Daughter personnel. The opening of Washington County Memorial Hospital took over providing health care. The Wallace store burned in 1972 and was razed after that.

The Daughters of Charity became interested in providing free health care to the people of Old Mines after purchasing Galilee, a summer residence and weekend vacation home located off of Highway 21 north of St. Joachim Church. The hewn-log structure was built in 1797; it is probably the oldest structure in northern Washington County. Located nearby are the remains of the Murphy lead furnace dating from the early nineteenth century now on Washington State Park property. As the number of Daughters declined, they sold the home in 1979 to Robert and Betty Renard, who intended to use it as a home for juveniles, but those plans never materialized. The continued used the house on weekends and made it available to parishes to use for retreats, days of recollection, and prayer days. St. Joachim Parish used the home for youth retreats, and the Rural Parish Workers brought young people there for recreation and prayer days. After the Renards died, their daughter, Peggy Droege, inherited the property and lives there full-time.

WASHINGTON COUNTY MEMORIAL HOSPITAL

Washington County Memorial Hospital was built in Potosi, Missouri, in 1963. While its staff treated basic non-life-threatening injuries at first, it served as a referral point for patients for other area hospitals: Barnes, Missouri Baptist, and Mercy in St. Louis. Over the years, it was renovated and expanded. From its basic beginnings, it became a medical care provider with twenty-five beds. Instead of having to travel to St. Louis for expert medical care, people from Old Mines have a good hospital only six miles south. Since 2018, the hospital had been administered by the Mercy Healthcare System.

ST. MICHAEL DISPENSARY

In 1971, under the guidance of St. Mary Health Center, St. Louis, the Rural Parish Workers opened St. Michael Dispensary in Fertile to serve the poor in Old Mines and the surrounding area. The Dispensary was located in the Maplewood School. Nurses (mostly nuns) from St. Mary Hospital volunteered to staff the clinic. Doctors from the Army and Air National Guard from St. Louis Lambert Airport were looking for opportunities on the weekends to practice medicine. The Rural Parish Workers set up the clinic in St. Michael House from 1990 to 1991. After the Army and Air National Guard discontinued its services, St. Mary Hospital recruited doctors from Jefferson Memorial Hospital in Festus to continue the clinic, which was held in the Maplewood School. After a few years, the clinic closed; doctor's preferred to see patients in their offices where modern medical equipment was available. Upon RPW recommendation, the patients were not charged for medical care. This continued for a few years on a limited basis.

OTHER HEALTH CARE

Also for a while, Sister Martha Heimer, who rented a log house on the Rural Parish Workers of Christ the King property, provided medical assistance to the poor on a limited basis in the 1990s.

Doctor Richard Davis retired from a successful chiropractic practice in St. Louis in 2009. He and his wife, Susan, moved to the Richwoods area, but made St. Joachim their parish. At the age of eighty-one, Davis felt that he had much left to give and was directed to the need of home-bound persons for chiropractic care. Thus, each Tuesday, before beginning his rounds, he would treat mobile patients in the Incarnate Word Center. Then, accompanied by Monica Pashia, a retired nurse and Rural Parish Worker oblate, he visited patients in St. Joachim Parish and elsewhere as word of his work spread rapidly by mouth. Davis was known for his gentle touch in relieving pain and for suggesting supplements that corrected imbalances of minerals in the body. In return for his services, he accepted the copay that insurances demanded along with homemade pastries and produce from gardens. After beginning with ten patients, by 2020 he had treated 150 patients. During the COVID-19 pandemic, his Healing Hands Ministry was put on hold except for a few patients he treated in his home.

Health Care

MOBILE CLINIC, MOBILE DENTIST

After Natalie Villmer, Directress of the Rural Parish Workers of Christ the King, approached then-Archbishop Robert Carlson of St. Louis in 2017 to speak about the needs in one part of the rural area of the archdiocese, Carlson found donors and made a plan for a mobile health unit for rural areas, especially Old Mines. Statistics show that the people living in Washington County and Franklin County lag behind the U.S. and Missouri on most health measures. In 2018, the Rural Parish Mobile Health Clinic was launched. A large metal garage was built on the site of the concrete basketball courts behind the St. Joachim School to house it. The mobile clinic contains a nurse's station between two doctor's offices and a cab for the driver. From the mobile clinic, patients without insurance are offered services weekly.

Patients register on the first floor of the Incarnate Word Center, previously known as the new convent, and see Sister Doctor Marie Paul Lockerd, RSM, and doctors and nurses from Catholic Hospitals in St. Louis. Lockerd is a Board Certified Family Practice physician and a member of the Sisters of Mercy of Alma, Michigan. The Rural Parish Mobile Health Clinic is its own 501C3 non-profit. As an outreach of Catholic Charities, it also serves the uninsured in St. Clair, Missouri.

On October 24, 2020, the Rural Parish Dental Clinic was blessed by Archbishop Mitchell Rozanski, who succeeded Carlson as archbishop of St. Louis. It offers services to those without dental insurance to those in Old Mines and other rural areas.

For Further Reading: *History of St. Joachim Parish: 1822–1972; 1723–1973*, Mark G. Boyer, *Historical Program-Pageant Book: 250th Anniversary, Old Mines, Missouri*, Natalie Villmer; *To Restore All Things in Christ*, LaDonna Hermann; Obituary for Mae Burford, Moore Funeral Homes; Serving the People of Washington County, *The Diggin's* 18:4.

18

Public Schools

On August 10, 1821, Missouri entered the United States as the twenty-fourth state and as the first one located entirely west of the Mississippi River in what had been part of the Louisiana Purchase of 1803. By 1818, the Missouri Territory had gained enough settlers to qualify for statehood. As the bill made its way through Congress, the issue of slavery was debated. What became known as the Missouri Compromise became law. Maine was admitted as a free state, and Missouri was admitted as a slave state to keep the number of free and slave states evenly balanced. The Missouri Compromise remained until 1854, when the Kansas-Nebraska Act repealed it. However, in 1861, when other slave states seceded to trigger the Civil War, Missouri chose to remain in the Union.

COMPULSORY SCHOOLING

In 1905, the Missouri legislators passed a law concerning compulsory schooling until the age of sixteen. In the Old Mines area, one- and two-room schoolhouses sprang up. Before the law it was too difficult for most parents to send their children to school because they lived in isolation too far away. Furthermore, there may be creeks to ford or pastures with charging bulls to pass through in order to get to a school on foot. In other words, absenteeism was high. Because the language spoken at home was French, when schools were erected and children began to attend them, English was the language of instruction. Most of the students knew no English, and they were forbidden to speak French while attending classes.

The one- and two-room schools were erected all over the area to meet the needs of the Old Mines population scattered all over the area. Thus, schools were built at Kingston, Racola, Od Mines, Fertile, Barytes, Tiff, Cadet, Aptus, Shibboleth, Cannon Mines, Fertile, Bellefontaine, and Mineral Point, to name a few. Students walked to school—some three to four miles—and after school they retraced their steps to their homes. Each school had one teacher, who taught all grades for all students. In Old Mines in 1980, Lawrence Z. Pashia remembered that Ellen (DeClue) Daugherty was the teacher. In Racola, Alla Boyer, Leah James, and Mr. Forbes were teachers. Because many children were employed in order to help support their families, truancy was often a problem, even though school was in session for only eight months. Many never graduated from eighth grade, and of those who did, few went to high school. If they chose to attend high school, they had to go either to Potosi or DeSoto.

The one-teacher, one-room schools were visited several times a year by a county superintendent of schools. According to Pashia, in Washington County, he was Orwell Fox; once a year he gave examinations and teaching certificates to teachers, who taught all grades and all subjects. Thus, some subjects were taught only two or three times a week.

The August 10, 1911, issue of the *Independent-Journal* indicated that Martha Wallace was teaching in Old Mines. The February 2, 1921, *Independent-Journal* identified a few teachers in some of the one-room schools for 1920–1921. Leo Politte was the teacher in Old Mines; Leah James, Rachel Bourisaw, and Alla Boyer were teachers in Racola; Sadie Richardson and Jessie Baker were teachers in Cruise; and Harry Hedley and George W. Cook were teachers in Fertile.

ONE DISTRICT

One-room schools continued until the early 1950s, when the State of Missouri stepped in and decided that education of students could be improved by combining some of the small schools into one district. In 1956, the K-14 district was formed from fourteen smaller schools: Kingston, Barytes, Racola, Maplewood, Cruise, Blackwell, Arnault Branch, Shibboleth, Cadet, Old Mines, Lower Bliss, Fountain Farm, Bellefontaine, and Tiff. While five schools—Kingston, Cruise, Bellefontaine, Cadet, and Lower Bliss—formed the Kingston-14 School District, the other nine schools were closed. In 1956, a new facility was built about one-eighth of a mile north of the old Cruise School (about four miles north of Old Mines village just inside the north end of the Old Mines Concession) to replace Cruise, Kingston, and Lower Bliss. In 1963, some rooms were heavily damaged or destroyed by fire, but all were repaired and rebuilt in 1970 with the addition of a multi-purpose room.

In 1956, the new school was named Cruise in honor of Cruise Higginbotham, who had owned the land upon which the old Cruise School had been erected. Once finished, approximately one hundred students attended the new school. In time, the Cadet school was closed and razed after 1973. The Bellefontaine school, which housed kindergarten and first grade until 1976, became the Head Start Center when kindergarten and first grade were moved to the K-14 campus. After 1973, the Head Start Center was moved to the main campus, and Bellefontaine was razed around 2002–2003. By 1973, the enrollment had grown to 465 students.

By 1979, the enrollment in K-14 School was approximately 350 students. By 1985, Building B construction began. Completed in 1986, it contained a full-size gymnasium and eleven classrooms. By 1989, enrollment reached five hundred students, and Building C, a double-wide modular unit that housed kindergarten classes, was added. During the 1991–1992 school year, Building D was built to house elementary classrooms, and, once the high school was opened, to house the fine arts and industrial technology programs. By 1993, enrollment had climbed to over six hundred students in kindergarten through eighth grade.

Because there was no high school, students chose to go either to Potosi High School or DeSoto High School; that arrangement cost the K-14 district over one million dollars a year! The dream of building a high school in the district began in 1994, when the foundations were poured for the Kingston K-14 High School; it became a reality in 1996–1997, when the first high school classes were held on the K-14 campus for freshmen and sophomore students. Those already enrolled in Potosi and DeSoto were given the option of staying where they were or coming to the new high school; approximately forty-six students made the decision to enroll in the new high school. In 1998, a junior class was added, and in 1999, the first senior class of Kingston K-14 was graduated. The class of 2000 was the first group of students to attend Kingston K-14 from kindergarten through grade twelve.

Enrollment continued to climb. In 1998, six modular units were installed to house elementary and special education classes, and in 1999, the Primary Building was erected; into that addition second grade students were moved near the end of the 2002–2003 school year. The modular units were removed during the summer of 2003 and replaced by a large, single modular unit to accommodate grades three through five. Another addition to the Primary Building began during the 2012–2013 school year to house elementary students; it was completed in the 2013–2014 school year. That addition allowed prekindergarten through fifth grade to be housed under one roof. The single modular unit became a storage building.

Enrollment continues to grow; with close to nine hundred students, as of 2021, and $8.8 million in yearly revenue, K-14 spends over nine thousand dollars on every student. More improvements are made; plans are in place for more buildings, more technology, and more educational opportunities to meet the ever-changing needs of society.

For Further Reading: The One Room Rural School and I, Lawrence Z. Pashia, *The Diggin's* 15:3; Wikipedia: K–12.

19

Old Mines Old Baptist Church

In the early 1800s, more people moved into the Old Mines area to mine lead, and some of them were Protestants, who wanted their own church. Thus, in 1833, the Old Mines Baptist Church was established on 2.75 acres of property about a mile north of St. Joachim Church off Highway 21 on the west side of the road. The church was a small rectangular, clapboard-covered building, about the size of the Lamarque School in Old Mines, painted white. It was covered with a corrugated tin roof. There were three windows with closeable shutters on either side, and entry was through a single door on one end.

    On the occasion of its one hundredth anniversary in 1933, Dr. E.S. Ewing addressed a meeting held on the lawn in front of the building, which was in very bad condition. Rev. Victor Connelly, pastor of the Bonne Terre Baptist Church, and five of his parishioners repaired the dilapidated building on November 19, 1942, and Connelly held a service in it on November 29, 1942, even though the church had been abandoned around 1937. He wanted to reestablish a Sunday School and mission church in it. Thus, he and his crew repainted the long, narrow, horizontal, wood planks on the exterior walls along with all the wood shutters on the six windows and cleaned the inside. Connelly's plans came to nothing in the strong Roman Catholic community of Old Mines. The church remained standing but unoccupied until the latter half of the 1900s, when it was completely razed.

    A part of the 2.75 acres of land deeded forever to this church is about a half-an-acre cemetery, in which many of the former members of the Old Mines Old Baptist Church are laid to rest. The oldest burial is listed as William Roderick, laid to rest in 1840 with no date or month given. The next oldest is Margaret Luisa (Periou) Roderique, who died August 7, 1840. The last burial to have taken place in the cemetery was Adam Franklin Barnes, who died on October 12, 1974; he was buried next to his wife, Ida Belle (West) Barnes, who died June 18, 1953. As well as can be determined, about 120 people are buried in the Old Mines Baptist Church Cemetery. The predominate surnames appearing at least twice or more, in alphabetical order, include Alderson, Barnes, Cain, Cole, Cook, De'Arment, DeClue, Gray, Hargus, Harris, Hartzell, Martin, Minx, Paul, Pinson, Polhemus, Portell, Roderique, Ross, Settle, Sherlock, Smith, Sparks, Torrence, Walton, and Wilkinson. All that is left of the once small, but thriving, Baptist community, is the one-half acre cemetery with its few gradually-deteriorating tombstones. Some relatives of those buried in it periodically remove the brush, briars, and weeds that tend to invade it. Around 2005, Paul (C.J.) Boyer organized members of the Old Mines community to clear trees and brush that obliterated many graves. That group continues to keep it clean every year.

For Further Reading: Washington County Cemeteries, Old Mines Baptist Church Cemetery; *The Diggin's*: Ancient Cemetery Restoration Project, 2:1; Baptist Church Burials, 20:1, 20:2.

20

250th and 275th Anniversary Celebrations

150TH ANNIVERSARY OF THE PARISH, 250TH ANNIVERSARY OF THE AREA

The years 1972 through 1973 marked the 150th anniversary of the founding of St. Joachim Parish (1822) and the 250th anniversary of the founding of Old Mines (1723). The two-year anniversary celebration began with the publication of the two-hundred-page *History of St. Joachim Parish 1822–1972; 1723–1973*. Written and edited by Mark G. Boyer, the spiral-bound book was published by Yearbook House, Kansas City, Missouri, in 1972. Boyer worked on the book during the summer of 1971 and completed it during his senior year in Cardinal Glennon Seminary College, St. Louis, Missouri. He employed the assistance of fellow seminarians with photography (Richard H. Risse, Denny Schaab), the cover (Mark A. Dolan), proofreading (Vernon J. Meyer, Jr.), secretarial work (Mary Ann Pratt), ad sales (St. Joachim School 7th and 8th grades and St. Joachim High School), and many others who contributed information and photographs, gave access to research files, or offered clarification in any way.

The theme tying together the various sections of the book was presented in the introduction written by Boyer: "Our history is a history of faith, a history of struggling, a history of service. It is a history of a simple people and their beginning-search-for-God. It is a history of a school, a history of a convent, a history of societies. It is most important of all a history of man [and woman] searching for God." At the time of its writing, the book located St. Joachim Parish within Old Mines. It contained a brief history of the area and a full history of the parish and St. Joachim Church. A short history of the Rural Parish Workers of Christ the King, a secular institute of women, occupied eleven pages of the work. The book contained the thirty-page parish census of 1890 taken by then-pastor Father E.T. Gallagher; readers could find the names of many of their ancestors in the census. There was both an essay and a photo essay on

Old Mines as it existed in 1972, and a list of the parishioners registered in the parish as of January 1, 1972. Seven pages were devoted to identifying vocations to priesthood, religious life, and secular institutes from the parish. The book concluded with a short history on St. Joseph Parish, Tiff, Missouri, a section to record Personal Family History, a list of ads and patrons, and an index.

On Wednesday, July 26, 1972, the pastor, Father Richard Suren, inaugurated the two-year celebration with a Mass of Thanksgiving in honor of St. Joachim and Anne, the traditional parents of the Blessed Virgin Mary. St. Joachim is the patron saint for St. Joachim Parish. After that morning Mass, the St. Ann Sodality served coffee to all in attendance.

The annual September 17, 1972, Fall Festival committee invited parishioners to don their 1800s clothes and share a dinner, visit the country store, enjoy a jeep ride, play social games, or try their skill at a turkey shoot.

On October 15, 1972, Suren celebrated the official 150th anniversary Mass with Cardinal John J. Carberry, Archbishop of St. Louis, presiding over the celebration and former pastors and associate pastors concelebrating: Fathers Edward Schramm, Anthony Jansen, Bernard Suellentrop, Alphonse Hoormann, and Joseph Capazzi. Also, in attendance was Father James Hanson, a native Old Miner. Following the Mass, a reception was held for the capacity crowd in the school hall.

Throughout the year of marking the twin anniversaries, two banners, made by Boyer, hung in the sanctuary of St. Joachim Church. One featured the shield of three fleur-des-les (French), a crossed pick and shovel (mining), the twin dates being marked, and a banner with St. Joachim. The shield was superimposed on an outline of the church. The other banner captured words from the introduction to the book: "... We are a people with a history ... of Faith." Below the words were: St. Joachim Parish, Old Mines. Throughout the year, especially for Easter and Christmas, the theme of being a people with a history of faith was the focus of bulletins and homilies by the pastor and associate pastor.

In the months leading up to the 250th celebration of the founding of the area, meetings were held to plan the Historical Pageant and all the activities that accompanied it. Funding was secured with several Moonlit Dances on the parish parking lot along with a fish fry sponsored by the Knights of Columbus. Souvenirs were made, dresses and bonnets sewed, and other things prepared in St. Michael House on the grounds of the Rural Parish Workers. Men, who wanted to participate in the whiskers' contest, grew beards.

On September 1 and 2, 1973, the 250th anniversary of the founding of Old Mines was celebrated. In preparation for that day, Natalie Villmer, an Old Mines native and a member of the Rural Parish Workers of Christ the King, wrote, after an extensive period of research, the seventy-six-page *Historical Program-Pageant Book*. The work contained congratulatory letters from Richard Nixon, president of the U.S.; Stuart Symington and Thomas F. Eagelton, U.S. Senators from Missouri; Richard H. Ichord,

250TH AND 275TH ANNIVERSARY CELEBRATIONS

U.S. House of Representatives; Christopher S. Bond, Missouri Governor; and Clifford W. (Jack) Gannon, Missouri House of Representatives. All around the ads in the book were excerpts of the history of the Old Mines area as gleaned by Villmer's research in 1972 and 1973.

On Saturday, September 1, 1973, the celebration began with a greeting from Marvin J. Politte, the chairman of the 250th anniversary celebration. After he presented government representatives—State Representative Clifford W. (Jack) Gannon and Magistrate Judge Larry Casey—Father Richard Suren welcomed everyone, blessed the Old Mines Flag—made by Mark G. Boyer—and the boy scouts raised it below the U.S. Flag. Then, at twelve noon on both days attendees could choose from a dinner, booths, games, exhibits—quilting, rug making, churning, a potter's wheel, pastry making—rides, refreshments, a log playhouse, and tours. There were demonstrations for making wood shingles, barite mining, blacksmithing, copper-smithing, etc. A museum of antiques was open at St. Michael House, Fertile, Missouri. At 7:15 p.m. both days a concert was held on an outdoor stage; at 8 p.m. on the same stage was presented a historical pageant, written by Villmer, which was followed by a fireworks display.

On Sunday, September 2, Charles R. Koester, Auxiliary Bishop of St. Louis, celebrated the 10:30 a.m. parish Mass, which was well attended. After that the festival began at twelve noon, as noted above. Over the two-day event, fifteen thousand people or more came to mark the birthday of Old Mines.

The chairperson for the two-day event was Marvin J. Politte; the vice-chairperson was Natalie Villmer; and the co-chairperson and treasurer was Lawrence Z. Pashia. Norman Wilson served as the special assistant to the chairperson, and Angela (Bequette) Portell served as the secretary. Richard L. and Rose (Daugherty) Villmer were chairpersons for the arts and skills exhibits and the anniversary booths. The associate pastor, Father James Moll, was the coordinator for the St. Joachim School festival booths. Theresa (Bequette) Coleman served as the ad-solicitation chairperson, while Nancy (Bone) Politte and Regina (Bequette) Brown served as publicity co-chairpersons. Aloysius (Hoot) Mercille was in charge of food arrangements, and the Lions Club of Potosi (Saturday) and St. Joachim Parishioners (Sunday) prepared the food. Transportation was under the direction of Vincent C. Paul.

The Historical Pageant, displaying scenes in the world, in Old Mines, and in surrounding areas from 1492 to 1973, was the highlight of both evenings. The pageant coordinator and technical director was Thomas G. Paul. The outdoor stage was designed by Mark G. Boyer, and its construction was under the direction of Burgess Barton. William Portell and Mrs. David Boyer functioned as stage managers. The pageant was directed by Incarnate Word Sister (Mary Leonard) Martha Ellen Maguire; she was assisted by Sisters Kathleen O'Driscoll and Loraine Bourisaw and Stephen and Joyce (Daugherty) Politte. Sister Beatrice Marie, CPPS, and Monica Pashia were the singing directors, and Marcia Ziegler was the dance director.

Old Mines residents, former residents, and friends made up the cast. Robert Villmer, Kenneth Barton, Monica Pashia, and Richard Villmer were the narrators. Background music was provided by Ronald Boyer, Donald Boyer, and Eddie Thurman. Lighting was handled by Mike Beiser; sound by Industrial Sound and Communication, Marion, Illinois; make-up by Linda Larson, Jefferson College; costumes by Joy Slayton, Mrs. James Politte; properties by Mrs. Burgess Barton. Villmer was assisted in research by David and Phyllis (Thebeau) Boyer and Mr. and Mrs. Eric Puronen.

The *Historical Program-Pageant Book* was printed by Holland Printing Service, Flat River, Missouri. After collecting and assembling photographs, memorabilia, and historical data in order to tell the story of Old Mines and St. Joachim Church, Villmer wrote: "The early days of Old Mines, as today, herald no spectacular deeds, no unusually outstanding events, but they do show us the strength of good people, of hardworking people, who pursued their daily tasks with faith in God and a merry heart, who stopped to chat, to assist, to pray, to console, to tell a story or play a harmless trick, to welcome a stranger, rejoice for a newborn baby, to sing a requiem, or to dance at a wedding. Love, faith, endurance, and happiness shine forth from the lives of those who kept Old Mines a spot on the map, a place by the side of the road, a community of people bound together by their love. It has been a joy to meet the old, as it is to greet the new. *Bienvenu la Vielle Mine!*" (Welcome to the Old Mine!)

For the anniversary, Phyllis Boyer composed the *Old Mines Song*. It is sung to the melody of the French National Anthem, the Marseillaise Hymn:

> All of Old Mines now join in gladness,
> Two hundred fifty years we grew.
> The young folks, old and middle-aged,
> Have worked our mines and tilled our soil.
> We saw the good times and the bad
> As we began our mining settlement
> With Renault in year seventeen twenty-three.
> We stayed and kept the village growing,
> With our faith in God never fading
> Two hundred fifty years!
> We lived and kept the faith
> May we endure in this loved place
> At least two fifty more.

175TH ANNIVERSARY OF THE PARISH, 275TH ANNIVERSARY OF THE AREA

The Sestercentennial (250th) Celebration of the Old Mines Area and the Sesquicentennial (150th) Celebration of St. Joachim Parish made people of the Old Mines Area more aware of the richness of their history. Thus, in 1997, the parish marked its

250TH AND 275TH ANNIVERSARY CELEBRATIONS

Dodransbicentennial (175th) Anniversary with a parish pictorial directory with the theme of strengthening the ties that bind. Besides photos of the families in the parish, the hard-bound book contained a short history of the parish and photos of various parish groups.

On Saturday, June 27, 1998, Old Mines marked its Bicenterquasquigenary (275th) Celebration, which began with the raising of the U.S. and Missouri flags, the presentation of a Proclamation from the Missouri House of Representatives Eighty-Ninth General Assembly honoring the establishment of Old Mines, a French community, and the singing of the National Anthem and the French Anthem. Alumni of St. Joachim Elementary and High School were invited to celebrate the Diamond Anniversary of the founding of the current school one year early. The Diamond Anniversary of the School occurred in 1999, since the school was opened in 1924 (+ 75 = 99).

Attending the celebration were State Representative of the 110th District Francis Overschmidt, Presiding Commissioner of Washington County Robert Simpson; Second District County Commissioner Gary Young; and Assessor Charlotte Boyer. Doug Karsch served as Master of Ceremonies, and Rose Ann Richards, chairperson for the event, accepted the Proclamation from the Missouri House of Representatives. Other committee members included Kathy Coleman, Virginia Pashia, Natalie Villmer, Christine Daugherty, and Doug Karsch. A memorial plaque, given in the name of Alice Widmer was accepted by the Rural Parish Workers of Christ the King and given to Joyce Politte, principal of St. Joachim School.

Following the opening ceremonies, friends and alumni of the school were invited to attend a reception, hosted by Phyllis Adams, in the auditorium. There, they could view pictures and displays and enjoy refreshments. Christine Daugherty collected most of the Eighth Grade Graduation pictures from 1928, displayed them, and took orders from others who desired a copy. Also, memorabilia from the 1973 Sestercentennial Anniversary pageant and festival were displayed. Kent Bone and Janie Skiles welcomed alumni to the Lamarque School, also known as Tin Can University, which had been restored and in which many alumni had attended during the course of their education. The alumni, friends, and others at the event attended the 5 p.m. Sunday Mass, after which they went to the Knights of Columbus hall for dinner and a dance.

The Old Mines Bicenterquasquigenary was also celebrated at the Old Mines Area Historical Society's October 4, Fete de L'Automne. The nine-page brochure produced for the celebration contained an article on the history of the French in Washington County by Kent Bone. He traced the mining done by Renaudiere before Philippe Francois Renault received a land grant to mind lead on June 14, 1723, for the village that ultimately became known as the Old Mine, today known as Old Mines. He also traced the various stages of development of the area and the ceding of the territory from France to Spain and back to France, who sold it to the U.S. Also included in the packet was information on the Renault family, Louisiana census records naming Renault, and notes on the Illinois census of 1732.

The Fete, held annually in Fertile, Missouri, featured a log home museum, a storyteller, genealogies of Old Mines families, antique farm equipment, a blacksmith shop, croquilloles, French pastry, cracklings, roasting ears, a bakery, French music, square dancing, a general store, a chicken and dumpling dinner, and more. The Old Mines Area Historical Society, the sponsor of the annual Fete de L'Automne, was itself an outgrowth of the Sestercentennial Celebration in 1973. See chapter 21 on the Old Mines Area Historical Society for more information.

For Further Reading: *History of St. Joachim Parish: 1822–1972; 1723–1973,* Mark G. Boyer; *Historical Program-Pageant Book: 250th Anniversary, Old Mines, Missouri,* Natalie Villmer; Alumni and Friends Celebrate 75th Anniversary of St. Joachim School, *The Diggin's* 4:3.

21

Old Mines Area Historical Society

ORIGINS

Four years after the Sestercentennial Celebration of the Old Mines Area, the Old Mines Area Historical Society was born. Because it made people aware of their history, preserving that history took on an urgency. Citizens who remembered the past were dying, and dying with them were many of the French customs. More than ever a sense of heritage and appreciation for it was needed, if it were going to be preserved.

Alice Widmer and LaDonna Hermann, both Rural Parish Workers of Christ the King, organized the first meeting of the Old Mines Area Historical Society in 1977. The first board of directors consisted of Alice Widmer, president 1977–1995; Fran(cis) Pashia, vice-president; Virginia Pashia, secretary; LaDonna Hermann, treasurer; and JoAnn Sullivan, assistant treasurer. The board members included, in alphabetical order: Peggy Alexander, Barry Bergey, Kenneth Bone, Ronald C. Boyer, Rosemary Hyde-Thomas, Robert Johnston, Jr., Francis Oates, Julia Olin, Anne Pashia, Edward Bernard Pashia, Kathy Pfeffer, Ruth Pfeffer, Eileen Villmer, and Natalie Villmer. The Old Mines Area Historical Society (OMAHS) was incorporated in 1977 as a non-profit organization with the purpose of preservation and promotion of the cultural heritage of the Mississippi Valley, especially the Old Mines area. All board members annually volunteer thousands of hours of work to make the OMAHS a viable organization.

After getting organized, the OMAHS built an archive building on ground leased to them by the Rural Parish Workers of the Christ the King in Fertile. The members established their headquarters in the archive building, which contains a meeting space, storage space, and a vault, where precious and valuable items are kept. After this work was finished, they moved a log cabin to the site from Cannon Mines, had a blacksmith shop constructed, and began an annual Fete de L'Automne on the first Sunday of October which is attended by thousands. The festivities begin with the raising of the French, Spanish, and U.S. flags, while the anthem for each, respectively, is sung or played. The one-day event features all types of French cooking—croquillones, pastries, bakery items, cracklings, roasting ears, etc.—French music provided by Dennis Stroughmatt and his band, and French arts and crafts demonstrated by locals. Those hosting the Fete dress in nineteenth century clothes to help set the mood for the Fall Festival. A museum featuring various topics of historical interest is set up in the Maplewood School adjacent to the grounds. Because the 2020 Fete had to be cancelled due to the COVID-19 coronavirus pandemic, board members sponsored A Taste of the Fete; they sold food on the Knights of Columbus parking lot with a drive through at the KC hall.

Those who attend the annual Fete de L'Automne receive an historical experience of the way people used to live in Old Mines, what they used to eat, and what they used to do to maintain their lives. It is also a community experience during which one can meet family members or engage in some genealogy provided by family surname by the OMAHS. By looking back at the past, people from Old Mines and elsewhere, who have some connection to Old Mines, can see how they got to the present. To this end, from 2014 to 2020, a touring history museum was established temporarily in several places in the area. For more information on the History Expo, see chapter 27 on Some Major Events in Old Mines.

SEMINARS, *THE DIGGIN'S*

Each year on the first Saturday in April, the OMAHS sponsors a French Seminar in St. Michael House next to the Fete grounds on the Rural Parish Workers' property. At the day-long seminar, speakers present lectures on a variety of topics, musicians play Old Mines French tunes, and storytellers weave French tales. Presenters and attendees come from all over the United States to participate in this annual event. Topics have included clothing, herbs, French gardening, and guns, to name a few.

The OMAHS publishes a quarterly newsletter titled *The Diggin's*. Members of the OMAHS receive the newsletter as part of their membership. *The Diggin's* was begun in the fall of 1995. Currently edited by Pat Moore, it contains articles on historical events and people, information on OMAHS projects, installments on censuses, original Old Mines Concession owners, medical records of soldiers, genealogy notes, pictures and copies of original documents, members' obituaries, and much more. Each twelve-page issue reports on the ongoing work and interest of the OMAHS.

The OMAHS board meets four times a year to conduct the business of the society. The by-laws, revised March 29, 2015, indicate that the board, including the executive members—president, vice-president, secretary, and treasurer—consists of fifteen members. Elected executive members serve two-year terms and may be re-elected.

OLD MINES VILLAGE

On April 30, 1999, the Old Mines Area Historical Society purchased fifty acres of property once owned by H(iginbottham) & P(olitte) Mining Company. The property, consisting of parts of lots 6, 7, and 8 of the Old Mines Concession, was once the site of a tiff mill, and it is located across Old Mines Creek directly east of St. Joachim Church. Since 1999, the OMAHS built a large pavilion on the property, graveled a parking lot, and moved four log houses from the area to the property to what is now known as the Old Mines Village (*Village de la Vieille Mine*). Two or three more disassembled log houses stored under the pavilion await reassembling on the grounds. The future plan is to finish the village and make it the site of the annual Fete de L'Automne.

On January 28, 2020, the OMAHS purchased twelve acres of property adjoining the fifty acres previously obtained. That property, located southeast of St. Joachim Church across Old Mines Creek and along Missouri Highway 21, consists of a log home built by Richard Juliette on what used to be the George Wallace property on Wallace Road. Gradually the home, now known as The Homestead, is in the process of replacing the OMAHS headquarters/archive building in Fertile. It will be used as a museum, offices, and storage for OMAHS records and other ancient items of interest.

Both the Old Mines Village and The Homestead on sixty-two acres of property are works in process. The goal is to recreate the feel of Old Mines as it would have been in the mid- to late-1800s. The cabins are all from the Old Mines area. Some of the logs are over 175 years old. While many of the homes have undergone changes, modifications, and additions through the years by the families who lived in them, they have been reconstructed as close to their original design as possible, while making allowances for preservation and maintainability. For example, the original roofs were made of hand split wood shakes, but modern metal roofing has been used to protect them from the elements. By moving its headquarters from Fertile to Old Mines, the OMAHS hopes to make its presence more visible.

REMAINING TO BE DONE

The goal for creating the Old Mines Village is to open to the public a temporary working village to demonstrate what life was like in the 1800s and 1900s. As already mentioned, more cabins/homes need to be reassembled. Electricity and water need to be brought to the site. Likewise, modern public restrooms need to be constructed. Lots of brush needs to be cut, modern roads need to be built, and parking lots need to be established. Walkways through the village need to be outlined and paved.

Work on establishing the museum in The Homestead continues. While some materials have been moved from the headquarters/archive building in Fertile, a lot more needs to be transported from that site to The Homestead. Solid fireproof file cabinets and a safe need to be purchased and installed in The Homestead to protect records and objects. Because history never ends, the OMAHS invites people to participate in its past, to get involved in the Fete and the seminars to learn about Old Mines' past, in order to live the present.

At the urging of this author, the appointment of a member of the OMAHS board or someone else to the position of Chronicler needs to be done. The role of the Chronicler is to keep a journal of events going on in the Old Mines area. In a journal, the Chronicler records the historical account of events taking place in the Old Mines area in chronological order. He or she is not responsible for writing a story about such events, but merely recording the event, the date, the place where it occurred, those participating in it, and the purpose of it. Of course, the Chronicler may clip newspaper articles, date them, and place them in the journal to supplement the record. The Chronicler continues to record information until he or she resigns the position. The journal is passed on to the next Chronicler. Once the journal is filled, it is given to the OMAHS to be kept in its archives, and a new journal is begun. Future researchers will be thrilled to find such a resource when narrating the history of Old Mines.

Also suggested by this author is the publication of a photo book to accompany this book. From the extensive OMAHS photo archives various pictures could be chosen to illustrate every chapter in this book. Furthermore, multiple photos could be selected to illustrate sections of chapters.

PRESIDENTS AND BOARD

The Old Mines Area Historical Society has benefited from strong presidential leaders. Alice Widmer served as president from the founding of OMAHS in 1977 to 1995. She was succeeded by Fran(cis) Pashia, who lead the society from 1996 to 2010. Vicki Puronen was president from 2011 to 2013, when Cindy Merx became president. As of the writing of this book, Merx continues to serve the OMAHS as president. Other current officers and board members as of 2021 are: Mary Rill, vice-president; Jeff Higginbotham, treasurer; Mary Roux, secretary; Mary Lou Darnell, Billy Emily, Zoe Martin, Pat Moore, Mary Norbut, David Pratt, Peggy Reichardt, Carrie Richards, Kris Richards, Janie Skiles, and Natalie Villmer, board members.

In 2027, the Old Mines Area Historical Society will mark its Golden Anniversary.

For Further Reading: *To Restore All Things in Christ*, LaDonna Hermann; Old Mines Area Historical Society, Inc., web page; *The Diggin's*: Future Site of la Village de Vielle Mine, 2:2; Editorial from the Editor of *The Diggin's*, 19:3; *Village de la Veille Mine*, 21:4; Eat My Dust Takes on a New Meaning, 23:1.

22

La Brigade a Renault

BEGINNINGS

Another result of the Old Mines Sestercentennial Celebration in 1973 in conjunction with the founding of the Old Mines Area Historical Society in 1977, was the beginning of the La Brigade a Renault in 1984.

After discussing the possibility, in 1984, Richard and Rita Juliette, Kent Bone, Regina Brown, James Bourisaw, Kay Bequette, Jerry Sansagraw, Bernadette Bequette, Carolyn Politte, and others met to evaluate the plausibility of organizing an event to further the rich heritage of Old Mines. At that meeting, a decision was reached to organize a non-profit club, which would be named La Brigade a Renault in honor of Philippe Francois Renault, who is credited with founding Old Mines village after getting a grant to mine lead in the area in 1723.

After reaching that decision, the group decided that they needed officers. Kent Bone was elected president; Richard Juliette, vice-president; Kay Bequette, secretary; and Carolyn Politte, treasurer. Since 1984, officers have changed. As of 2021, Tim Daugherty serves as president; Richard Juliette, vice-president; Dennis Boyer, secretary; and Mary Rill, treasurer.

OLD MINES RENDEZVOUS

Once the decision was made to found La Brigade a Renault and the first officers were elected, the rest of 1984 and the early part of 1985 were spent raising funds to host what has become known as the Old Mines Rendezvous. It was first held in May 1985 on the grounds of St. Joachim Church, Old Mines. The first rendezvous brought over thirty primitive camps to the fields, while many area residents also participated in the event. Shooting matches were held, primitive crafters displayed their wares, and a variety of eighteenth-century-style shops were set up by merchants.

Near what was the Daly Store (razed in 2019; the Daly house was razed in 2018), a clay bread oven was erected with the help of two Canadian French craftsmen: George Bernell and Mike Abeare. That oven was the first one of its type to appear in Old Mines in nearly one hundred fifty years. Regina Brown, Ann Pratt, and Donna Malloy baked and sold what has come to be called Heritage Bread. For the first few years, they baked the dough on grape leaves, as that was the old custom. After that, bakers began to place the dough in tin pie pans. Also, inside the Daly Store, a group of women engaged in traditional quilting. In the evenings, the store became the site for a music festival with food being served to attendees. That first La Brigade a Renault Rendezvous was considered an outstanding success by all involved.

RENAUDIERE MEAT SHOOT AND RENDEZVOUS

Such success resulted in the first Winter Shoot held in February 1986. The club members, with the help of area residents, hosted the Renaudiere Meat Shoot and Rendezvous. That event, named after the first French miner in the area, Philippe de La Renaudiere, resulted in the scheduling of two events every year: the Winter Shoot in February and the Rendezvous in May. The weather, of course, influences workers, campers, merchants, and the general public's support of the events. For a few years inclement weather caused the cancellation of the Winter Shoot. The Winter Shoot was held almost continuously from 1986 to 2020. The Rendezvous was held continuously from 1985 to 2019. COVID-19 caused the cancellation of the Winter Shoot in 2021 and that of the Rendezvous in 2020.

RENDEZVOUS VILLAGE AND BREAD OVENS

As more and more people began to attend both events, a village was erected on the lower field behind (west of) the Daly Store. In 1986, a two-story cabin from Richwoods was donated to the Brigade; it was disassembled in Richwoods and reassembled on the lower field of the church in Old Mines. The Villmer cabin, the one farthest west from Highway 21, became the site for the women to mix bread dough; thus, it is now named the Bread Cabin.

With the facilities for bread-making moved to the Bread Cabin, the bread oven was relocated from the Daly Store to the east side of the Bread Cabin. A high-pitched roof was erected over it to protect it from the weather. However, it caught on fire and burned down. A new oven was built by Benny Thebeau, a local stone mason, who fashioned a stone base for the oven. Then, he placed a clay dome on the stone base. As the demand for the Heritage Bread continued to grow during events, Thebeau enlarged the stone base, removed the clay dome, and built two stone ovens on the double base. Then, he erected a pavilion over the two ovens large enough to cover them and to provide shelter for bread bakers.

On the other side of the Bread Cabin, Bill Polhemus donated a cabin in which his parents had lived. Occupying the middle of the rendezvous grounds, it is called the Registration Cabin since that is where shooter registrations take place. It is located to the east of the ovens. The cabin that is furthest east was donated to the Brigade by Glenn Osia; it is known as the Presidential Cabin. Some past presidents of the Brigade have lodged in it during events. It is also used to lodge out of town helpers.

Thus, the three cabins and ovens form a small village that becomes the focal point for the annual Winter Shoot and the Rendezvous. According to the members of the Brigade, the cabins require a lot of upkeep, which means time, energy, and money. Over a five-year period, a new subfloor was installed in the Bread Cabin, and a porch was added to the rear. A new floor and back porch were added to the Registration Cabin. And the Presidential Cabin was essentially rebuilt.

The Daly Store, which had stood on the church property for over one-hundred years and closed a number of years ago, was given by the pastor of St. Joachim Parish to the Brigade for its use at the time of the Brigade's inception. Father Robert Johnston was a staunch supporter of the Brigade's plans and events. The store became the site for the Brigade's annual Workers' Appreciation Dinner with a dance and party. Some of the participants in the Winter Shoot used it as a sleeping quarter. In the course of time, the store became unsafe to use. Furthermore, in the span of six months, it was struck by automobiles twice. After this, the pastor of the parish decided that it needed to be removed. So, in 2019 it was razed. Events that had been held in it were moved to the Incarnate Word Center, which had been the new convent dedicated in 1968.

SHOOTING RANGE

A few years after the Brigade was organized, it purchased five acres of property across the Pat Daly Road, south of the church and school grounds and to the west of the old cemetery, to use for its events. After purchasing the five acres, the property owner donated an additional five acres, which became the site of the shooting range. Because Johnston had allowed the Brigade to erect three cabins on parish property with the agreement that up to a total of seven could be added, the Brigade donated the ten acres to the parish. Besides being used as a shooting range, some of the property is used for parking for events.

During the two annual events sponsored by the Brigade, camp fees are collected from participants and merchants. For the Winter Shoot, sometimes referred to as the Renaudiere Black Powder Shoot, participants pitch camps around the cabins and on the lower school playground area. For those not desiring to dress in period clothing, a modern camping area is laid out in the baseball and soccer field to the far west of St. Joachim Church and School. Black powder shooting matches are held, along with fire start with flint and steel and trap set in February and knife and hawk throwing and fire start with flint and steel in May. In recent years, an archery shoot has been introduced. A fee is charged to the shooters, who are placed in one of three categories: men, women, and youth. The fees are used to purchase prizes awarded to the winners of shoots and event expenditures; some prizes are donated by local merchants and individuals. No entry fee is charged to the public, who can purchase food and soft drinks and enjoy music and dancing. Nationally-known musicians have performed at the rendezvous, as well as local ones. Children from St. Joachim School have sung some of the French songs handed down from their ancestors.

RENDEZVOUS HISTORY

The La Brigade a Renault Rendezvous, sometimes referred to as La Fete a Renault, is called a rendezvous, a French word meaning a coming together. Originally, it was used by French fur traders, who lived like mountain men. After a year's worth of trapping in what is now the western United States, they gathered at a designated place in the west to trade their furs with merchants for supplies for the next year. The golden era of fur trade occurred from 1780 to 1840. Sometimes a rendezvous might last a month with food, dancing, and socializing. The May Rendezvous becomes a festival complete with visiting, drinking, eating, traders, games, and dancing. The Brigade stages a living history reenactment with its two-day event. Many members of La Brigade a Renault Rendezvous belong to other groups of reenactors who share an interest in history of the Old Mines area and other areas.

Through the two annual events, members of the Brigade, volunteers, participants, and the enthusiasm of the general public and parishioners reveal a community interested in three-hundred years of Old Mines history. Through their gatherings, they teach younger generations about old Old Miners and what they faced in shaping this part of the U.S. that became the State of Missouri in 1821. The events also instill pride in those who come from the oldest settlement in Missouri. By presenting living reenactments of history, the Brigade encourages the next generations to participate and join in the efforts not to forget their heritage.

For Further Reading: La Brigade a Renault web site.

23

Lead and Barite Mining

LEAD MINING

From the time of Philippe Francois Renault in 1723 to the time of Moses Austin in 1800, lead was mined with a pick (axe) and a shovel and, maybe, a sledge hammer. Thus, the mines were called diggings! There were several kinds of lead deposits worked by miners. Sometimes large strata of lead several feet thick was mined. Large fissures, called caves, were also mined, along with small fissures, called loads. Miners excavated potters ore, called galena, gravel ore, or floats, and sparry matter called tiff. An individual miner usually excavated a shallow pit, which was eight- to ten-feet in diameter and usually not more than eight feet deep. As the mine got deeper, a windlass—an apparatus for moving a bucket of lead out of a hole with a rope attached to the bucket and the other end attached to a wooden horizontal cylinder itself attached to a platform over the hole and rotated by the turning of a crank—might be used to bring the lead to the surface. Two men usually worked a digging when using a windlass; one with pick and shovel loaded the bucket in the mine, and one at the surface hoisted the ore to the ground, where he separated the ore from clay and other rock.

In either case, once the lead ore was extracted from the veins on the surface of the ground or a few feet below the ground, the ore was placed in a bucket or a basket and carried or hauled to a smelter in a cart. The individual miner got paid for the ore by the owner of the smelter, if he had dug the lead from his own land. If, functioning as an individual contractor, he had dug the lead from someone else's land, he got paid by the owner for the going rate. If the miner worked for a company owning a smelter, then he got a salary for mining set by the company.

In the earliest days of mining, the lead ore was smelted in one of two ways. The first type of smelter was named a log-heap furnace. The ore was mixed with logs, which were set on fire. The fire burned the lead out of the ore. Once the fire burned out and the lead cooled, the lumps were gathered, sometimes recast into small bars, placed in leather pouches or baskets, and carried by pack animals to the Mississippi River to be placed on ships headed to New Orleans.

Another type of smelter was called the log furnace; it was a further refinement of the log-heap furnace. After building on a sloped hill a smelting chamber out of stone or brick to contain the heat, oak logs were rolled into it with split logs set vertically on top of them. Ore was piled on top, and more logs were placed on top of the ore. The fire was started. As the fire burned, the ore melted, and the lead ran out from a grooved opening in the bottom of the stone or brick hearth. About 50 percent of the lead was extracted from the ore in the twelve- to twenty-four hours it took to complete the smelting process. Once all was cooled, the lumps of lead were gathered, sometimes recast into small bars, placed in leather pouches, and carried by pack animals to the Mississippi River to be stored and then placed on ships headed to New Orleans. The log furnace was further refined by making a groove in the stone or brick hearth so that the molten lead would flow into a mold placed at the lower end of the groove.

A log heap furnace was the least expensive to build. The log furnace needed to be built on a hillside slope so that the molten lead could run out of it. While it was more expensive than the log heap, the basic cost involved would have been making bricks or gathering stones and cutting or fathering oak logs. Such log furnaces were not permanent structures; thus, they could be built wherever there was mining and easily replaced when they wore out.

When Austin arrived in what is now Potosi, he introduced what was called the ash furnace. This smelting process began with the ashes left in the log furnace; those contained coarse ores which the log fire could not extract. The ashes were crushed and placed into the ash furnace. A log fire was built above the ashes on the roof of the stone or brick chamber. The fuel was isolated from the lead—making it a reverberatory furnace—and yielded around 15 percent more lead. The ore was smelted by the heat that was reflected off the walls of the furnace. After the fire was started, it took about two hours to recover the molten lead. The ash furnace supplemented the log furnace, and it could run continuously rather than intermittently.

By the mid-1830s, a better smelter was making its appearance. It was named the scotch hearth furnace, the American scotch hearth furnace, and the blast furnace. The centerpiece was a stone or brick rectangular box which was several feet square with a back and sides. The front panel had a groove which sloped to a melting pot outside the furnace box. A pipe entered the lower portion of the rear of the box so air could be forced into the furnace to produce heat; often a water-powered, steam-powered, or horse-powered bellows was used. Into the box was placed small pieces of ore mixed with wood or charcoal. A stone or brick chimney was built over the box to insure a good draft. Once the fire was started, the forced air created a high and even heat. The molten lead flowed from the box and down the groove on the front into a melting pot from which it was ladled into pig molds, creating elongated rectangular bars of lead.

Lead and Barite Mining

More ore with wood or charcoal could be added to the box to keep the process going until the box filled with residue and needed to be cleaned. This type of furnace recovered 80–90 percent of the lead. By 1858, in Washington County, there were sixteen scotch hearth furnaces, one log furnace, and eleven unclassified furnaces—most likely individual inventions based on one or other or a mixture of features of the four types of smelters.

In Old Mines in 1855, there were two scotch hearth furnaces (American scotch hearth furnace, blast furnace): Long's furnace and C. White's furnace, which was a double scotch hearth. The scotch hearth furnaces were replaced or converted to air furnaces in Missouri beginning around 1874. The M and S Union Company (also known as the Union Mining and Smelting Company) furnace and the L.J. White furnace were air furnaces in Old Mines. Also, there may have been a furnace owned by James D. Lowry, but the type is not known. However, by the 1860s, when the lead blast air furnace was invented, the lead market had collapsed in Old Mines; the surface ore had been depleted, and most miners were not interested in sinking deep shafts into the earth. Nevertheless, the sparry matter called tiff, often tossed aside by the miners, became a new mining venture.

The lead that had been transported using pack horses, then wagons once roads were constructed, to ports on the Mississippi River—Kaskaskia, Fort de Chartres, Ste. Genevieve—by the early 1800s could be hauled over the Selma Road, which at first connected the Shibboleth Mines to Herculaneum. That road was later extended through Old Mines to other roads connecting furnaces and villages through the area. The goal was to get the lead to the Mississippi River; from there it could be sent to various markets, such as New Orleans and St. Louis. Shipment by railroad began in the 1850s, including, ultimately, the line that ran through Cadet.

Lead was pressed into flat sheets and used for roofs. Gutters were made from lead. The shot in a bullet was lead. Pewter housewares contained lead. Once indoor plumbing was invented, most water lines and pipes were made of lead. Glazes put on pottery contained lead. Most paints and protective coatings contained lead. Burial vault liners were made of lead. Leaded glass and crystal, obviously, contained lead. Once the automobile needed a battery, a lead-acid battery became a standard ignition tool. Lead was used to shield from radiation in medical analysis and video display equipment. It was the primary ingredient in solders, and it was added to gasoline. After it was discovered to be toxic and removed from paints, glazes, water pipes, gasoline, etc., it continued to be used in ammunition, oxides in glass and ceramics, casting metals, and sheet lead.

BARITE (TIFF)

As the surface mining of lead ran out, in the mid-1860s the mining of barite was taking off. What had been considered waste in lead mining—called tuff—became tiff. A commercial application was found for the soft-non-metallic mineral known as barite, locally known as tiff. Having a reputation as the most lasting of all white pigments, it could be used as a filler in plastics, paper, paint, putty, and rubber. Barite was found in linoleum. It was also valuable in producing chemicals, in refining beet sugar, in the preparation of cosmetics, and when x-raying the digestive system. However, its most important use, discovered around 1926, was as a weighting agent in drilling oil wells through the mud.

Once there was a use for barite, the tailings from the surface lead mines were revisited by the same hand miners to extract the tiff. The lead diggings became barite diggings. Barite that had been left behind when lead was mined was gathered from tailings. New deposits were often found when farmers plowed their fields and turned over pieces of barite. Some miners would take a steel bar and drive it into the ground, withdraw it, and inspect the tip to see if it had white residue, which would indicate the presence of barite near the surface. Other miners would sink a small hole into the ground using a pick and shovel in the hope of finding barite in the red clay.

All of the barite produced before 1937 was by hand mining. Landowners would lease their property to tiff diggers, who paid a royalty to the landowner for the barite they mined. The digger, using a pick and shovel, sank a three- to five-foot pit into the soil. If barite was found, the miner continued to dig down. He was usually assisted by a partner or a member of his family. The windlass, used to mine lead, was used to mine barite. In the shaft, the digger placed the barite in a bucket; the person on the surface hoisted it to the ground, where he or she laid it on the ground or on boards to dry; it could also be dried over an open fire. Once the barite was dry, it could be cleaned. Using a small hammer, it was broken into smaller pieces which facilitated the removal of clay and other impurities. Then, it was placed in a rattle box, which looked like a baby's cradle. By rocking the barite back and forth, forcing it against the metal spikes inside the box, more clay could be removed.

Once the barite was cleaned, it was placed on a wagon or in a cart drawn by mules or horses and brought to merchants running country stores. There it was weighed and sold in exchange for commodities or a check. In Cadet, Long's Store, located near the railroad, served as a major depot for barite. At the peak of the hand-mining days, 250 to 275 wagons a day would pass through the scales at the store. The tiff remained stockpiled at the store until it was sold to a buyer who had access to a railroad or, in Long's case, loaded onto railroad cars, which took it to a customer or a larger company for further processing. When it reached its destination, it was ground, washed to remove any remaining clay, treated in lead-lined tanks with sulfuric acid to remove iron oxide (a bleaching process), washed again to remove the acid, dried, and packed in barrels and sacks to be sold and used.

When mechanized mining came into existence about 1924, shovels, powered by steam, gasoline, or electricity, with large dippers loaded barite onto railroad cars, whose tracks had been extended into mining areas, and a gasoline-powered locomotive hauled the car to a washer plant for milling. That process consisted of washing the ore to remove the clay, then breaking the large pieces into smaller pieces. Then, the ore was placed in a wheelbarrow or wagon and hauled to a gasoline-powered washer where any remaining clay was removed. Finally, the barite was shaken to pack it tightly in barrels and sacks. That type of washer was portable, and it could be moved from one site to another as needed. There was a permanent washer like the above-described one in Old Mines. It was during the mid-1920s that the Eagle-Picher Company and the National Pigments and Chemical Company built the first permanent barite washing plants in the Old Mines area.

A log washer was used often near plants that had ramps for rail cars. The barite was dumped out of the bottom of the rail car through bars covering a thirty-foot-long log washer, which consisted of paddles rotating around a log axis. With the addition of water, the paddles removed the clay from the tiff. The water and clay flowed to a tailings or mud pond. The ore was then crushed, and the barite was concentrated into barrels and sacks.

During the Great Depression and recession (1929–1938), the washer plants closed, and all barite mining was done by hand again. In the 1940s, the mechanization of barite mining returned to a larger scale than it had ever been, while hand mining regressed. Power shovels dipped the ore out of the earth and loaded it onto trucks. The trucks hauled it to washer plants, which were portable or permanent. The ore was dumped into hoppers, which fed it to a crusher. Then, after it was broken into smaller pieces, a strong jet of water blasted the barite to remove the clay. Then, it went to a log washer, where any remaining clay was cleaned. All clay ended in a tailings pond. Following a final grinding, the tiff went through a classifier, after which it was packaged for shipment.

Barite that was going to be used for oil drilling was not bleached. It was ground dry. Barite that was going to be used in applications other than oil drilling was ground while it was wet, thickened, bleached—using a hot solution of sulfuric acid—vacuum filtered, dried in a kiln, and bagged.

While barite mining methods did not change much into the late 1950s, prospecting was often done using backhoes and power augers. When tiff was found, diesel- or gasoline-powered shovels stripped away the land to a depth of ten to fifteen feet. Trucks continued to haul the ore to a washer. Often a rotating breaker screen was used to reduce the size of the ore. A jaw crusher was also used for this purpose. Large quantities of water were required for milling the barite; this meant that tailings and wastewater had to be contained behind dikes, which were built across small valleys. The height of the dike was increased as more and more tailings were sent to the pond and more and more earth, which had been stripped, came to the plant. After a very heavy rainfall in the 1950s, a dike located near Old Mines Creek burst and sent a wall of water and mud rushing down the stream. One home built near the creek was demolished by the flood, and one person was killed. The body was not found for several days. See chapter 27 on Some Major Events for more information on this. By 1972, front end loaders were used in addition to shovels.

In 1957, production of barite peaked at 382,000 tons. While it continued to be mined in small quantities, its many uses were replaced by other synthetic materials. For all practical purposes, barite mining came to an end in 1998, even though a grinding plant was still operating in Washington County in 2000 and in 2009 for the very limited amount of tiff still being mined.

In 1972, after recognizing that the tailing ponds contained about thirty-percent of the barite that had not been collected during the milling process, the Missouri Geological Survey began investigating recovery methods. Four ponds were used as a sample; the survey discovered that in the sixty-seven existent ponds, the tailings consisted of thirty-nine million tons averaging 5 percent barite. More barite was mined than lead! Thus, for all practical purposes, by 2000 the mining of lead and barite had come to an end in Old Mines. Those who had been employed in the mining industry had to seek other places for work.

For Further Reading: *Historical Program-Pageant Book, 250th Anniversary, Old Mines, Missouri*, Natalie Villmer; Wikipedia: Southeast Missouri Lead District, Reverberatory Furnace, Windlass; Lead Industry, encyclopedia.com; United States Department of the Interior, National Park Service, National Register of Historic Places, George Cresswell Furnace; U.S. Army Corps of Engineers: A Cultural Geographical and Historical Study of the Pine Ford Lake Project Area: Washington, Jefferson, Franklin, and St. Francois Counties, Missouri; U.S. Department of the Interior, U.S. Geological Survey: Geology and Mining History of the Southeast Missouri Barite District and the Valles Mines, Washington, Jefferson, and St. Francois Counties, Missouri; Uses of Lead, Geology.com; Excerpts from: The Geology, Mining, and Preparation of Barite in Washington County, Missouri, A.A. Steel, *The Diggin's* 22:1; The Tiff Diggers, *Missouri Life* 4:2.

24

Old Mines French Language

OLD MINES FRENCH

The first men and women who first set foot on the soil of Old Mines came from France, and they spoke French. The area in France from which they came dictated the way—syntax, pronunciation, use of words, accent, etc.—they spoke French. This is easily understood by those who speak English in Boston compared to those who speak English in Dallas compared to those who speak English in Louisiana. All speak English, but it is not exactly the same. Furthermore, English in the United States is not the same as English spoken in Britain. As other French-speaking people moved from Canada to Old Mines and from Louisiana to Old Mines, the form of French spoken in Old Mines took on its own unique flavor.

Once English-speakers arrived, it developed further, even incorporating English words and phrases into its usage. In the end, it became an amalgam of Old Norman French, Native American languages, and frontier English. One must also keep in mind that Old Mines was an isolated village for the most part; thus, while it maintained its French heritage, it continued to develop and change among those who spoke French. Furthermore, since it was an oral language without a comparable written form, the only way to learn it was from those who spoke it.

The unique form of French found in Old Mines is referred to as Missouri French, Pap-Paw French, Creole French, Canadian French, French Patois, and Old Mines French. While it is generally phonetically similar to other North American varieties of French and shares many lexical similarities, it remains unique to the area in which it developed. It continued to be the only language spoken by the residents of Old Mines well into the 1930s. Furthermore, it has the distinction of being one of only three French dialects believed to have originated in the U.S. In order to simplify this chapter, the phrase *Old Mines French* will be used exclusively.

DEMISE OF OLD MINES FRENCH

Four factors caused the demise of Old Mines French. First, what changed the speaking of French in Old Mines was the 1905 Missouri law legislating compulsory schooling for children until the age of sixteen. While French was being spoken at home, in the one-room schools that developed after the law went into effect, the language was English. Officials from the State of Missouri along with teachers saw the French language as a barrier needing to be overcome in order to assimilate Old Miners into the broader society and culture. Authority determined that speaking only English would help remove some problems that were considered to be inherent in indigenous French culture.

From 1905 to 1920 a majority of French children in Old Mines knew no English before beginning first grade. While they spoke French at home, they were required to speak English in school. Gradually, those who attended school became bi-lingual, speaking French at home and English at school and other places where the primary language was English. By 1937, a visitor to Old Mines estimated that about 90 percent of Old Miners spoke both French and English, but in 35 percent of homes only French was spoken.

The second factor assisting in the demise of Old Mines French was the development of major highways and rail lines, both of which connected the isolated village to the larger area. While Old Miners were still speaking French, those living in other towns were speaking mostly English. When Old Miners travelled and spoke French, they were not easily understood by the majority of those they encountered. So, they began to learn and speak English.

The third factor causing the demise of Old Mines French follows upon the second. As English took root in other villages and towns, and as children learned and spoke only English in schools, those who continued to speak French faced scorn and ridicule for their strange tongue that few, if any outside the village of Old Mines, could understand. It didn't take long for the speaking of Old Mines French to become associated with ignorance, non-education, and backwardness. In other words, speaking Old Mines French became a stigma. Thus, learning English and speaking it became a matter of survival.

The fourth factor that caused the demise of Old Mines French and the rise of English is the result of changes in economic and political structures both locally and regionally (state). Economically, mining and farming were the primary ways people made a living. At first, they mined lead, and, when the strip-mining of lead gave out, they mined barite (tiff), which also ultimately came to an end. General or home farms supplied food—meats and vegetables—which could be smoked, salted, or cured and canned for use throughout the year. There were others who served as mill owners/operators, blacksmiths, general mercantile store owners/workers, and other types of odd jobs. In terms of political structures, Washington County, in which Old Mines exists, became a county in 1813. Missouri entered the Union in 1821. On both levels of those political structures, the language spoken was English, and one fulfilled his or her political responsibilities by speaking or writing English.

Those who have studied Old Mines French often add other factors that contributed to its demise. Some include intermarriage with English speakers, English media, conscription of young men in two World Wars, and economic opportunities outside the village which required the English language.

Using the 1910 U.S. census information, Michael L. Olsen—in a University of Georgia paper in linguistics—proposes that because fifty-one residents of Old Mines had an ancestral connection to France (that is, having one or both parents born in France), many who reported speaking English lived in households where many more spoke French. He argues that for many of the reasons noted above for the demise of Old Mines French, the 1,711 residents of the Old Mines area spoke the language at home and passed it on as the first language to their children. In other words, the records of the 1910 census underrepresent the degree to which Old Mines French was spoken at the time.

OLD MINES FRENCH DOCUMENTED

In 1930, a French professor named William Marion Miller visited Old Mines. At that time, he determined that the largest concentration of French speakers existed there. He published an article, "Missouri's 'Paw-Paw' French," in the *French Review*. Prior to Miller's work, the existence of Old Mines French was largely undocumented and unnoticed. From 1934 to 1936, Joseph Medard Carriere made several trips to Old Mines to study the French dialect and to collect folktales spoken in French by storytellers. His study of the dialect consisted of recording seventy-three folk tales from local storytellers. He estimated that about six hundred families still used the dialect at that time. In 1937, Carriere published the book *Tales from the French Folk-lore of Missouri*, and in 1939, he wrote the article "Creole Dialect of Missouri" in *American Speech*. In the article, he observed erosion of the lexicon and the introduction of grammatical structures reflective of increased usage of English.

Carriere was quickly followed by Ward Allison Dorrance, who documented the language and culture of the isolated village of Old Mines and Old Mines French, which was declining rapidly. In 1935, he published the book *The Survival of French in the Old District of Sainte Genevieve*. J.T. Miles reported in "History and Customs of Washington, Iron, St. Francois, and Ste. Genevieve Counties" (a typescript in Washington County Library, Potosi, Missouri) that by 1937 about 90 percent of Old Miners were bilingual.

In the late 1940s and early 1950s, electricity made it to the Old Mines area. Different sub-villages saw the wires strung from pole to pole at different times along the roads. When trees needed to be cleared to prepare to plant the poles and then string the wires, it took longer to get electricity to homes in the hollows. While battery-powered radios had brought English stories into village homes before the advent of electricity, electricity enabled televisions to bring English stories with characters acting the parts on screen. Whereas people in the past gathered around a storyteller to listen to tales told in Old Mines French for entertainment, with the advent of radios and television in the late 1940s and 1950s they gathered around a radio or a television to listen to stories told in English. Those who lived miles away from a power line continued storytelling in Old Mines French for several more decades.

By 1950, those who were 50+ years old spoke French among themselves, especially when they did not want their grandchildren to understand what they were talking about. The children (20+ years old) of those who were 50+ years old in 1950 could understand the French, but they could not speak it. And the grandchildren (born in 1950) of those 50+ years old in 1950 could neither speak nor understand it. Only the oldest people, whose English was poor, spoke French regularly to each other. Applying this to his own family, this author's maternal great-grandmother and grandparents spoke both French and English; they spoke French when they did not want him to know what they were talking about. This author's mother could understand what they were saying, but she could not speak French. By the time this author entered the picture, only English was spoken in his home. Thus, by the 1960s, no one remained who spoke only French; English became the language used by everyone.

Clyde O. Thogmartin visited the Old Mines area sometime before 1970, when he wrote his doctoral dissertation, later published as a book, *French Dialect of Old Mines, Missouri.* After completing his PhD in Romance Linguistics, he worked as a French Professor at Iowa State University in Ames, Iowa. Old Mines French had become stratified by age; the only fluent speakers were the oldest of the community. He attributed the influx of English media, the conscription of local men into the World Wars, and economic opportunity away from traditional mining as contributing to the demise of Old Mines French.

In 1977, Gerald L. Gold, a Canadian anthropologist studying the socio-cultural situation of the French minority, visited the Old Mines area. In 1979, he published the article "Lead Mining and the Survival and Demise of French in Rural Missouri" in *Cahiers de Geographie du Quebec,* in which he documented how movement away from family and child labor in lead and barite mining coincided with the loss of Missouri French. He also suggested that the 1970 census statistic of 196 native French speakers in Washington Country underrepresented the true number of Old Mines French speakers.

In the summer of 1977, Rosemary Hyde Thomas, a professor of English from St. Louis, came to Old Mines to begin a three-year study of Old Mines French. She wanted to listen to others speak it and to speak it herself. Thus, in September 1977, after conducting some interviews to find material, she offered a free class to anyone who wanted to learn or to relearn the old French dialect. Eight native speakers of Old

Mines French served as assistant teachers. She surfaced around thirty-five people, all of whom were at least sixty years old, who remembered Old Mines French from one degree to another. The result was an Old Mines French textbook; Thomas took the oral language and put it in written form. By 1979, the weekly classes consisted of professional instruction with eight core lessons attended regularly by twenty people. This led Thomas to publish her dissertation, *Some Aspects of the French Language and Culture of Old Mines*, in 1979, for her doctorate from St. Louis University. Thomas concluded that Old Mines French disappeared as a result of public roads, compulsory English education, English enforcement by parents, and intermarriage with other English speakers.

Nevertheless, as Thomas's classes continued, participants remembered situations, customs, and stories that many had long forgotten. By the summer of 1980, Thomas devoted the interviews to one topic: old French stories. Each of the thirty-hours of interviews gathered over three months was tape-recorded and transcribed word for word on paper. One activity of the interviews consisted of translating Carriere's stories from Old Mines French into English; Carriere had transcribed the stories he had collected and published in 1937 exactly as he had heard them in the Old Mines French dialect. Since the dialect was only oral, Carriere had no standard to follow when transcribing them, so he used unique words, constructions, and spellings as he heard them. About 75 percent of Old Mines French can be understood by those who are fluent in standard French. The result of Thomas's work was the publication of *It's Good to Tell You: French Folktales from Missouri* in 1981. The 246-page book primarily consists of twenty-one folk tales in English with Old Mines French as Carriere recorded them in the 1930s.

In *Status and Function of Languages and Language Varieties*, a collection of articles published in 1989 and edited by Ulrich Ammon, a German linguist and sociologist from the University of Dusseldorf, it was estimated that only a handful of elderly speakers of Old Mines French in isolated pockets remained. However, in 2014, several were found for an interview with National Public Radio host Robert Siegel. Kent Bone, who learned the local Old Mines dialect—described as a linguistic bridge, melding a Canadian French accent with a Louisiana French vocabulary—was interviewed along with then seventy-eight-year-old Cyrilla Boyer, who knew some of the Old Mines French but not enough to be fluent. She narrated how in the 1920s and 1930s, students who spoke French in the classroom were punished; thus, parents no longer passed on the language to their children. In general, according to NPR, most speakers knew only a smattering of words and phrases by 2014.

Another person interviewed by NPR was Dennis Stroughmatt, who was referred to as Old Mines French's ambassador to the outside world. He first visited Old Mines in the 1990s to complete a folklore class project while he was a student at Southeast Missouri State University in Cape Girardeau, and he became hooked on learning the language, going to Old Mines every weekend for two years to learn Old Mines French and traditional fiddle tunes. After graduation from Southeast Missouri State, he spent some time in Lafayette, Louisiana, becoming more fluent in French. Then, he earned a Master of History degree at Southern Illinois University in 1999. That same year, he attended the University of Quebec at Chicoutimi, Canada, where he was awarded a Certificate in Quebec French Language and Culture. In the NPR story, Stroughmatt explained that Old Mines French, often referred to as Paw-Paw French—named after a wild, local, fruit-bearing tree—has a big accent. He also expressed his hopes that the language would survive.

An Associated Press story in 2014 and updated in 2016 estimated that fewer than thirty people in Old Mines were fluent in Old Mines French. Stroughmatt tries to keep the language alive through history and music. He has recorded the histories of the elderly, uncovered scratchy wax cylinder recordings, and become a modern-day storyteller. He learned fiddle-playing from two Old Miners and continues to play and sing French tunes in Old Mines French. Scott Gossett, who studies francophone literature at the University of Missouri, explained in 2014 that the reason for the decline of Old Mines French—and ultimately its disappearance—is that there has never been a continuous academic study of it. He explained that one cannot teach an unwritten language; one learns a spoken language from those who speak it. Furthermore, when Old Mines French gave into English, not only did the language change, but the people and the reality of their lives changed, too.

As of the writing of this book in 2021, there are very few people living in Old Mines who speak Old Mines French. Most of those who knew the language have died, and the dialect has been buried with them. By the time the next generation appears in Old Mines, Old Mines French will have totally disappeared with those last few who knew it.

For Further Reading: Wikipedia: Old Mines, Missouri; Missouri French; Missouri's Paw-paw French Dialect Fading into Silence, Bridgit Bowden, Jake Godin, Ryan Schuessler, Al Jazeera English; Missouri French: A Race to Record Rare U.S. Dialect before Last Speaker Dies, Associated Press; Census Mining in Old Mines, Missouri: Reconstructing a French Community, Michael L. Olsen; Saving a French Dialect that Once Echoed in the Ozarks, Robert Siegel, NPR; Preface in *It's Good to Tell You*, Rosemary Hyde Thomas; A la Recherche de Pawpaw French: Classroom Activities, Eileen M. Angelini; Dennis Stroughmatt: Biography; Clyde Orville Thogmartin, Obituaries, Ames Tribune; Gerald Louis Gold, UQAC (Universite du Quebec a Chicoutimi); *The Diggin's*: 275 Years of the French in Washington County, Kent Bone, 4:2; Joseph Medard Carriere (1902–1970): "Collector" of Missouri French Folklore, C. Ray Brassieur, 11:1.

25

French Customs, Practices, Ways of Life

There were a variety of French customs, practices, and ways of life that existed at one time and then disappeared, or that continued well into the 1960s, or some that even continue today. The early settlers of Old Mines were bearers of the French culture they brought with them across the Atlantic and by way of Canada and Louisiana to Old Mines. Among these, in alphabetical order, are the following:

Baskets: Baskets were often woven together from oak, hickory, or ash trees. The wood chosen was due to its strength and pliability. Saplings about four to six inches in diameter were cut and split in eighths, and splints were cut or pulled off parallel with the grain of the wood. After soaking the splints in water to make them even more pliable, they were woven into the desired basket shape. For larger baskets, willow could be used because it was lighter.

Blacksmithing: Until the invention of motor cars, the blacksmith was the most important person in Old Mines. He made the metal rims that cover the wooden wheels on wagons and carts. He shod horses, made picks, shovels, hoes, hammers, nails, chains, and more. Equipment required for mining and farming was produced by the blacksmith, who also produced the implements for the kitchen: pot, kettle, and spit. His fire, often fueled by charcoal, was quickened by a large leather bellows. His tools included a forged iron anvil, hammers, tongs, and more. He often functioned as the farrier or shoer of horses. Gunsmithing was a specialized branch of blacksmithing.

Blessed Candles: Candles, blessed and obtained on February 2, the Feast of the Presentation of the Lord (known as Candlemas), could be lit to protect the home from a storm. Blessed candles were also lit and placed on either side of a crucifix when a priest brought communion to the homebound.

Blessing: Depending on the family, on either Christmas Day or New Year's Day the patriarch—if there was no patriarch, then the matriarch—gave a parental blessing to his (or her) family. In some cases, the person giving the blessing knelt and prayed while candles were lighted near a holy picture. After the prayer, he (or she) would rise and pronounce a blessing on the members of the family. In other cases, those desiring to receive the blessing knelt before the seated patriarch or matriarch giving it. He or she would put his or her hands on the head of the person to be blessed and invoke a blessing upon the individual.

Bouillon: A house party, in which a soup (broth) made from boiled chicken (or beef) was served to guests, was call a bouillon. Bread, stale or fresh, could be torn into small pieces and put into the broth. Once crackers became commercially available, around 1900, they could be crumbled into a bowl of bouillon, sprinkled with pepper, and eaten. After eating, those present could play card games, such as pinochle, pitch, or euchre.

Brooms: No matter if the house had a dirt floor or a wood floor, a broom was needed to sweep it. Brooms could be made from buck brush, a wild shrub that grows two- to three-feet tall, which was tied tightly onto the end of a pole or stick. Brooms could also be made by shaving splints from a straight oak or hickory branch to within a few inches of the end, then folding them back and bunching them over the end of the branch. By the 1840s, people began to plant boom corn to harvest and make brooms. Brooms were used to sweep the house and to sweep the yard of leaves and grass. Eventually, brooms could be bought at the hardware store.

Burial: Before undertakers or funeral homes became popular, someone in the community would volunteer to make the coffin for the body of a deceased person. While some members of the family washed and dressed the body, other members went to the cemetery and dug the grave for it. Once the coffin was finished, the body was placed into the box, which was set on two chairs or two sawhorses, and displayed in the home for a day or two. Family, friends, and neighbors would stay up all night with the deceased, who would remain in the home until the funeral. On the day of the funeral, the top of the coffin was nailed or screwed on and hauled to church in a wagon. Pall bearers carried the coffin into the church and set it upon the bier. After the Mass, it was carried to the cemetery to the place where the grave had been dug and lowered into the grave using several ropes; the ropes were placed under the coffin with a man on each end of the rope. Together the men let the ropes slip through their fingers until the coffin reached the bottom of the grave. Then dirt was shoveled into the grave; no outer vault was used. Over the course of the years, as the wood rotted and the body returned to the earth from which it came, the grave would cave in. More soil would then be put in the hole to level the ground.

Buying on Time: The owners of general stores often permitted customers to buy on time. What this meant is that the customer was able to take home the goods and foodstuffs with the promise to pay later. The owner kept a ledger or record book of what he or she was owed and by whom. After getting a paycheck, people would make a trip to the general store and pay for what they had bought on time.

Christmas Caroling: Sometime before Christmas, usually the Sunday before, students from St. Joachim High School would meet in the school and prepare to go caroling to those who were homebound. A school bus, usually driven by Vincent Paul, along with the pastor of the parish, would pick up all participants and haul them over the highway and backroads to those confined to their home. After arriving, all would enter the home and crowd in together to sing two to four Christmas carols to all present. This was an anticipated event for all homebound and those who lived with them. After all the stops were finished, the bus would deliver the students to the school, where hot chocolate and cookies were served.

Christmas Treats: While individual families had special cakes, cookies, and pastries they prepared for Christmas, in general it was only at Christmas that one could buy oranges, peanuts, and hard candy.

Christmas Tree: Until artificial Christmas trees came on the market, French people took an ax into the woods and chopped down a cedar tree (or a pine if one could be found), which was brought into the home a few days before Christmas and lodged in a bucket of rocks filled with water. Before artificial decorations were available, the tree was decorated with fruit, popcorn strings, and candles, which were lit only once or twice; often a flaming tree had to be dragged out of the door to save the home! After artificial trees and decorations became available, the box of decorations was hauled out of the closet and electric lights were put on the tree, followed by ornaments and tinsel. The bucket, which held the tree, was wrapped in a piece of cloth (usually an old sheet), and gifts large and small were placed under it, until Christmas eve or Christmas day, when they were distributed and opened.

In the earliest days of the French in Old Mines, Christmas trees were not often used. The French did cut and bring evergreen branches into their homes, hanging them on the walls or making a wreath from them and hanging it from the ceiling or the rafters.

Clothes: Before clothes were made commercially and sold, they were made at home. Sheep were grown, and their fleece was sheared from them. The wool for yarn was first carded—the fibers were combed with cards, brushes resembling curry combs of the stable, so that all of the fibers were going in one direction. The wool was then hand spun on a spinning wheel to provide yarn. If the yarn was to be colored, it was dyed with natural dyes, such as indigo for blue, madder for red, walnut hulls for brown and blacks, pokeberries for pinks and lavenders, and hickory bark for yellow. After it was dry, the yarn was set up on a loom and woven into cloth of various types. Out of the cloth, people made dresses, shirts, pants, etc.

Crocheting: Dresser scarves, doilies, and pillowslips were often crocheted; crocheting is a process of creating or adding to textiles by using a crocket hook to interlock loops of yarn, thread, or strands of other materials. The name is derived from the French term *crochet*, meaning *small hook*, which can be made from metal, wood, bamboo, or plastic. While many doilies were totally crocheted, dresser scarves and pillowslips often featured crocheted fringes. Rugs were made from strips of rags tied together into a long length of fabric and crocheted or hooked.

Drive-In: The Starlite Drive-In, originally named the Cadet Drive-In, opened in 1952 in Old Mines. It was and remains a favorite place to go on the weekends to see a movie. Even though it was closed in 2009, it reopened in 2010 and continues to show modern movies April through October. In 2013, Honda sponsored a contest to give America's favorite drive-ins digital projectors, which would allow them to stay in business as the Hollywood studios transitioned from film reels to high-tech hard drives. The Starlite Drive-In was one of nine national winners. In 1968, Terry Mercille bought the Starlite from Henry and Dorothy Blunt. In 2009, Terry's sons—Kevin, Doug, and Rob—inherited the Starlite. Located off of Highway 21 in Old Mines, the drive-in's two screens can accommodate five hundred cars.

Easter Chicks and Ducks: Another custom was getting chicks and/or ducks for Easter. After they were hatched, they were dyed pastel blue, green, red, yellow, and pink and sold in a variety of stores. Chicks and ducklings needed to be kept warm and given food and water; often they were placed in a cardboard box near a stove and covered with a towel at night. Once they were big enough to be put outside in a coop, they went there. Over the course of several weeks, they grew feathers and the pastel dyes disappeared. In a few months, they were taken out of the coop and placed in the chicken yard attached to the shed, where they roosted at night and, if hens, left eggs in the nests during the day. They, of course, could also be slaughtered and eaten!

Easter Eggs: On Holy Saturday, the day before Easter Sunday, both children and adults would gather around the table to dye hard-boiled eggs. Before the availability of kits of Easter egg dyes, people colored eggs using dyes made from coffee, plants, and Kool-Aid. They put the dyes in tea cups or mugs and they used a teaspoon to lower one egg at a time into each cup being sure that it was submerged completely into the dye until it was colored. Once colored, the egg would be lifted out of the dye and rolled onto an old dish towel to dry. After all were dry, the colored eggs were placed in a bowl or basket set on the table.

Easter Eggs Hunt: On Easter Sunday morning adults might hide the eggs in the house or outside for the children to find. Taking a basket or a bowl, the children would search inside the house or outside in order to find and gather the colored eggs.

Easter Water: When attending Mass on Easter Sunday, it was customary to bring an empty bottle. Once Mass was finished, people brought their empty bottles and jars to the huge tub of water in the sanctuary of the church. Known as Easter water, that water had been blessed during the Easter Vigil the (day or) night before. Once the bottles were filled with Easter water, they were taken home, and sometime on Easter Sunday water was sprinkled by one member of the family on all others, and all over the house, inside and outside, as a protector. It was also sprinkled on chicks, ducklings, dogs, cats, and livestock and on coops, barns, and sheds.

Egg Fighting: This was a popular Easter Sunday activity after Easter Mass on the grounds of St. Joachim Church. People had various ways to make the shell of the egg hard, such as covering them with salt for a month before Holy Saturday, when they were boiled and colored. On Sunday they were brought to church. People would wrap their hand around an egg in a fist with only the top of the egg showing. One person would hit the tip of another's egg with his or her egg. The object was to crack the opponent's egg. If one end cracked, it could be turned over to the other end, and the fight would continue. The egg that cracked on both ends was won by the person whose egg did not crack. Such egg fighting, also called egg cracking, went on until there were only a few people left with non-cracked eggs. Of course, someone might try to cheat by using a wooden egg! Egg fighting also occurred at family meals after everyone sat down around the table, but before the eating of the Easter feast began.

Embroidery: The craft of decorating fabric or other materials with thread or yarn is known as embroidery. People in Old Mines would often embroider dresser scarves, pillowslips, and tablecloths. Using a needle to apply colored thread to create a design on an item, embroidery could also be used to add beads, sequins, and other decorative items found in a household linen closet, cabinet, or cedar chest.

Foods: Among the traditional foods were **croquinoles** (*crocquecignoles, croquesingoles, croxignoles*), a twisted and crispy fried dough fritter coated with sugar or a glaze; **cracklings**, fried pork skins; **boules de pain**, round loaves baked in outdoor ovens; **sauerkraut**, made from cabbages in the garden that were thinly sliced, placed in a large pottery crock filled with rock salt water, and weighted down in the water with a plate that had a clean rock set on it; various kinds of **cookies** and **pies**; **jams** and **jellies** made from wild berries and fruits; **galettes chouazes**, a type of fried biscuit; **lost bread**, stale bread soaked in milk and egg batter and friend (French toast); **chicken and dumplings**; **Navy beans** and **cracked hominy** (dried corn kernels soaked in lye, rinsed, and heated in a kettle till it plumped, then canned or dried) cooked with a ham bone; **fried potatoes**, thinly sliced potatoes cooked in lard in an iron skillet; **brine pickles** made from sliced cucumbers from the garden, placed in a large pottery crock filled with rock salt water, and weighted down in the water with a plate that had a clean rock set on it; **drip milk**, clabbered milk left in a bowl overnight and poured into a clean pillowslip hung outside to drip (cottage cheese); and a number of ways of preparing **wild game**—deer, boar, rabbit, squirrel, etc.—and **wild greens**—polk, sourdock, carpenters square, watercress, wild onions, lambsquarter, wild lettuce, wild mustard, etc.—and wild mushrooms (morels). **Wild onions** were often cooked with scrambled eggs. Other wild greens were tossed together, like a salad, and hot bacon grease was drizzled on them. **Wild mushrooms** could be dipped in batter and friend in an iron skillet or cooked with scrambled eggs.

Fruit Trees: Most yards had fruit trees in them. Peach, apple, and plum trees were grown for their fruits. Jellies, jams, and wine could also be made from their fruits. Some people also had a vineyard for growing grapes and making wine; others harvested wild grapes and elderberries to make wine. From trees growing in the woods, pawpaws were harvested in the fall; the yellow-green to brown fruit, having a sweet, custard flavor, could be eaten raw or used in ice cream and baked desserts.

Another wild tree from which fruit could be harvested was the persimmon. In the fall, the green fruit turns orange and wrinkled; it can be eaten after it is picked, or it can be mashed to remove skins and seeds and used to make sweet breads.

Games: Children often played cowboys and Indians outside. All the children had holsters and guns that fired caps. Hide and seek, wolf on the ridge, and leapfrog were played by boys and girls. Boys played marbles, drawing a circle in dirt and trying to knock out of the circle the marble of an opponent or trying to knock into the circle the marble of an opponent. During World War I and II, boys played war; they made mud balls about one inch in diameter, let them dry, chose teams, chose a Kaiser, and, while the Kaiser ran from one side to the other, threw the dried mud balls at him in the hope of hitting him. By the time they reached junior high, most boys owned a bee-bee gun. Inside children played checkers, Chinese checkers, cards—rummy, pinochle, euchre, and solitaire—Battleship, and Monopoly. They may have owned a farm barn, complete with all kinds of toy animals, or an electric train made out of metal. The engine pulled several cars around a metal track and puffed smoke out of its stack. Most children had a bank in which to drop coins; at first the banks were made of metal and in the shape of an animal, such as a dog or cow; later banks were made of plaster and then plastic. Other games might include an erector set with bolts and nuts and metal pieces from which things could be built, jacks, pick-up sticks, baseball, horseshoes, a sled. Today, children play computer games. Adults, who often played euchre, continue to do so today as members of weekly clubs.

Gardens: Flower gardens of peonies, sweet William, Iris (often called flags), and petunias along with lilac, bleeding heart, and other annuals planted from seed, like zinnias, graced the front and sides of most homes. Usually, flower gardens were outlined with rocks of all shapes, sizes, and colors. In between the garden rock outlines, the ground was swept with a hand-made buck-brush broom to keep the walkways clean. Somewhere within the wood palings fence could be found a seven-sisters rose bush. Other plants could also be found in the flower beds, and later the wood palings fence gave way to wire fence stapled to fence posts, which had been cut from (cedar) trees, buried upright in the earth, and pounded with the sledgehammer to drive them deeply into the ground.

Somewhere behind the house or located at the side of the house was the large vegetable garden, which was plowed in the spring to create furrows for seeds, after having the wood ashes from the stove(s) thrown on the soil throughout the winter. Lettuce, radishes, onions, cabbages, corn, beets, green beans, potatoes, sweet corn, and cucumbers were planted. Seed potatoes were cut into pieces and dropped into preprepared holes. Depending on the family, tomatoes could also be planted in the vegetable garden—along with wheat, barley, pumpkins, watermelons, and muskmelons (cantaloupes)—which had to be fenced to keep animals out of it, since all was open range for stock. Some gardens also contained tobacco and cotton. Green beans, pork, and new potatoes were often cooked together. Much, but not all, of what was

French Customs, Practices, Ways of Life

grown in the vegetable garden was canned for the winter and placed in the root cellar, where jars of berries, fruits, and vegetables were available for winter eating.

Before the first frost, green tomatoes were picked and ground in a meat grinder. Seasonings were added, and the mixture was put in jars. The Spanish pickles were stored in the pantry or root cellar.

Children were often sent to the garden to pull weeds. In some families, this was considered a fitting punishment for children who had done something wrong!

Gristmill: Before there was a general mercantile store in which a person could purchase flour, people ground wheat and corn at home using an improvised mortar and pestle. Later, there was a gristmill in Old Mines, where grain—wheat and corn—was ground into flour, which could be used to make bread and cornbread. Gristmill refers to the grinding equipment as well as the building. Gristmills were located near water, which powered a water wheel, which was attached to a rotating stone with a series of wooden gears. The grain was lifted in sacks onto the sack floor at the top of the mill, often using a hoist. After the sacks were emptied into a hopper, the grain fell down through a hole in the moving runner stone at the bottom of the mill and was ground between the runner stone and the stationary stone. Both stones had their faces cut with a pattern of groves called furrows. The furrows worked liked scissors, which cut and ground the grain into flour, which fell into an output hopper, where it was collected and put into sacks.

Groundhog Day: Groundhog Day is an annual observance on February 2. In order to avoid the seven years itch—seven years of hard times, barely scratching out a living—one was encouraged to eat crepes (pancakes and sausages) on this day. The belief was that if one made and ate crepes, the actions would bring good fortune and a good wheat harvest. Gradually, the act of the groundhog seeing his shadow came to mean thirty days of winter remain; if he did not see his shadow, spring was near. In Catholicism, this day is known as the Feast of the Presentation of the Lord or Candlemas, because at Mass on this day candles are blessed for use in church and in the home. They were believed to offer special protection from storms and lightning when burned.

Hog-Slaughtering: Once it turned cold enough to freeze meat, those who had pigs to butcher would gather together at one place. After killing the pigs, they would be hung so that the blood would run out of them. Then, while the men cut the various parts of meat off of the carcass, salted it, smoked it with hickory wood, and let it hang in the smokehouse, the women would grind parts into sausage and fill the washed intestines (casings) with it. The fatty parts were cut into small pieces and rendered in a huge iron kettle sitting on a hot fire. The grease, called lard, was collected and stored in pottery crocks or metal containers. The pieces left from the rendering were called cracklins (the forerunners of pork rinds), which were eaten. From the ears, tongue, feet, other cuts (and sometimes heart) mixed together with gelatin, head cheese (not dairy) was made. The recipe varied from one cook to another. After it was gelled, it was sliced and eaten cold alone, on bread, or on crackers. An alternative to adding gelatin was the simmering of the pig's head which produced a stock naturally gelatinous. When added to the other ingredients, once all cooled, a cheese-like loaf was formed and could be sliced. Out of the blood, mixed with rice, cabbage, and other items, blood sausage was made and stuffed in the cleaned large intestine (natural casing) of the hog.

Horseshoes: With two iron stakes driven into the ground and worn horseshoes as game pieces, two teams of two people attempted to pitch the horseshoes while standing at one stake to the other one in the hope of getting them around the other stake. Points were awarded for ringers, leaners, and sliders. While people still play horseshoes today, they no longer have the worn shoes from their horses to use. Modern horseshoes are now a lawn game with stakes set in a lawn or sandbox traditionally placed forty feet apart. The shoes are more stylized U-shaped bars, about twice the size of an old horseshoe.

House-Raising: If someone needed help to build a house or a barn, the men living close would help erect the logs. Two kinds of house-raising could occur. Early in the history of Old Mines, log houses were built with the logs placed vertically next to each other. Later, logs were notched and placed horizontally on each other. Those building the house could get the outline or frame done in a single day. One must keep in mind that in the eighteenth and nineteenth century, people built small houses, some only one or two rooms. While the men erected the logs, the women cooked a meal for them. A lot of visiting also took place at a house- or barn-raising.

Once the house was erected and a wood-shingle roof covered it—later tin would replace the wood—the owners would fill the spaces between the logs inside with chinks, pieces of wood cut with one very narrow edge (like an ax) and pushed into the spaces between the logs. Then, earth was mixed with straw and spread over the logs and chinks (daubed) to create a very smooth mud wall. Once the mud dried, the walls were whitewashed with lime. Later in time, a thin wallboard could be tacked over the lime and papered with brown wrapping paper, newspapers, or wallpaper. The wide-boarded floors were covered with handmade rugs.

Usually, a porch was added to the house. During hot times, that is where people would sit to cool off. The logs on a covered porch could be treated the same way as the logs inside the house, or they could be left like the rest of the outside walls to turn a dull gray from exposure to the weather.

In Catholic homes, the walls inside were covered with religious pictures, and there may be a dresser turned into a type of altar with small statues of the Blessed Virgin Mary, the Holy Family, a saint, and a blessed candle or two. Furniture was often handmade, but later secondhand furniture or store furniture was purchased for the interior of the room(s).

Every house had at least one chimney and some had two. The lower portion was made of stone, and the upper portion was made from bricks. Not only was the chimney used to burn wood for heat, but it was also the place where food was cooked. Once both wood-burning for heat and wood-burning for cooking stoves were invented, chimneys went out of use. Stove pipes usually rose directly through the ceiling and the roof to the outside. Later, stone or concrete flues were built, and stove pipes went into them to vent the smoke to the outside.

Internet: While those in the last century knew nothing about it, internet service came to Old Mines in early 2000, and the advent of Face Book and other social media began. In 2020 broadband cables were laid for faster and more efficient internet. Computers became another necessary household appliance. While people became more connected through the internet, they also became more socially isolated; they no longer had to get out of their houses to connect to others.

Joyeux Noel: The standard French word for Christmas is Noel. The greeting given by one person to another on Christmas day was *Joyeux Noel* (Joyous Christmas! or Happy Christmas!). In some communities, *Bonne Christmisse* (Good Christmas!) could be heard.

Kerosene: Kerosene, also known as coal oil, paraffin, and lamp oil is a combustible hydrocarbon liquid derived from coal or petroleum. A light yellow-brown in color, it was purchased from a general store by the gallon and pumped from the supply drum into the customer's metal container. At home it was poured into the glass or pottery base, fount, of a kerosene lamp. A wide, flat, cotton wick or mantle was placed in the fount and fed through a lamp burner attached to the top of the fount. The top part of the wick extended out of the wick tube of the lamp burner, which included a wick-adjustment mechanism that controlled the flame. Adjustment was done by means of a small knob operating a cric, a toothed metal sprocket bearing against the wick. The kerosene was drawn upward by capillary action. Also attached to the fuel tank were four prongs to hold the glass chimney or globe, which acted to prevent the flame from being blown out and enhanced a thermally induced draft. The glass chimney needed a throat, or slight constriction, to create the proper draft for complete combustion of the kerosene. The mantle or wick holder had holes around the outer edges. When the lamp was lit and a chimney was attached, the thermally induced draft drew air through those holes and passed over the top of the mantle. This had a cooling effect and kept the mantle from over-heating. When the lamp was lit, the kerosene that the wick absorbed burned and produced a clear, bright, yellow flame. Electricity made the kerosene lamp obsolete, although many people kept them to be used when the electricity went out.

Lent and Carnival: Lent began on Ash Wednesday, which is calculated by the moon. Easter is always the first Sunday after the first full moon following the Spring Equinox. Lent is counted back six Sundays before Easter Sunday and the Wednesday before the first Sunday of Lent is Ash Wednesday. The day before Ash Wednesday is Carnival (meaning *to take out the meat*). Today it is known as Mardi Gras (Fat Tuesday). A very long time ago, no meat was eaten at all during Lent by Catholics. So, the day before Lent began, all meat and meat products were eaten. Such strict abstaining was gradually tempered to the abstaining now done only on Ash Wednesday, Fridays of Lent, and Good Friday. From time to time, Mardi Gras has been celebrated in Old Mines with merrymakers dressed in costume and a meal served in the school cafeteria.

May Crowning: In St. Joachim Church in early May, the Blessed Virgin Mary was crowned with a ring of fresh flowers. At first, Catholics would gather for this ceremony in church, where they recited the rosary before Mary was crowned by a young woman chosen to do so. Once a large statue of Mary was erected in the church yard, a procession was held from the church or school to the statue while reciting the rosary. Sometimes, school students were assigned a single prayer—such as a Hail, Mary; an Our Father; or a Glory Be—to say. Once the procession reached the statue and gathered around it, the young woman, clothed in a prom dress and escorted by a young man in a suit, walked up the steps and over the platform to the statue of Mary, upon which she placed the crown of flowers. Once plastic flowers—then silk flowers—were invented, they were used in the crown. The young woman chosen to crown Mary considered it a singular privilege.

Meal-Eating Order: Before large homes were built, on special occasions, when a number of adults were present—like Christmas, Easter, an anniversary, etc.—adults sat down to eat the meal first, while the children waited until the adults were finished and left the table. Later, the practice developed of having a children's table, at which children ate at the same time as the adults did. And in some families, the children were fed first, then dismissed, so that the adults could sit longer and enjoy the meal and the conversation that accompanied it.

Meat (Hunting): Before there was refrigeration, there was fresh meat. People hunted squirrels, rabbits, opossums, racoons, and other small and edible game. Small game, once killed, needed to be skinned, cooked, and eaten because there was no way to keep the meat from spoiling, unless it was made into sausage and smoked or preserved in some other way. Besides being good food, rabbit furs could be sold. Chickens could be slaughtered, but they had to be plucked, cooked, and eaten the same day or the meat would spoil.

Memorial Day Observance: After Mass on Memorial Day, a procession is formed of those who desire to walk to cemetery 3 while reciting the rosary and carrying plaques with the names of those who served in World War I and II. The cross and the church and U.S. flags lead the procession. When the rosary is completed, the pastor blesses the graves of those buried in the three St. Joachim Church cemeteries with a focus on those of veterans and those who died serving the country in a branch of the armed services.

Musical Instruments: The most popular instrument played by the French was the fiddle (violin), which one learned to play from an elder. Other instruments played were the French harp (harmonica), accordion, banjo, and guitar; one learned to play these from someone who already knew how to play them. A few families had a piano, which only a few people played. While individuals could play alone at home, they came together to play together for dances, square dances, wedding receptions, and other occasions.

Nativity Scenes: Some homes displayed Nativity scenes for Christmas. Located on the fireplace mantel, a sideboard, or a corner table, there could be found baby Jesus, Mary, Joseph, shepherds, sheep, wise men, and a camel. At first, the figures were made out of wax, which, of course, easily melted in the summer. Later, they were made out of plaster, which, if dropped, shattered into many pieces. Then, once plastic was invented, the figures appeared in painted plastic, which didn't melt or break when dropped. The figures were placed in a creche, usually, with maybe a few branches of cedar or pine. Or, they may have been placed beneath the Christmas tree. In some families, the baby Jesus was not added to the creche until Christmas Eve or Christmas Day.

Nicknames: There are hundreds of nicknames that were used to distinguish two to six people with the same first and last name. A nickname distinguished one Joe Boyer from another Joe Boyer, or one Pete Boyer from another Pete Boyer, etc. The nickname may have arisen from the father's name, from a certain characteristic of the person, or from something in which the individual was involved.

Outhouses: Outside toilets with either one or two places to sit were built of logs or boards about one hundred feet from the house over an excavated hole. Corn cobs, a Sears catalogue, or a Montgomery Ward catalogue served as toilet paper.

Palm Sunday: On the Sunday before Easter, Palm Sunday, palms were blessed only at the earliest Mass and then left on tables for people attending later Masses to pick up and take home. Palm branches were brought home and placed behind a cross or a picture of a saint. If one knew how to do so, he or she might weave the various strands of the branch into a cross or something else. During lightning and thunder storms, palm branches were burned in an ash tray or bowl to drive away the lightning and thunder and protect the house.

Picnic: During the summer, an annual picnic was held on the church grounds, often on the Fourth of July. While the women prepared chicken salad sandwiches and a meal to be served to those desiring to purchase either, the men tended to booths featuring games, like toss the ring on a Coke bottle, knock down the stacked milk bottles with a baseball or softball, or with a small net dip a fish out of a shallow pool and get a prize indicated by the number on the bottom of the fish. There were chances to buy on raffles for quilts or decorated dresser scarves. Bingo was played for cash, embroidered pillow slips, or other kinds of prizes. Children could ride a pony, and adults could ride a horse. In the evening, a square dance was held. The proceeds from the picnic were used to help pay the priests' salary, the nuns' salary, and other church expenses. The church picnic was the top social event of the year drawing home many who had moved away.

The summer picnic gradually turned into the Fall Festival, held in early September. What the picnic was to previous generations, the Fall Festival has come to mean for current generations. Skits, music programs, and bands have been added. Families who have moved away come back to Old Mines to catch up with childhood friends, relatives, and staff at St. Joachim. The Fall Festival is the second largest fundraiser for the parish and the school (The annual school auction holds first place). It is a community event involving grandparents, parents, students, teachers, etc. People come from other states to attend it. People look forward to it, and they are disappointed when it did not occur, such as when the remnants of a hurricane brought lots of rain to Old Mines and the festival had to be cancelled or when it was cancelled because of the 2020 coronavirus (COVID-19) pandemic. The Fall Festival gathering raises awareness of the history that made the people of Old Mines who they are today.

Porches: Older homes had porches built on the front and often on the back. Modern homes have private decks on the backs. Sitting on the front porch and/or the back porch was a practice common well into the last century. Relatives often came to visit unannounced, especially on Sunday afternoon or evening, and all adults would sit on a porch and share news, gossip, and stories. While the adults would talk, the children played various games in the yard. In the heat of the summer, people sat on the porch to cool in the breeze and rest from physical labor.

Postman: Known as mail carriers today, the postman of the past picked up the mail at the Cadet post office, where it was delivered by train, and brought it to the post office in the Wallace Store, which was destroyed a long time ago. He could also provide taxi service in his wagon for anyone needing to travel from Cadet to Old Mines. Once the mail was sorted and placed in mail boxes in Wallace Store, it could be picked up by the villagers. Of course, once automobiles were invented and Missouri Highway 21 was built, people erected mailboxes on the side of the road, and the postman delivered the mail from Cadet to the mailboxes.

Quilting: Quilting was done by women. Once a woman put a quilt on a frame, she might invite her neighbors to come and help her make a quilt. While a finger with a thimble pushed a needle with thread through the top, stuffing, and lining of the quilt—making small stitches in a design indicated by the owner—women would pass around information. Once all finished, they might enjoy dinner together. A quilting club was formed at St. Joachim; women made quilts for monthly raffles and fall festival raffles.

The top of the quilt was usually patchwork, indicating the scraps of cloth were pieced together to form it. Under the top was an insulating layer or bat, such as wool, cotton flannel, or felt. The bottom layer or back of the quilt was another piece of cloth, sometimes a sheet. Quilting was the process of sewing together all three layers. If the cover was not quilted, then it was tacked with thread tied at intervals on the top of the quilt.

French Customs, Practices, Ways of Life

Rail-Road Lumber: Men who worked in the DeSoto Railroad Shop could haul home tung-and-grove wood flooring that was taken out of box cars during repair. The used lumber was reused to build barns, sheds, and other types of outbuildings. Some would use the cheap lumber to repair their homes or to build an addition to it.

Rail Splitting: When a new fence was to be erected, a man's neighbors were often invited to help with the splitting of rails. Before the invention of barbed wire or woven wire fence, most fences were made of rails, ten- to twelve-foot-long cedar logs that were split lengthwise into three, four, or six rails—maybe more depending on the diameter of the log—or poles. After laying the ground chunk, the first rail on the ground, a zigzag outline was created. Then, the logs were stacked on top of each other with each section at about a 45-degree angle until the piled logs reached the desired height. At the junction where logs were woven together, posts were placed on either side of the rails to keep them in place and could be tied at the top with wire or rope where they crossed each other to keep them in place.

Rationing: During World War II, many items were rationed to the general public because they were needed by the soldiers fighting the war. Items such as sugar, meat, coffee, butter, cooking oil, canned milk, canned goods, gasoline, and rubber were available only with stamps issued by the government. Every citizen was issued ration books, which contained removable stamps good for such items mentioned above. Once the stamps were used for specific products, no more could be bought until a new ration book was obtained.

Saddler: Those who owned horses that were ridden needed saddles, and the person who made them was called a saddler. Saddles were made from wet green cattle leather that was fastened to a wood structure called a tree. As it dried, the leather contracted and strengthened the structure. The saddle could be embellished with carving, tooling, and other decorative attachments. Cattle hides were tanned by soaking them in either a mixture of hardwood ashes and water or rubbing them with the animal's brains to remove the hair. After tanning, the leather was used to make saddle bags, harnesses, stirrups, and other riding equipment.

Santa Claus: Before the standardization of Santa Claus in his red suit and black belt and boots, he was often displayed dressed in other colors, like blue and green. During the weeks before Christmas, he might spy on children, leaving treats for them on the fireplace, table, or window sill. After all the children were sound asleep on Christmas Eve, Santa visited the home, leaving a small gift for each child. Toys were made of wood or metal before plastic was invented.

Sewing: Before the first foot-operated sewing machine was invented, sewing was done by hand with a needle (steel or sharpened small bone) and thread. Many items were made out of cloth flour sacks or feed sacks. Some were made out of tanned leather of various kinds. Cloth was purchased from the general store by the yard, and out of it shirts, pants, and dresses were created. As children outgrew their clothes, they were slightly altered or repaired and passed on to the next child. Once the peddle-operated, metal, sewing machine made it to Old Mines, it took less time to make the clothes that were worn. And, of course, once the electric-powered sewing machine was invented, sewing, once a necessary skill for survival, became a form of artfully crafting clothes of all shapes and kinds for the family.

Shiveree (Shivaree, Chivaree): A group of neighbors would often conspire to sneak up on the home of newlyweds after midnight on the day after their wedding. The leader of the group would scream, which was the signal for all the others to yell and bang pots and pans and fire shotguns and pistols into the air, creating a ruckus until the couple appeared at the door. In some cases, the newlywed husband was put on a heavy plank and paraded around by the men, while the newlywed wife was placed in a wheelbarrow and paraded by the women. After this, the couple was congratulated by the group and refreshments may have been served. The word *shiveree* is the anglicized version of the French *charivarie,* which means a mock serenade for newlyweds. This custom may have been brought to Old Mines by the Canadian French. The modern version of shiveree is the custom of tying tin cans together and hitching them to the newlyweds' car to make a loud clanking as they drive away from the ceremony or reception. In Old Mines, shiveree was practiced primarily for couples of whom one or both had been previously married.

Shoes: Because shoes were expensive to buy and most villages did not have a cobbler, many people wore them only in the winter. They were barefoot the rest of the time.

Showing Respect: No one ever would have thought of calling an elder by his or her first name. Aunts and uncles always would be called Aunt Mary or Uncle John both in talking to her or him or talking about her or him. Grandmothers were addressed as Grandmother Alice or Granny Alice, and Grandfathers were Grandfather Bill or Grandpa Bill. People who were not related, were referred to as Mrs. Jane or Mrs. DeClue or Mr. Robert or Mr. Hahn. For women who had never been married, respect was shown by calling the woman Miss Louise or Miss Mary.

Shrines for the Blessed Virgin Mary: In the 1970s, there developed the custom of preparing a shrine in honor of the Blessed Virgin Mary. Usually, a statue of Mary was placed outside the home in a garden or a grotto made of wood or stone. Ultimately, as people removed the old bathtubs from their homes or acquired one elsewhere, they discovered that burying them lengthwise about halfway in the ground created the perfect white grotto for a concrete statue of Mary or a large blue statue of Our Lady.

Slaves: John Smith T, Etienne and Marie-Louise Lamarque, and others in Old Mines owned slaves. However, the life of the Missouri slave was different from those in the cotton-growing region further south. In Old Mines, a large number of families owned one or two slaves, often a man and woman who were married to each other. The slaves were usually domestic help; the woman served as a cook or maid, and the man worked wherever he was needed, usually mining. Where the slaves worked the land on a farm, they were more like farm hands than plantation workers. As farm hands, they labored in the fields besides their owners and their sons. On January 1, 1863, President Abraham Lincoln set free all slaves.

Soap: Before bars of soap could be purchased in a general store, most people had to make their own. After saving the ashes, on soapmaking day someone poured water through them in order to get a lye solution, which was combined with lard or grease and boiled down in a large metal pot over a fire in order to get lye soap. The liquid mixture was poured into molds and dried.

Sorghum-Making: After planting sugar cane in the spring, the making of sorghum would begin in September or October. Children could be sent into the sugar cane field to strip the blades off of the cane using a stick, paddle, or knife and to cut off the tops of the cane containing seeds. Adults would cut the canes and haul them out of the field in wagons to the mill, where they were fed into a press or grinder pulled by mules that squeezed all the juice out of them; the juice, green in color, ran into a large flat pan, which was set upon a fire in a three- to four-feet wide, five- to six-feet long, four feet deep furnace built in the earth. As the sorghum boiled, the green foam was skimmed off. It was stirred with large wooden paddles. Once it was cooked and cooled, it was stored in glass or metal containers.

Springs and Spring Houses: The springs that feed Old Mines creek are found all along its eight-mile length from its origin in Frogtown, just south of Old Mines proper, to where it empties into Mineral Fork. People would walk to the spring closest to where they lived carrying a bucket or two, which they filled from the spring and carried back to the house. That water was used for drinking, cooking, washing, and bathing. It was heated on the wood stove for the usual Saturday bath in a washtub placed in the kitchen. Frequently, all members of the family used the same water, taking turns by age or some other designated method.

Because springs were the source for clean water to drink, people used to build log spring houses, small sheds, either over the springs or over the area where the spring began to flow toward Old Mines creek or another small stream that flowed into Old Mines creek. The spring houses kept debris out of the spring. Into the cold water flowing through the spring house, people used to store milk, cream, butter, cottage cheese, and anything else that they wanted to keep cool, such as melons and berries.

Square Dances: In time past, people gathered together in a home or a pubic hall to have a square dance. Those who knew how to play a musical instrument provided the accompaniment for the dancers. At a minimum, only a fiddle was required. Elements from traditional French dances were brought to Old Mines by French settlers in the eighteenth century and developed through the past three hundred years. Basically, a square dance requires four couples arranged in a square with each couple facing the middle of the square. A caller may indicate what the dancers are to do, or all the dancers may agree to the moves. Such folk dancing or traditional square dancing has been influenced today by western square dancing.

Storytelling: Before radios and television came to Old Mines, entertainment came from listening to storytellers. A grandfather or father of a family who was reputed to be a good storyteller taught his grandson or son the oral stories. Such a master storyteller held a special place in the culture of the Old Mines area. Because the stories existed only in the memory of the storytellers, they changed as they were told, because no one hears what another person says; he or she filters what is heard and tells it differently. Thus, in the stories, details change and episodes change depending upon the storyteller. In the 1930s, some stories were recorded by professors in French and later translated into English. More can be found on storytelling in chapter 24 on Old Mines French Language.

Summer Kitchen: During the French, Spanish, and American governments, food was cooked in the fireplace, and outside during the summer. Once wood-fired cook stoves were invented and made their way to Old Mines, food was prepared on the top of a cast iron stove. It wasn't long before people began erecting a summer kitchen. This was a room connected to the house in some way or a smoke house not too far from the house. A wood-fired, cast iron stove would be placed in the summer kitchen and all cooking would take place there in order to cut down on the heat in the house. Once the food was cooked, it was brought into the house. Some summer kitchens were large enough to house a table and cabinets in which pots, pans, skillets, and cooking utensils were kept. The canning of fruits and vegetables often took place in the summer kitchen.

Telephones: In the mid-1950s, dial telephones began to be installed in the rural areas of Washington County. At first, the telephone company was resistant to stringing the wires needed for dial telephones throughout the area. However, some people—such as Verna M. Boyer in Brown Hollow—insisted that telephone cables could be placed on the electric poles already in place. In the beginning, there were often eight to ten families on a party line. A caller had to pick up the phone and see if anyone was talking to another party before getting a dial tone and being able to dial a number. After that, private lines were developed, and then home telephones became rare with cell phones, which came to the area in 2005.

Television: Three broadcast channels from St. Louis were available to those who owned a television in the late 1940s and 1950s. They needed to have an antenna on the roof of their home high enough to pick up the signals; a cable from the antenna to the back of the TV was converted from signal to black and white picture, then eventually to color, if the TV had that capacity. Around 2000, satellite TV was able to supplement the local channels, and dishes made it possible to tune in to hundreds of new offerings. Likewise, when TV signals switched from analog to digital, old tubular TVs needed to be replaced with larger screens on narrower, smart TVs.

Threshing: Threshing, the removal of the seeds from the stalks of wheat (or corn), is done by a thresher, a piece of farm equipment. Before such machines were invented, threshing was done by hand with flails. Once the hose-drawn thresher was invented in the latter part of the eighteenth century, it didn't take long before it was steam powered and engine powered. The thresher was hauled to the farms of those who grew wheat (or corn), where it separated the seeds from the stalks (or corn from the stalks). Then, it was taken to the miller, who ground the grains of wheat into flour to make bread and the corn kernels into cornmeal to make cornbread.

Washboards, Wringer Washing Machines: Laundry was done in a washtub filled with warm water either heated on the stove inside the house or in a large iron kettle over an open fire outside the house. After placing a washboard, a wooden-framed corrugated piece of metal on which clothes could be rubbed to help get them clean, into the tub, the scrubbing of dirty clothes with soap began. Once the dirty clothes were declared to be clean, they were rinsed in a washtub of cold water, wrung out, and hung on a clothesline to dry. The invention of wringers that could be attached to the washtub meant that more water could be extracted from the clothes by passing them through the hand-cranked device which consisted of two rollers. Once electricity was available, the washboard and wringer became obsolete. People could buy a wringer-washer. The electric motor put the agitator into motion to clean clothes, and the electric wringer removed most of the water and soap from them as they passed through the rollers out of the washer into the rinse tub. Then, by moving the wringer, the clothes could be passed through the rollers again from the rinse tub to the clothes basket awaiting them; the basket was taken to the clothes line, and the clothes were hung out to dry often using one or other type of clothes pins.

Water Witching: Also known as dowsing, water witching was a skill using a forked stick, called a divining rod, made of hazel, willow, peach, elm, or another tree, which, when held in both hands, dips over a water source. Water witching produced the location for wells dug in areas where there were no springs and the water source was unpredictable. Once water was found and a well dug, the sides of the well were reinforced with rock to keep the earth from caving in the well.

White Sheets and Underwear: Until late in the twentieth century, all sheets were made of white cotton. After washing them and hanging them on a clothesline to dry, if one wanted the wrinkles removed, they had to be ironed. Before the invention of electric irons, heavy iron irons were placed on the hot surface of a wood stove where they were heated and then passed over the sheet lying on a towel which had been placed on a table or on an ironing board. As the iron cooled, it had to be replaced on the stove and reheated to be used again. Some people owned two irons, so that one could be heating while the other one was being used. With the invention of wrinkle free cotton, commonly called permanent press, by Ruth Benerito in the late 1950s, not only were permanent press white sheets widely available in the 1960s, but they also were produced in a variety of colors. The production of fitted sheets, invented October 6, 1959, by Bertha Berman, enabled a bottom sheet fitted with elastic corners to stay attached to the mattress, while a top sheet was placed under the quilt or blanket.

What is true about sheets is also true about underwear, primarily boxer shorts or briefs and T-shirts for men and panties and braziers for women. All that underwear was once white. With the invention of permanent press, underwear began to be produced in prints and colors in the 1950s and 1960s. What is today called underwear, in the 1800s, women wore a chemise, drawers, bloomers, and in the winter woolen knickers and vests. Men wore pantaloons under their short breeches, using silk or wool stockings to cover their legs. Under their long breeches, they wore knee-length drawers made out of white linen, cotton, or wool; they looked like a white drapery knee-length boxer with drawstrings at the waist and the knees.

Whittling: Using a knife, a whittler did more than just create a pile of wood shavings. He often passed the time by making toys, animals, and bird figurines. Small decorative items placed in the home were often the work of a skilled whittler.

Wood-Cutting: The source for heat in most homes was a fireplace, then a wood-burning stove, which burned wood that had to be harvested from the forests. Even after fireplaces gave way to wood-burning stoves, trees needed to felled and cut into the right size of pieces for the fireplace or stove. Some people believed that wood-cutting was best done in December or January before the sap began to rise from the roots of the tree causing it to produce leaves. The hope was to avoid creosote, which emerged from the wood when it was burned and stuck to the sides of the chimney and the stove pipes. Creosote could catch on fire and burn in the chimney, stove pipe, or flue and sometimes catch the house on fire.

Wood Shingles: Before tin and asphalt shingles, most roofs were made of wood. Using a two- to two-and-a-half-foot-long cedar, red oak, or cypress log, a froe would be placed at half-inch intervals and pounded into the log with a mallet as the shingle would split off. When enough shingles had been made, they were seasoned or dried to prevent their warping. Once that had occurred, the first row of shingles was pegged or nailed in place on the roof joists at the edge of the roof and the next rows likewise, overlapping the previous row and interspersed over the cracks between shingles in the previous row. Sometimes, wood shingles or shakes were weighted with poles.

Workplaces: By the late 1940s and early 1950s, when barite mining was coming to an end, many men drove to DeSoto, Missouri, to work in the Union Pacific Railroad Repair Shops. Others drove to Potosi, Missouri, to work in the Brown Shoe Factory. Women often worked in FoJo Studio, a photo lab in DeSoto, at the Shoe Factory, or in numerous other stores or shops in either city. By the 1960s, some people were driving to St. Louis five days a week to work in any number of manufacturing jobs at MacDonald Aircraft, Chrysler, Boeing, and other large plants. While the Union Pacific Railroad Repair Shops in DeSoto continues to employ people, as does Walmart and Arch Johnson Rock Quarry, others find work in Potosi at the Red Wing Shoe Factory, Purcell Tire, Walmart, JV Construction, YMCA of the Ozarks, or any one of many fast-food places. With the opening of the Potosi Correctional Center in 1989, hundreds of jobs became available to care for the eight hundred death row, maximum

French Customs, Practices, Ways of Life

security, and high-risk male inmates in the maximum-security prison. In the 1980s, many women found work in schools, hospitals, banks, and stores, while men entered the construction industry. In the second decade of the twenty-first century, new careers opened in HVAC, nursing, therapy, radiology, etc. Self-employed Old Miners worked from home in insurance, marketing, and sales. Others found jobs with Ameren Electric, County Schools, JV Contracting, Washington County Hospital, etc. Today, a great number of St. Joachim parishioners are retirees.on the next line insert the following:

Hat/Cap Doffing: While driving by the church, men used to take off or lift and tilt their hats or caps as a mark of respect.

For Further Reading: Cinema Treasures: Starlite Drive-In; DriveInMovie.com: Starlite Drive-in; Prize Projector Means New Dawn for the Starlite Drive-in, Joe Williams, *St. Louis Post-Dispatch*; Wild Edibles, Larry R. Beckett, *Missouri Conservationist* 82:3; *The Diggin's*: Excerpts from Kaskaskia Under the French Regime, Natalia Maree Belting, 3:4; Candlemas, Groundhog Day, Kent Bone, 4:1; Continued Excerpts from History and Customs of Washington, Iron, St. Francois, and Ste. Genevieve Counties, J.T. Miles, 6:2; Old Mines Remembered, M. Louise (Boyer) Osia, 8:3; *Noel et Bonne Annee*, Sally Borgerson, 8:4; Mardi Gras in Old Mines, 12:1; Pawpaw-French Creole Cooking, Kent Bone, 13:1, 13:2; The Saga of a Barn, 13:1; The One Room Rural School and I, Lawrence Z. Pashia, 15:3; Take Out the Meat, Pat Moore, 24:1; Wikipedia: Split-Rail Fence, Threshing Machine; III. The Character and Culture of the Missouri French, IV. The Fairy Tales in the 1930s, in *It's Good to Tell You*, Rosemary Hyde Thomas; How to Make Hand-Split Wooden Shingles (Shakes), Robert Simonson, Mother Earth News; The Old Custom of Shiveree, Steve Roark, Union Outside; Shivaree: The Traditional Hazing of Our Newlywed Ancestors, The Findmypast Team; *Historical Program-Pageant Book: 250th Anniversary, Old Mines, Missouri,* Natalie Villmer.

26

La Guillonee

FRENCH CUSTOM

One of the best remembered French customs is *La Guillonee* (*Guignolee, Guiannee*), which is marked on December 31, New Year's Eve. Originating in the Middle Ages in France, this custom was brought to the United States by French settlers in Old Mines and from Canada and New Orleans. In feudal times, peasants would gather at the home of their feudal lord, and, if he was impressed by their singing, he would treat them to food and drink. As the custom developed beyond the Middle Ages, small bands of singers began to visit their neighbors in a village, like Old Mines, and at a nod from the leader, they would begin their song outside a home. If the houseowner opened the door and invited them in, they would finish their song. If the door was not opened, then the troupe of singers would move on to the next house in the village. When invited in, the singers would request a treat—meat, chicken, cake, pie, etc.—which would be brought to a designated home or hall for the *La Guillonee* Ball, often held on January 6, the twelfth and last day of Christmas. All attending the ball would share in the food that had been collected; this event is known today as a potluck dinner.

In Old Mines, the potluck with dance was often called the King's Ball, because it was held on the day marking the appearance of the magi to the child Jesus. The magi, often in the past referred to as three kings, presented three gifts to the King of kings. At the ball on January 6, a queen was chosen to preside. A bean found in a large cake eaten at the ball determined who the next queen would be at another ball held in two weeks. The balls continued every two weeks until Ash Wednesday.

Here is the English translation of *La Guillonee* by Mrs. Joe D. Casey from Old Mines French which appeared in the *Independent-Journal* on January 18, 1951:

La Guillonee

Good evening, master, mistress, dear
And everyone that lives here too;
For on the last day of the year,
The *Guillonee* is to us due.
If you should feel like giving us any kind of treat
We only ask you to bestow a small chine-piece of meat.
A chine-piece of meat is no great treat.
Ten feet long is all it need be
But we will make it ninety feet
Of rich and savory fricassee.
If nothing to us you are willing to give, then let us know;
We only ask that you to us your oldest daughter show.
We will give her a pleasant time,
And we will nicely chafe her feet.
We will let her have a jolly time,
And we will quickly warm her feet.
When I was in the midst of the woods,
I was in the shade;
I heard the cuckoo and the turtle dove cooing in the glade.
Nightingale of the verdant wood,
Ambassador of lovers gay,
Go tell, from me, my own true love,
To have a joyful heart always.
Tell her always to have a joyous heart, never to grieve,
The girl that never had a lover, say how does she live?
Her thoughts of love keep her awake
And chores away gentle sleep.

Epilogue:
And now, good company we pray
That you will kindly us excuse:
If we have foolish been and gay,
It was to drive away the blues.
Good-night, master and mistress, dear,
And everyone that lives here, too,
On the last day of the parting year
The *Guillonee* is to us due.

A story of *La Guillonee*, sung on Friday evening, December 31, 1915, appeared in the *Potosi Weekly Journal* on January 6, 1916. Louis D. Bone reported that he and his family were awakened around 11 p.m. by the stomping of feet on the porch of their home and singing. All got out of bed, lit a lamp, got dressed, and opened the door to admit the singers, who packed the room. They were accompanied by someone playing the violin and the guitar. After Bone and his family promised to donate something for the ball, all left. However, Bone's wife invited them to come back and sing the song again. Then, she treated them to cake, fruit juice, and apples in the basement of their home. After enjoying the refreshments, the troupe left.

La Guillonee belongs to a genre of customs known as begging quests. Other begging quests include Mardi Gras, Carnival, Christmas Caroling, and Halloween, among others. What all begging requests have in common is a group leader, a specific song (or songs) that is sung, and disguises and costumes to provide anonymity. French peasants from the Middle Ages would not recognize *La Guillonee* as it evolved in the U.S.

In a January 3, 1938, *St. Louis Post-Dispatch* article, Etienne Edouard Roussin recounts the singing of *La Guillonee* as part of a folk festival celebrated in Richwoods, Missouri. He explains how at dusk on New Year's Eve children and youth gathered at a predetermined meeting place from which they set out with three fiddlers and a leader to make the rounds of the town. As the group went from house to house, they requested a donation for the ball. He also mentions that in some places money or clothing was collected for the poor. In the manner of Christmas carolers, all sang the song. Roussin reports that while the members of the troupe dressed tacky, they did not travel in masquerade costume. Around midnight, the event was finished, and all retired to their homes to await the predetermined date for the ball.

In the article, Roussin states that he had heard that the custom in some places was to warm the feet of the oldest daughter before the open fireplace, even though the lyrics of the song refer to warm her feet by dancing. In Richwoods, according to Roussin, the custom was to exact a promise from her to attend the upcoming ball. He also explains that the chine-piece of meat refers to the backbone or spareribs from a pig which were roasted and served at the ball. Finally, he explains that the name *La Gaiannee*, one of the spellings of the event, means gay or happy year. In 1938, the author of the article mentions that a Father Gilbert M. Fess, a professor of French at the University of Missouri, was planning on making a recording of a fiddler playing the song.

In that same newspaper article, an English translation of *La Guillonee* appears. While it is very similar to the one found above, there are a few differences.

> Good evening, master, mistress, dear,
> And everyone that lives here, too;
> For on the last day of the year,
> The *Guillonee* is to us due.
> If you should feel like giving to us any kind of treat,
> We only ask you to bestow a small chine-piece of meat.
> A chine-piece of meat is no great treat,
> Ten feet long is all it need be,
> But we will make it ninety feet
> Of rich and savory fricassee.

La Guillonee

If nothing to us you are willing to give,
Then let us know;
We only ask that you to us your eldest daughter show.
We will give her a pleasant time,
And we will nicely chafe her feet,
We will let her have a jolly time
And we will quickly warm her feet.

When I was in the midst of the woods,
I was in the shade;
I heard the cuckoo and the turtledove
Cooing in the glade.
Nightingale of the verdant wood,
Ambassador of lovers gay,
Go tell, from me, my own true love,
To have a joyful heart always.
Tell her always to have a joyful heart,
Never to grieve
The girl that never had a lover.
Say how does she live?
Her thoughts of love keep her awake
And do not allow her to sleep.
Her aimless love keeps her awake
And chases away gentle sleep.

Epilogue:
And now, good company,
We pray that you will kindly us excuse;
If we have foolish been, and gay.
It was to drive away the blues.
Goodnight, master, mistress dear,
And everyone that lives here, too;
On the last day of the parting year,
The *Guillonee* is to us due.

As Roussin mentions above, it seems that the custom of begging for the poor, while singing a song, is another variant of how *La Guillonee* was celebrated in some places. Another variant states that the poor begged food and drink from the wealthy, who had some to spare during the winter. And still another variant states that young men were seeking donations for Twelfth Night, that is, January 6, when the ball was held, or the young men were visiting the homes of young women seeking a future bride. Women began to join the groups in the twentieth century.

Wikipedia presents a shorter version of the lyrics of *La Guiannee*:

Good evening master and mistress,

And all who live with you.
For the first day of the year,
You owe us *La Guignolee*.

If you have nothing to give,
A chine of meat or so will do.
A chine of meat is not a big thing,
Only ninety feet long.

Again, we don't ask for very much,
Only the oldest daughter of the house.
We will give her lots of good cheer,
And we will surely warm her feet.

Now, we greet you,
And beg you to forgive us please.
If we have acted a little crazy,
We meant it in good fun.

Another time we'll surely be careful
To know when we must come back here again.
Let us dance *La Guenille*,

—*La Guenille, La Guenille*!

RECORDING THE CUSTOM

By the 1950s, *La Guillonee* was quickly disappearing in Old Mines. While it still was sung in a few places, the people who knew the memorized song and the fiddlers who knew how to play it were dying. Their children didn't know Old Mines French. Plus, traveling from home to home singing a song on New Year's Eve had been replaced with traveling to a New Year's Eve party to dance to the music of a band, while enjoying alcoholic refreshments!

The gradual disappearance of *La Guillonee* got the interest of Father Edward A. Bruemmer, pastor, and Father Joseph Capizzi, associate pastor of St. Joachim Parish from 1955 to 1961. Capizzi made arrangements with Frank Eschen of KSD Radio and TV in St. Louis to come to Racola, a sub-village of Old Mines, to the home of Ralph and Theresa Coleman to record *La Guillonee* in their front room in October 1956. Ralph served as the fiddler for the then-recently revived group of Old Mines singers who knew the Old Mines French song. Eschen, who died in 1960 at the age of fifty, covered special events and subjects related to religion for KSD. As a Catholic, he had some connection to Capizzi (whom he referred to in a letter as Cap), who orchestrated the taping that resulted in five hundred 45-RPM vinyl records being pressed and sold. One side of the record features Eschen explaining the custom and song. The other side of the record presents the recording of *La Guillonee*. Ralph Coleman is the fiddler,

Steve Thebeau is the group leader and soloist, and the group consists of Nicholas Thebeau, Joseph Thebeau, Edgar Bequette, Roussan Bequette, Magdalena Thebeau, and Lourdes Bequette.

On November 29, 1956, Capizzi confirmed the order for five hundred records to be produced by Technisonic Studio in St. Louis. In the letter, Capizzi indicated that the label on both sides of the record should be *Joachim Records*. One side would contain "Narration by Frank Eschen (in English)" and the other side would contain "*La Guignolee* (in French) by the Old Mines Singers." Eschen wrote to Capizzi on December 6 1956, informing him that he had recorded the narration for the record in the office of a Father Schwienher at the League of the Sacred Heart. Schwienher then took the narration to Bud Harrison at Technisonic Studio to be dubbed onto the record. Eschen also informed Capizzi that by doing this he had saved him a $12.50 studio fee at Technisonic.

Kent Bone, in the fall 2003 issue of *The Diggin's* (9:3), reported that he had sought a copy of the record throughout the 1970s and 1980s, when Old Mines French was in serious decline. Many people told him they had a copy, but no one ever delivered one to him. Finally, in 1995, Gary Vaught from DeSoto brought him a copy that he had found in a box of old Christmas records that had once been in a jukebox. Dennis Stroughmatt, who has an interest in Old Mines French, offered to have the record transferred to a CD. Mike Lescelius of Misunderstudios, Murphysborough, Illinois, performed the technical work of getting the record to a digital master of the 1956 recoding with Bone's plan to rerelease the song.

With the support of the Old Mines Area Historical Society, *Disques Assimineur* was chosen as the label for this and any future media projects sponsored by the OMAHS. The label refers to *disques*, the French word for disc or record. *Assimineur*, coined by Ray Brassieur of the University of Louisiana at Lafayette, refers to another name for Old Mines French: Pawpaw French. *Assimine* is the Franco-Algonquin word for the fruit of the papaw tree—pawpaw—and mineur is the French word for miner. Put together, they form *Assimineur*, basically Pawpaw (French) Miner!

The CD cover was designed by people working at PRO CD in Kirkwood, Missouri. The photo chosen for the cover was Zedore Coleman sitting in front of a split picket fence playing his fiddle. Zedore is the grandfather of Ralph Coleman, who played the fiddle for the record. Accompanying the CD is a booklet, co-produced by Bone and Natalie Villmer, which contains an English translation of the song, a biography and photo of Eschen, a collection of essays dating from 1867 that illustrate the custom in its mid-Mississippi context as well as in the larger scheme of French North America, and some written correspondence between Eschen and Capizzi, who, after he left Old Mines, joined the U.S. Navy and drowned in an accident. The CD made its debut in October 2003.

In the 1970s, the OMAHS attempted a revival of *La Guillonee*. Natalie Villmer taught it to St. Joachim School students for about ten years. For three to four years, it was performed in the homes of area residents with Anna Pashia as leader, at the Rendezvous with students, and at the Fete de L'Automne. However, it was too late for a new generation to embrace it. Old Miners had been assimilated into an English-speaking culture, in which New Year's Eve dances coupled with a total loss of Old Mines French meant the demise of this custom. Furthermore, in Old Mines, singers would often blacken their faces with soot from the wood stove or shoe polish. Today, such black face is not politically acceptable by African Americans, although in Old Mines such an action most likely referred to the death of the current year.

For Further Reading: *The Diggin's*: La Veillee de le Jour de L'an, La Guillonee, Kent Bone, 6:4; French New Years Custom Survived in Old Towns, 6:4; The Private Recording Label of Old Mines Area Historical Society, Inc., "Tune from the Pawpaw Patch," 9:3; Keep the Music Alive, 18:3; *La Guillonee: A French New Year's Eve Custom and Song: A Collection of Stories 1855–2009, Vol. I*, Kent Bone, Natalie Villmer; *History of St. Joachim Parish: 1822–1972; 1723–1973*, Mark G. Boyer; *Historical Program-Pageant Book: 250th Anniversary, Old Mines, Missouri*, Natalie Villmer.

27

Some Major Events

CYCLONE 1911

On April 19, 1911, a cyclone, a huge and powerful storm, passed through Cadet, Missouri, where it did considerable damage to property and destroyed an immense amount of valuable timber. After coming from the west and moving to the east, it cut a wide swath through the forest before leveling barns, houses, and removing roofs. It also moved a building off its foundation about four inches, while doing damage to several more homes and buildings.

CYCLONE 1917

On May 31, 1917, a cyclone passed through Washington County, Missouri, leaving seven people dead, many injured, and wrecking homes, businesses, fences, orchards, and crops. The greatest damage was done in Mineral Point, where the entire town was destroyed. The powerful, three-eights-of-a-mile-wide storm traveled in a northeast direction. Homes, stores, and barns were destroyed. Large swaths of timber were blown down.

The railroad track one-fourth of a mile south of the Mineral Point station was curved sixteen inches out of line. That caused the north bound passenger train number 22 to stop about one half of a mile south of the station. After the cyclone passed, some of the 6,500 passengers on the train assisted in the rescue work in a driving rain and hail storm. Some of the injured were put on the train and taken to the YMCA building in DeSoto, where they received medical care.

Eighty-three homes were destroyed; thirty homes were damaged; and 149 people were declared to be homeless. The loss of property, crops, orchards, and live stock was estimated to be from $150,000 to $200,000.

FLU PANDEMIC 1918 AND 1921

The 1918 influenza pandemic was caused by the H1N1 virus with genes of avian origin. There is no universal consensus regarding where the virus originated; during 1918–1919, it spread worldwide. It was first identified in the U.S. in the military in the spring of 1918. About five hundred million people worldwide became infected with the virus; in the U.S., 675,000 people were infected with the virus. At the time, there were no vaccines to protect against influenza infections, and there were no antibiotics to treat secondary bacterial infections that are associated with it. All people could do was isolate, quarantine, practice good personal hygiene, use disinfectants, and limit public gatherings. Young adults were those most seriously affected.

Lawrence Z. Pashia remembered that many people died in Old Mines. In 1980, he said that as an altar server in St. Joachim Church, he participated in as many as four funerals in one day, while the priest, Father John Daly (1916–1928) went on many sick calls. He also recalled burying two people who died from the flu in the same grave. It was very contagious.

In 1921, another flu epidemic struck the area, but not as many people died as in the epidemic of 1918. According to Burlin Boyer, an undertaker in Desloge, Missouri, this flu epidemic affected children. He reports that he and his father, C.Z. Boyer, also an undertaker, buried thirty-five children in 1920; 38 in 1921; 33 in 1922; 27 in 1923; 24 in 1924; and 21 in 1925. In addition to the flu, children died of scarlet fever, pneumonia, diphtheria, small pox, and meningitis.

OLD MINES CREEK FLOOD 1957

After a very heavy rain during the day and night of June 29, 1957, a dike containing the wastewater from milling barite or tiff broke in Old Mines and sent a wall of red muddy water surging north in Old Mines Creek. Albert Battreal died in the flood, as it completely washed away his home. His body was found several days later downstream covered in debris near Racola. In Racola, Roy Amsler filed a claim in St. Louis circuit court for twenty thousand dollars damages and forty-thousand dollars punitive damages against National Lead Co., Magnet Cove Barium Co., and Homer Politte, Henry Hartzell, Willard Politte, and Leonard Howell, mining land owners or mining operators in the Old Mines-Racola area. Amsler owned a tavern and motel in Racola. He claimed that he and his wife stood waist-deep in the flood water surging through his tavern and living quarters. Besides the damage to the tavern, two small cottages at the rear of the tavern were washed away by the flood. Amsler claimed that his car was damaged. Several other homes also suffered damage by the water, which left deposits of heavy red mud from the tiff ponds.

Some Major Events

TORNADO 1969

Probably the most natural devastating event to occur in Old Mines' history was the tornado that hit Frogtown on June 22, 1969. The tornado, a violent, twisted funnel of high-speed wind, was on a twelve-mile path that touched the ground south of Old Mines village and west of Missouri Highway 21. It hit and destroyed the home of Roy and Opal Pratt, killing fifty-two-year-old Roy and their eight-year-old son, Francis Paul. It injured Opal and five of their other children: Wayne, Freda, Ann, Mary, and Dorothy. They were taken to St. Luke Hospital and Children's Hospital in St. Louis to be treated for head injuries, broken limbs, and other serious injuries.

Eight other homes in the same area were destroyed: Mr. and Mrs. Raymond Boyer, Mr. and Mrs. Matt Boyer, Mr. and Mrs. Elmer Dean, Thomas Matt Roderick, Clyde Boyer, Edythe Miller, Everett and Ruby Miller, and Mr. and Mrs. Columbus Boyer. Houses were completely removed from their foundations. Walls exploded from the force of the wind, and roofs caved in. Four other homes suffered major damage, four had minor damage, and thirty-four outbuildings were destroyed.

Debris was strewn in all directions. Cars and trucks were blown a hundred yards away, and some were crashed into trees. Many trees were stripped of their branches or had debris wrapped around them. Electric poles were toppled over roads. At least twenty people were injured.

The people of Old Mines began to rebuild the day after the tornado. A trust fund was established for the Pratt family. The Knights of Columbus gathered clothing to distribute to those who had lost everything. Furniture depots enabled those who found new places to live to furnish their houses and apartments. The Red Cross helped with food, clothing, and collection of donations. Repair crews formed to fix homes that had minor damage. Gradually, over the course of the year cleanup was accomplished and rebuilding was begun in Frogtown.

DRUG-LINKED KILLINGS 1974

Four young men, who died under suspicious circumstances in the Old Mines area, were most likely murdered, according to the *St. Louis Post-Dispatch*, August 11, 1974. Two women, who had lived in Potosi, volunteered information to the Florissant Police Department about the drug traffic in Washington County. While local law enforcement at first thought that the deaths were accidents, the women said they were murders. Bruce Williams, David Coleman, David Pratt, and Kelly Koch died under suspicious circumstances. Coleman drowned in a small pond, and Williams and Pratt were hit-and-run victims. Koch died when his car ran into a tree. The women named twelve persons who were involved in drug trafficking in Washington County.

GREAT FLOOD 1993

The Great Flood of 1993 primarily concerned the Mississippi River and the Missouri River from April to October of that year. However, when the Mississippi River flooded, it caused the Meramec River, one of its tributaries to flood. In turn, the flooding of the Meramec River caused Big River, one of the Meramec's tributaries, to flood. With Big River flooded, the Mineral Fork, one of Big River's tributaries, flooded. And, if Mineral Fork flooded, then one of its tributaries—Old Mines Creek—was not able to empty into the Mineral Fork. Thus, water rose, was backed up, all the way from the Mississippi River to Old Mines. Fifteen to twenty billion dollars in damages occurred over an area 745 miles long by 435 miles wide, totaling about 320,000 square miles. The flooding lasted from one hundred days in some places to two hundred days in other places. Homes were destroyed, fifteen million acres of farmland were inundated, and two whole towns were relocated to higher ground. Thirty-two people lost their lives to the floods. Even after the water was gone, large amounts of sand were left to cover farmlands and homes.

THUNDERSTORM WIND GUSTS 2003

On May 6, 2003, thunderstorm wind gusts uprooted and damaged hundreds of trees from just north of Potosi to Richwoods, which lost electricity due to downed power lines. Washington State Park was closed for seventeen days after the storm because of all the tree damage. The property belonging to the Rural Parish Workers of Christ the King also sustained tree damage. As the storm moved to DeSoto, the winds continued to damage trees and cause power line damage. The thunderstorm winds approached one hundred miles per hour; they destroyed six homes, majorly damaged twenty-seven homes, and minorly damaged 111 homes. Many businesses schools, and churches suffered roof damage. Heavy rain caused flash flooding, with up to four feet of water on Main Street in DeSoto. Some people referred to this storm as a cyclone, but the National Oceanic and Atmospheric Administration (NOAA) identified it as thunderstorm high wind gusts.

BICENTENNIAL OF WASHINGTON COUNTY 2013

On August 17, 2013, the Bicentennial of Washington County was celebrated in Old Mines on the campus of St. Joachim Church and School. Washington County was erected on August 21, 1813. The chairperson for the celebration, John Robinson III, and the committee decided that it was best to hold the bicentennial celebration in the oldest settlement of the county (and the State of Missouri) instead of marking it in the county seat, Potosi. Robinson served at the Master of Ceremonies for the raising of three flags—French, Spanish, and United States—by members of La Brigade a

Renault in the area on the church property where they host their rendezvous twice every year. Speeches were given by the Counsel Honoraire de France, the Honorable James Mueze, who came to the celebration; by Representative Ben Harris and Senator Gary Romine, and others.

Potosi Mayor T.R. Dudley narrated a history of Washington County, noting the presence of Native Americans, French miners seeking lead and barite, and more. Following the speeches, attendees could see historical cultural exhibits, eat authentic foods, see crafters at work making candles, sewing and spinning, making rope, and baking bread, view period clothing and living history displays of old guns and trapping equipment, play games, and more. Dennis Stroughmatt and Ozark Mountain Strings provided music for the event. The planning committee from Old Mines included Mary Norbut, Monica Pashia, Natalie Villmer, Dennis Boyer, and Richard Juliette.

WASHINGTON COUNTY HISTORY EXPO 2019, 2020

The first Washington County History Expo (History and Tourism Fair) was held from 1 to 4 p.m. on February 22, 2015, in the Lions Den in Potosi. The second one followed in 2016 and the third in 2017. Weather caused the cancellation of the fourth in 2018. The fifth expo was held on February 24, 2019, in St. Joachim School auditorium in conjunction with La Brigade a Renault Winter Shoot. Not only did it celebrate the history of the area, but it featured the Old Mines Area Historical Society's focus on publications and history, the Mine a Breton Historical Society's focus on artifacts and photos, and the Village of Caledonia Historical Society's focus on its 200th anniversary. The sixth expo was also held in conjunction with La Brigade a Renault Winter Shoot on February 22, 2020, in St. Joachim School. The highlights of that expo were presentations on Missouri State Parks and the opportunity to see the Rural Parish Mobile Healthcare Clinic.

The purpose of the free expos was to meld history and tourism by presenting displays sponsored by various Historical Societies in Washington County: Bellevue Valley, Mine a Breton, Old Mines Area, Valley of Caledonia, Washington County Chamber of Commerce, and Potosi Lions Den. The displays and demonstrations vary from place to place. The expo is designed to help those who want to learn more about area history, genealogy, tourism, and local business. Artisans, authors and publications, genealogical and historical societies, business, civic, historical, public, and tourism groups are present at the expos. The organizers of the expo hope to get the traveling exhibit back on the road for 2022.

CORONAVIRUS PANDEMIC 2020-2021

On February 11, 2020, the World Health Organization (WHO) named the disease that was first identified in December 2019 in Wuhan, China, COVID-19, meaning coronavirus disease 2019. In March 2020, WHO declared coronavirus to be a pandemic with severe acute respiratory syndrome; it is spread through the air from one person to another through breathing, coughing, sneezing, or speaking and enters through the mouth, nose, or eyes. It may also be spread through contaminated surfaces. Preventative measures included social distancing, wearing face masks in public, ventilation and air-filtering, hand washing, disinfecting surfaces, and self-isolation for those who were exposed or symptomatic. In January 2021, vaccines began to be approved and distributed to prevent the disease.

In the Archdiocese of St. Louis, the archbishop ordered a lock down of all churches under a stay-at-home order on March 17, 2020. St. Joachim parishioners could not attend Mass or receive sacraments except by invitation of the pastor. On May 19, 2020, churches reopened under specific guidelines of safe distancing, wearing of masks, a percent of occupancy, removing participation aids, and sanitizing facilities.

In St. Joachim Church, every other pew was roped off to facilitate safe distancing. Parishioners wore masks into church, during Mass, on the way to communion, and when leaving the building. The priest also wore a mask when in close proximity to others and when distributing communion. Volunteers wiped and sanitized the pews after each Mass. Parishioners who ventured to attend Mass had to rely on online bulletins or pick-up paper bulletins and other communication from the rectory porch. Participation aids were given to parishioners, who were instructed to take them home and bring them to church every time they came to Mass.

RCIA baptisms and full receptions at Easter, first communion, and confirmation were postponed. RCIA baptisms and full receptions occurred on the Vigil of Pentecost, May 30, 2020. First communion, scheduled for May 3, was moved to June 14. Confirmation, scheduled for May 19, took place on June 28 by the pastor, Father Anthony Datillo. To practice social distancing and at the same time accommodate the crowds, first communion and confirmation were live streamed to tents pitched in the parking lot. Ronald Boyer, who live streamed Sunday Mass to you tube and face book, making it possible for those who stayed at home to view Mass on their home computer, tablet, or smart phone, set up the live stream to parishioners gathered under the tents. Those attending the sacramental celebrations under the tents came to the church door to receive communion.

By using all recommended COVID-19 precautions, the Parish School of Religion, RCIA, and St. Joachim School began again in August 2020. PSR continued to November 11, when the number of students in quarantine required a month-long break; on December 9, PSR was back in session. St. Joachim School also adjourned a couple of times due to staff infection and once due to the number of quarantines; it resumed on December 9, 2020.

COVID-19 changed St. Joachim Parish. Because the obligation to attend Sunday Mass was suspended, attendance greatly decreased, especially among young families. Members of the older generation, who were more at risk, were advised to stay home. Some of them attended weekday Mass because there were fewer people in attendance. From March through May 2020, funerals were held in the cemetery with a Memorial Mass scheduled at a later date. Drive-by wakes became common. Several parishioners died after being infected with coronavirus.

Because of coronavirus, the September 2020 Fall Festival was cancelled, along with the St. Ann Turkey Bingo and Craft Festival and the Pro-Life Dinner. Parish meetings were cancelled. To avoid the virus, people stayed isolated in their homes. They wore masks when in public. There were periodic shortages of food, paper products, and sanitizing supplies in local stores. And, of course, all had to refrain from hugging or touching others.

As of the writing of this book, while vaccinations are taking place, more than 121 million cases of coronavirus have been confirmed worldwide with 2.69 million deaths. Some of life is very gradually getting back to normal. Mask-wearing, social-distancing, and sanitizing remain in effect. The end of the virus remains in the future. The hope is that vaccines will keep it under control.

For Further Reading: Wikipedia: Great Flood of 1993, COVID-19 Pandemic; History of 1918 Flu Pandemic, Centers for Disease Control and Prevention; The Biggest Flu, Beth W. Orenstein, Everyday Health; *The Diggin's*: Cyclone Passes through County, Killing Many, 8:1; The Early Days of the Undertaking Business, 12:3; Bygone Days, Lawrence Z. Pashia, 15:4; Our Towns: Cadet in the News, 20:1, 21:1.

28

Wars and Soldiers

REVOLUTIONARY WAR

While the French had been in what became the State of Missouri as early as 1719 mining lead, they did not participate in the Revolutionary War (1775–1783) because that took place on the east coast of North America in the thirteen original colonies, located a long way east and across the Mississippi River. After a series of British Parliament acts that angered the colonists, the first continental congress assembled in Philadelphia in 1774; as a result, the Revolutionary War began in 1775, and, after the second continental congress in Philadelphia in 1775, the colonists formed the United States and declared their independence from Britain on July 4, 1776. In St. Joachim Cemeteries there is buried only one man who fought in the Revolutionary War: Thomas Madden.

WAR OF 1812

The same is true of the War of 1812 (1812–1815), when the U.S. declared war on Britain and attempted to conquer what is now Canada. The war ended with no gain on either side. However, some people from what is now Canada may have escaped the war by migrating south into what was the Louisiana Territory.

On August 10, 1821, Missouri entered into the United States, but that had little immediate effect upon those living within the boundaries of the twenty-fourth state to enter the union. Known as the Missouri Territory before it became a state, it was part of the 1803 Louisiana Purchase.

Wars and Soldiers

MEXICAN-AMERICAN WAR

After the U.S. annexed Texas, the Mexican-American War (1846–1848) began. Mexico sent troops to attack U.S. troops, and congress declared war. The war ended with Mexico ceding the states of California, Utah, Nevada, as well as parts of New Mexico, Colorado, Arizona, and Wyoming. This was another example of a war that was fought too far away for French settlers in Old Mines to know too much about. In St. Joachim Cemeteries, there is only one man who fought in the Mexican-American War: Elijah Godat Bequette.

AMERICAN CIVIL WAR

The first war to make its way to Old Mines was the American Civil War (1861–1865). The issue was slavery. Eleven southern states, known as the Confederacy, did not want slavery to be abolished. Under the leadership of President Abraham Lincoln, a member of the Republican Party, slavery was at first not to be expanded, and then it was abolished. The union, consisting of northern states, won the war, which ended forever the practice of slavery.

Just as the nation was divided on the issue of slavery, so were citizens living in Old Mines. Its earliest settlers had owned slaves. Around Cadet, Missouri, Sam Long was captured by union soldiers as he made his way home from his store. They tied him to a tree and shot and killed him because someone had accused him of having slaves hidden in his home along Big River. His body was found by his family three days later. While standing in front of his fireplace in his living room in his home in Fertile, Missouri, George Higginbotham was shot by bushwhackers. At Racola, Missouri, the Coleman store was ransacked by soldiers on their way down Old Mines Creek, while up the creek soldiers came into the log home of James Dean and threatened the family with harm. They left quickly, after hearing gun shots in Old Mines, and escaped harm.

St. Joachim Cemeteries contain the graves of some who fought in the American Civil War. Below is a list of those who served their country and are buried in St. Joachim Cemeteries, in alphabetical order up to December 2016: Francis Zeno Bequette, Thomas Joseph Cyrill Bequette, Felix Mathew Bouchard, Peter Bourisaw, Tojule Bourisaw, Benjamin Boyer, Elisha Boyer, Felix Boyer, Ferdinand A. Boyer, Fred K. Boyer, Jacob Boyer, John T. Boyer, William Cyprian Boyer, Richard Brimm, Alois Coleman, John Dean, Felix DeCleau, John DeClue, Felix Douglas, Paul Dumphy, Joseph Rosatti Govero, Joseph B. Hanson, William Thomas Hopkins, James Juliette, Jules Juliette, John Calliot LaChance, Richard O'Brien, J.N. Paul, Cyprian N. Politte, David Politte, Joseph Politte, Louis Abraham Politte, Michael Politte, Neree Nurial Rosemond Politte, Henry Pratt, Antoine Reando, Patrick Sheehan, John Tebeau, Paul Joseph Napoleon Trokey, and Michael Ward.

After the Civil War ended, men who fought in it returned to Old Mines to farm or to mine lead. The tiff that the miners had been discarding when mining lead was discovered to be valuable; thus, a new industry of mining barite (tiff) was born. Other people grew wheat, tobacco, sugar cane, corn, and other items to make a living. Some hunted and fished.

The next national fight is known as the Spanish-American War (1898). Because the U.S. supported the Cuban struggle for independence, Spain declared war on the U.S. The war lasted only a short time, and, after the peace treaty was signed, the U.S. gained the Philippines, Puerto Rico, and Guam. Like many previous wars, this one had little to no effect on Old Miners.

WORLD WAR I

However, World War I (1914–1918) did affect the people living in Old Mines. Young men were summoned to serve their country after the U.S. joined the allies (Russia, Britain, France, Japan, and Italy) to defeat the central powers of Germany, Austria-Hungary, Bulgaria, and the Ottoman Empire. Some, who spoke French, became interpreters in France. Many Old Miners are buried in foreign soil that had been tilled by their ancestors. Those who came home to Old Mines narrated how those in other countries lived in addition to all they had seen while being trained in the U.S.

St. Joachim Cemeteries contain the graves of some who fought in World War I. Below is a list of those who served their country and are buried in St. Joachim Cemeteries, in alphabetical order up to December 2016: Chester Joseph Bourisaw, Frances James Boyer, Harry Wilfred Boyer, Joseph H. Boyer, Walter Richard Boyer, Joseph Ben Coleman, Patrick Edward DeClue, Curtis White Eakin, James E. Hopkins, Isaac James Jullerate, Festus Joseph Lalumondiere, Thomas Edward Nephew, Joseph Wilfred Osia, Rolla Joseph Pashia, Anslen Portell, Peter S. Robart, Morgan Joseph Ronquest, Thomas Walter Sampson, Cecil G. Schmidt, Sr., and Edward A. Swantner.

WORLD WAR II

From 1939 to 1945, the U.S. was involved in World War II, and young men were drafted into service after Germany invaded Poland. The enemy, named the axis powers, consisted of Germany, Italy, and Japan; the allies consisted of Britain and Russia. Once Germany and Japan capitulated in 1945, the war ended in Europe, but it changed the lives of those who returned to Old Mines. Mechanization became the order of the day. Families bought cars, trucks, and radios. Many such items were bought on what was known as "on time." That meant that regular payments were established, usually monthly, until the item was paid in full. Electricity poles and lines began to be erected and strung through Old Mines. The practice of going to bed at dusk and rising at dawn was erased by the electric light. Opportunity for employment increased, while the road to get to it—Missouri Highway 21–was improved.

St. Joachim Cemeteries contain the graves of many who fought in World War II. Below is a list of those who served their country and are buried in St. Joachim Cemeteries, in alphabetical order up to December 2016: Louis Edward Baker, Harold M. Barlett, Clifford D. Bequette, Howard J. Bequette, Joseph Roy Bequette, Sylvester C. Bequette, Bernis M. Bone, Jesse E. Bone, Floyd Francis Bourbon, Alfred Wilfred Bourisaw, James M. Bourisaw, Willard P. Bourisaw, Carl I. Boyer, Daniel Thomas Boyer, Sr., Edmond L. Boyer, Francis George Boyer, Francis Lucian Boyer, Harold W. Boyer, Howard Lucian Boyer, Sr., John Melvin Boyer Sr., Joseph Boyer, Lawrence Edward Boyer, Jr., Raymond Carter Boyer, Terrence Gene Boyer,

Adrian Glennon Coleman, Alphonsus J. Coleman, Bernard Adrain Coleman, Sr., Chester Paul Coleman, Clyde J. Coleman, Francis I. Coleman, Ignatius Joseph Coleman, Joseph E. Coleman, Sidney Vincent Coleman, James Edward Courtaway, Joseph Francis Courtway,

Clarence DeClue, David E. DeClue, John Lawrence DeClue, Vincent M. DeGonia, Marion Andrew Govero, Edgar Lee Hammond, Jack Lee Hammond, Sr., Walter Vincent Kincaid, Bernard Harold Koch, Matthew W. Koch, Robert E. Luther, Leo Guy Mercille, John R. Minx, Jr., Everett Joseph Missey,

Edward R. Nephew, Homer C. Nephew, Carl Joseph Osia, Clarence L. Osia, Ralph P. Pashia, Roy William Pinson, Edwin Willis Politte, Charles Allen Portell, George Henry Portell, Malcolm Martin Portell, Thomas Edgar Portell, Elijah Louis Price, Elliott Bernard Price, James Clayton Rawe, Sr., Walter D. Reando, Lawrence R. Recar, Lloyd Joseph Robart, Howard E. Ross,

Edward Burnham Sansoucie, Elmer R. Sansoucie, James A. Sansoucie, Joseph Bryan Sansoucie, Nichols Edward Thebeau, Ralph A. Thebeau, Walter Sherman Thebeau, Irvin Joseph Thebo, Orville Jethro Valle, Burnham Joseph Villmer, and Leo B. Young.

KOREAN WAR

Five years after the end of World War II, the U.S. entered into the Korean War (1950–1953). North Korea invaded South Korea in 1950, and nations allied with the U.S. intervened with the South. Meanwhile, Russia and China supported the North. Again, young men from Old Mines were drafted into service. The Korean conflict ended in 1953 when the demilitarized zone was established.

St. Joachim Cemeteries contain the graves of some who fought in the Korean War. Below is a list of those who served their country and are buried in St. Joachim Cemeteries, in alphabetical order up to December 2016: Paul L. Bourisaw, John A. Boyer, Leo S. Boyer, Ralph Stanley Boyer, Clyde J. Coleman, Ferd F. Coleman, John Leroy Coleman, John Paul Coleman, James Courtois, Donald Raymond Cwiklowski,

Cornelius A. Daly, Maurice G. Daly, Thomas Glennon Davis, Donald James Mercille, Norman E. Minx, Glen Francis Osia, Joseph Melzo Osia, Lawrence Edward Parks, Harold Joseph Pinson, Sherman M. Portell, Chester Phillip Reando, Larry James Riddle, Rousan Joseph Thebeau, and Charles Junior Ward.

VIETNAM WAR

Six years later, the Vietnam War began (1959–1975). The forces of North Vietnam were joined by the Viet Kong, Khmer Rouge, China, Russia, North Korea, and Pathet Lao to fight the anticommunist forces of the U.S., South Vietnam, South Korea, Australia, Philippines, Thailand, New Zealand, Laos, and the Khmer Republic. The war ended when North Vietnam won and Laos, Cambodia, and South Vietnam became communist states. Young men from Old Mines were drafted into service; some of them died for the freedom of other nations.

St. Joachim Cemeteries contain the graves of some who fought in the Vietnam War. Below is a list of those who served their country and are buried in St. Joachim Cemeteries, in alphabetical order up to December 2016: Donald J. Boyer, Paul Richard Coleman, James Dale Fenwick, Robert Vernon Malloy, Lawrence Edward Parks, Ronald Joseph "Brazz" Politte, Ronald Joseph "Ronnie" Politte, Michael Malcolm Portell, and Marvin Paul Singer.

GULF WAR

In 1990, the Gulf War began (1990–1991). The draft had disappeared in the U.S. Now, it was a volunteer army, navy, air force, marines, and coast guard. The United Nations authorized thirty-four nations to remove Iraq from Kuwait. Those who had volunteered for service found themselves deployed to fight Iraqi forces. Kuwait was liberated in 1991. In St. Joachim Cemeteries, up to December 2016 there is one grave of Austin David Pratt, who fought in the Gulf War.

WAR IN AFGHANISTAN

Ten years later, the U.S. entered into War in Afghanistan (2001–present). Beginning on October 7, 2001, the objective of the volunteer U.S. forces was Operation Enduring Freedom: It was an effort to drive al-Qaeda and Taliban forces from power in Afghanistan. Some young men and women from Old Mines fought in this war and eliminated or downsized enemy forces. However, from time to time, forces increased and had to be driven back or eliminated again. This is the longest war in which the U.S. has ever been engaged.

Wars and Soldiers

PEACETIME MILITARY SERVICE

St. Joachim Cemeteries contain the graves of some who served in the military during peacetime. Below is a list of those who served their country and are buried in St. Joachim Cemeteries, in alphabetical order up to December 2016: Adrian Julian Boyer, Foster Joseph Coleman, F. Regis Daugherty, Gale Roy Hardin, James D. Kay, Lynn Charles McMahan, Patrick N. Missey, Gloria Marie Owens, Paschal Pashia, Robert Anthony Politte, Victor Paul Politte, Michael Ellis Portell, Louis Edward Rolling, Kenny Sansoucie, Jimmie Dale Thebeau, Keith Randall Thebeau, Edward S. Todd, and Alex Paul Yarbrough.

BURIED IN ST. JOACHIM CEMETERIES 2017–APRIL 2021

From January 1, 2017, to April 30, 2021, the following were buried in St. Joachim Cemeteries: Donald B. Bourbon, Alfred Boyer, Joseph W. Boyer, Joy W. Boyer, Jeffrey Coleman, Robert S. Mercille, Burnam D. Pratt, James Rawe, Michael R. Riddle, Ronald W. Thebeau, and George E. Wall, Jr.

OLD MINERS IN THE ARMED FORCES

In alphabetical order, the following from the Old Mines area served in the U.S. armed forces:

Thomas M. Allen, Chad J. Aubuchon, Leon J. Aubuchon, Josh Aubuchon, Miles Aubuchon,

Daniel Battreal, Ralph F. Battreal, William Battreal, Christopher Bequette, Howard Bequette, Joseph R. Bequette, Lennis Bequette, Mike Bequette, Steve Bequette, Bernis Bone, James E. Bone, Jesse Bone, Joey Bone, Lewis Bone, Virgil Bone, Donald Bourbon, Floyd Bourbon, Frank Bourbon, George A. Bourbon, Aloysius G. Bourisaw, Alphonsus J. Bourisaw, Clement C. Bourisaw, James H. Bourisaw, James K. Bourisaw, Kenny Bourisaw, Ping Bourisaw, Willard P. Bourisaw, Bernard J. Boyer, Charles F. Boyer, Donald T. Boyer, Edward Boyer, Francis Boyer, Francis A. Boyer, Francis C. Boyer, Francis M. Boyer, Francis G. Boyer, Gary Boyer, Harold Boyer, Homer Boyer, Howard L. Boyer, Jeff Boyer, John J. Boyer, Joseph Boyer, Joseph P. Boyer, Joseph R. Boyer, Kenneth Boyer, Lawrence E. Boyer, Leo B. Boyer, Lynn Boyer, Richard Boyer, Robert (Bud) Boyer, Vincent L. Boyer, Wilfred Boyer, Woodrow E. Boyer, Zeno Boyer, Wilfred E. Brakford,

Ralph Charboneau, Adrian G. Coleman, Bernard Coleman, Bernard L. Coleman, Bradley Coleman, Caryle Coleman, Charles Coleman, Chester Coleman, Clyde Coleman, Earl J. Coleman, Everett V. Coleman, Foster Coleman, Francis R. Coleman, Glennon Coleman, Ignatius J. Coleman, Jack Coleman, James C. Coleman, James R. Coleman, Joseph L. Coleman, Kenny Coleman, Leon Coleman, Michael Coleman,

Paul R. Coleman, Ray Coleman, Roy J. Coleman, Sidney V. Coleman, Stanley Coleman, Stanley F. Coleman, Harold T. Courtaway, James E. Courtaway, Joseph Courtaway, Nelson P. Courtaway, Bernard Courtois, William Crippen,

Cornelius A. Daly, Maurice Daly, Joseph G. Daugherty Sr., Milton Davis, Conley J. Dean, Gussie Dean, James L. Dean, Joseph L. Dean, Alois J. DeClue, Clarence DeClue, Harry DeClue, James L. DeClue, John L. DeClue, Julie DeClue, Leonard DeClue, Paul F. DeClue, Raymond DeClue, Stanley DeClue, Thomas D. DeClue, Thomas F. DeClue, David DeGonia, Joseph T. DeGonia, Vincent DeGonia,

Raymond Emily, Raymond Emily, Sr., Scott Emily,

Lawrence Flynn, Paul Flynn,

Kenneth Gaylord, Kenneth J. Gaylord, Larry Godat, Aloysius Govero, Lawrence Govero, Adrian Guenther, George Guenther,

Chris Hahn, Paul Hanson, Henry S. Hartzell, John Q. Hochstatter, John C. Huskey

Leo Jackson, Robert Johnston, Darian Juliette, James Juliette, James K. Juliette, John Juliette, Richard Juliette, Thomas Juliette, Tyler Juliette, Vincent R. Juliette,

Edward B. Keen, Andrew Kincaid, John Kincaid, Jordan Kincaid, Walter V. Kincaid, Boniface Knott, Bernard H. Koch, Harold J. Koch, Joe Koch, Karl Koch, Leo A. Koch, Matthew Koch, Richard Koch, Rose Ann Koch, Wayne Koch,

David Lalumondiere, Festus J. Lalumondiere, George Lalumondiere, Joseph Lalumondiere, Willard Lalumondiere, Chadbourn G. Long, G. Chad Long, Morris Long, Robert E. Luther,

Arthur Martin, Walter Martin, Leonard K. Maxwell, Roger McMahan, Donald J. Mercille, Doug Mercille, Leo Mercille, Oliver G. Mercille, Raphael J. Mercille, Robert Mercille, Buford Minx, Clifford Minx, Clifford Missey, Edward Missey, Everett Missey, Hubert Missey, Joseph M. Missey Mark Missey, Patrick N. Missey, Roger Missey,

Donald Neff, Edward R. Nephew, Thomas E. Nephew, Vincent T. Nephew, (Francis) Pete Nicholson,

Carl J. Osia, Clarence L. Osia, Francis Osia, Glen F. Osia, James R. Osia, Russell Osia,

William Pace, John A. Parker, Donald Pashia, James Pashia, James E. Pashia, Joseph Pashia, Lucian H. Pashia, Monica Pashia, Paschal Pashia, Paul Pashia, Philip Pashia, Ralph Pashia, Rolla J. Pashia, Kenneth Payne, Steve Peyton, Daily Pinson, Dorsey J. Pinson, Homer Pinson, Roy Pinson, Seth Pinson, Vincent Pinson, Charles Politte, Daily S. Politte, Edwin W. Politte, James D. Politte, James F. Politte, James L. Politte, Jimmy Politte, John Politte, Joseph Politte, Lawrence Politte, Lisa (Nickelson) Politte, Lester Politte, Malcon Politte, Marvin J. Politte, Miranda (Kintzler) Politte, Patrick Politte, Steven A. Politte, Walter Politte, Willard Politte, Zach Politte, Carl J. Portell, Charles Portell, Donald L. Portell, Edgar T. Portell, Floyd F. Portell, Homer Portell, Martin W. Portell, Malcom Portell, Raymond Portell, Robert Portell, Thomas E. Portell, Tim Portell, Austin D. Pratt, Burnham Pratt, Charles Pratt, Clarence J. Pratt,

David F. Pratt, Helen Pratt, Michael E. Pratt, Robert L. Pratt, Ellion B. Price, John A. Price, Lige L. Price, Ron Pruitt,

James C. Rawe, Chester P. Reando, James Reando, Thomas Reando, Walter D. Reando, Walter J. Reando, Jr., Glen Recar, Laurence Recar, Andrew Ricketts, Michael Riddle, Henry Robart, Ivan J. Robart, Loyd J. Robart, Peter S. Robart, Bernard C. Roderick, Charlie Robert, John Robert, Morgan J. Ronquest, Howard E. Ross, Loran Rundell,

Christopher Sampson, Jerry P. Sampson, Paul Sampson, Thomas W. Sampson, Calvin C. Sanders, Bobby Sansoucie, Chester Sansoucie, Edward B. Sansoucie, Elmer R. Sansoucie, James A. Sansoucie, Kenny Sansoucie, Lindell Sampson, Frank Sancegraw, Jerry Sansegrah, Cecil Schmidt, Jr., Patrick Schulte, Ralph Schulte, Jim Shepherd, Lloyd Shepard, Doug Short, Joseph M. Singer, James Skags, Bobby G. Skiles, Edward Skiles, Donald L. Smith, Sr.,

Brandon Tefenauer, Adrian L. Thebeau, Anastie Thebeau, Charles Thebeau, Donald G. Thebeau, Donald J. Thebeau, Elmer M. Thebeau, Frank Thebeau, Henry S. Thebeau, Homer Thebeau, Irvin J. Thebeau, James D. Thebeau, James S. Thebeau, John Thebeau, Joseph O. Thebeau, Keith R. Thebeau, Leonard Thebeau, Leroy J. Thebeau, Nelson F. Thebeau, Nicholas Thebeau, Ralph A. Thebeau, Raymond Thebeau, Ronnie Thebeau, Rousan J. Thebeau, Vincent Thebeau, Walter S. Thebeau, Irvin Thebo, Michael Thurman,

Orville Valley, Hubert Van Beven, Alva Veach, Charles Veach, David Veach, John Veach, Mark Veach, Aloysius Villmer, Burnham Villmer, Thomas Villmer William Vineyard,

John Warden, Dallas Warren,

Luke Yarbrough, Owen Yarbrough, Raleigh Yarbrough, Luckey Yates, Norval J. Yates, and Leo Young.

For Further Reading: History of American Wars, Gettysburg Flag Works.

29

St. Joseph Parish, Tiff, Missouri

BEGINNINGS

In the early 1900s, Father Luke J. Kernan, pastor of St. Joachim Parish (1901–1912), made trips to Tiff, Missouri, to celebrate Mass in the home of Frank Boyer, a two-room log structure. Kernan went to Tiff to minister to the growing number of Catholics in the barite-mining village there.

The early community at Tiff was begun when John Campbell came from Buffalo, New York, to organize a corporation named the South East Missouri Barytes Company. He sold shares to local land owners and built the earliest barite (tiff) washer in Tiff. Campbell bought land containing barite along with other land upon which he constructed approximately forty homes for miners. He also bought a home for himself, located across the road from St. Joseph School, along with a company store. Miners took their salary in merchandise from the store. The tiff washer Campbell built was located in the same general vicinity as the store.

Once Campbell's operations were under way, Mass and sacraments were celebrated by Kernan in the hall above the company store until the first church was built. The first step to building a church was taken by the archbishop of St. Louis, John Joseph Glennon, who bought about a third of an acre from Campbell's company for the erection of a church on June 10, 1905. Under Kernan's leadership, a wood rectangular building with a bell tower was constructed by "Coot" Cole. Parishioners entered it from ground level and sat in bench-like seats. At the back of the building was a sacristy, which the priest entered by way of outdoor stairs. In the winter, the church was heated with a wood stove located in the rear of the building, which was dedicated to St. Joseph.

A simple, plain altar was located at one end which identified the sanctuary. Father Tim Dempsey of St. Patrick Church, St. Louis, donated vessels and vestments.

Either Kernan or a Redemptorist priest from Mount St. Clement College in DeSoto, Missouri, came to the church to celebrate Mass or sacraments, often spending the night in Campbell's home.

Mary Magdalene Boyer served as the first organist in the church, even bringing her own organ to the church until parishioners could afford to buy one. Ben R. Boyer donated property for a cemetery. Thus, people came from the surrounding villages of Blackwell, Barytes, Bellefontaine, Cadet, Cannon Mines, Fertile, and Shibboleth for Mass, sacraments, and St. Joseph devotions.

PARISH FOUNDED

In 1918, Father John Cook (1918–1923) was sent to St. Joachim Parish as the associate pastor to Father John Daly (1916–1928). Cook took an immediate interest in the mission parish. In May 1923, he oversaw the separation of St. Joseph Parish from St. Joachim Parish, and he was appointed its first pastor. Cook moved into the basement of the wood church while he planned and built a rectory and a school with the assistance of parishioners living in the area. Alla Boyer, who had been teaching in public schools, moved to St. Joseph School to teach, while also serving as Cook's housekeeper.

On a Friday evening in Lent 1935, following the Stations of the Cross, the wood church caught on fire and burned. Everything was lost, including parish records. Cook made plans to build a new stone church to replace the one that had been destroyed. On August 9, 1936, the first Auxiliary Bishop of St. Louis, Christian Winkleman, officiated at the laying of the cornerstone for the new church; ten priests were also present for the ceremony, which was followed by a picnic sponsored by the women of the parish.

Cook served as the architect and contractor for the new church, even doing much of the work himself. He employed John Norris from DeSoto as a stone cutter who taught his craft to Henry Bourisaw and Andrew Aubuchon. The stone was obtained from a site near Washington State Park. Earl Bohn, also from DeSoto, was employed as the carpenter; he taught Lucian Aubuchon, Harry Aubuchon, Steve Boyer, Charley Boyer, Elmer Boyer, Edward Boyer, Wallace Boyer, and Tom Daugherty woodworking skills and how to mix concrete. When it was finished, the church cost the parish about six thousand dollars.

At the time that St. Joseph Parish was being founded, the Blessed Virgin Mary had appeared to Lucia dos Santos and Francisco and Jacinta Marto in Fatima, Portugal, at the Cova da Iria on May 13, 1917. After careful investigation by the Church, the first and the five apparitions which followed it were declared worthy of belief on October 13, 1930. On May 13, 1946, Pope Pius XII granted a canonical coronation to the venerated image enshrined in the Chapel of the Apparitions of Fatima. To commemorate the apparitions, a shrine was constructed in front of St. Joseph Church depicting the initial apparition of the Our Lady of Fatima to the three children.

Religious instruction was conducted in homes; lay men and women taught the Catholic faith to children and adults. Upon completion, they were presented to the pastor for further instruction. Mamie (Myrtle) Bouchard taught during Cook's tenure as pastor. Later, Daphne Farrell continued the process. Today, students attend parish school of religion classes in St. Joachim Parish.

For income, the parish depended upon socials, picnics, fish fries, and square dances. Music for square dances was furnished by Pete Burford's band, while the floor was managed by Winfield Young. A fall festival was held on September 26, 1948, to commemorate the twenty-fifth anniversary of the erection of St. Joseph Parish.

PASTORS

Cook, who served as pastor for those twenty-five years, was replaced on October 16, 1948, by Father Alphonse Hoormann, who served the parish until June 1955, when he was named pastor of St. Joachim Parish. Hoormann was followed by Father Francis Matyas, who served until 1961. Matyas's successor was Father Albert Danter; he was pastor until 1966, when St. Joseph Parish became a mission of St. Joachim Parish under the leadership of Father Bernard A. Suellentrop, who was assisted by Father Anthony J. Jansen.

Under Suellentrop's pastorate, St. Joseph Parish formed a parish council in May 1969 to assist the pastor in management of the parish. Bernard Roderick was the first council chairman, followed by Glennon Daugherty and Richard Villmer. Lindell Johnson served as treasurer and maintenance supervisor of buildings, grounds, and cemetery, as well as playing the organ for some services. The parish council continued in existence until 1987. Today, instead of a parish council, a parish meeting is held at least twice a year to plan and review liturgies and attend to building maintenance, parish grounds, and the cemetery.

FIFTIETH ANNIVERSARY

On Sunday, August 12, 1973, the parish marked its fiftieth anniversary with an outdoor Mass celebrated before the front doors of the church. The large crowd of attendees were seated in folding chairs on either side of the front walkway. Auxiliary Bishop of St. Louis, Charles R. Koester, presided at the Mass. The then-current pastor of St. Joachim Parish, Father Richard Suren, and the then-current associate pastor, James Moll, concelebrated along with Danter, Suellentrop, and Jansen. Also present were Msgr. Joseph B. Winter, dean, and Cook. Hoormann delivered the homily. Father Mark G. Boyer, then a seminarian, served as Master of Ceremonies for the Mass; he was assisted by Vernon J. Meyer, another seminarian. Bernard Roderick and Glennon

Daugherty were the lectors; Thomas Daugherty served as thurifer; while Timothy Daugherty carried the cross and Randy Politte and Kenny Barton served as acolytes. Anthony Daugherty carried the book for the bishop, while Dale Politte assisted with his crosier, and Neil Thebeau with his miter.

Music for the Mass was provided by Joyce Politte. The choir—Stephen Politte, Marcella Boyer, Regina Pinson, Cathy Daugherty, Bernadette Daugherty, and Connie Daugherty—led the singing.

Just as the Mass ended a storm broke. Those who had brought picnic baskets moved to the upper classrooms in the school building. On the lower floor, an old-fashioned country chicken and beef supper, orchestrated by Myrtle Bouchard and ten other volunteers, was served to the bishop and priests.

RENOVATIONS

Since marking its fiftieth anniversary in 1973, some major renovations have been done to the church. The wood front doors with vertical narrow glass panels have been replaced with metal doors. The original tile floor was replaced with laminate flooring. The purple cloth drapes that hung all around the apse of the church were removed, and the apse walls were painted. Air conditioning was installed, and a metal roof was put over the slate roof. At the front of the church a restroom was added, and a concrete handicapped-accessible walkway outside the front of the church was completed. Improvements to the church were the result of parishioners', family members', and friends' generous donations.

Since 1966, after St. Joseph Parish became a mission of St. Joachim Parish, the rectory has served as a rental house. The school, which had been used for parish council meetings, business affairs, Vacation Bible Schools, and Boy Scouts and Cub Scouts, for the most part remains unused.

At the time of the writing of this book, there are twenty to twenty-five families attending St. Joseph Church. Music for Mass is provided by Regina (Daugherty) Pinson. There is no choir. And people wonder what the future of the parish might be.

Before the 2020 COVID-19 pandemic, monthly Eucharistic Adoration was held. Likewise, holyday Masses were celebrated. And with the assistance of retired Father Richard Tillman, Paschal Triduum services were celebrated. Once the pandemic began, it became difficult to practice social distancing because of the small size of the church. And with elderly parishioners it was important to stay home to avoid the virus.

While the parish has remained a strong faith-filled community of dedicated Catholics, who continue to share generously of their time, talent, and treasure, the number of parishioners has continued to drop over the years due to mortality, the lack of local employment, and the rise in the number of inactive Catholics. Until the late 1980s, there were enough parishioners to fill two weekend Masses; after that a single Saturday evening Mass was sufficient. In other words, St. Joseph Parish faces the dwindling number of Catholics that can be seen around the United States.

In 2023, St. Joseph Parish celebrates its centennial. At the time of the writing of this book, no plans have been made to mark its one hundred years.

MILITARY SERVICE

St. Joseph Cemetery, Tiff, Missouri, contains the graves of some who have served in the military. Below is a list of those who served their country and are buried in St. Joseph Cemetery, in alphabetical order, according to the war, and up to December 2016.

World War I (1914-1918): Oliver Joseph Aubuchon, Joseph Charles Bequette, Joseph Anastia Degonia, and Curtis White Eakin.

World War II (1939-1945): Harry F. Aubuchon, Lawrence Francis Aubuchon, Cletus S. Boyer, Glennon James Boyer, Herbert Lawrence Boyer, Irvin Andrew Boyer, Michael Claude Boyer, Vincent William Boyer, James A. Degonia, Joseph Thomas Degonia, Sr., Joseph Melvin Missey, and Bernard Whaley.

Korean War (1950-1953): Frank Joseph Boyer, Glennon James Boyer, Joseph Melvin Missey, Joseph Milton Missey, and Bernard James Neubrand.

Vietnam War (1959-1973): Joseph Milton Missey and Lindell Paul Sansoucie.

Peacetime Military Service: Murrell J. Boyer and John Henry Mercer.

For More Information: *History of St. Joachim Parish: 1822-1972; 1723-1973*, Mark G. Boyer; *Historical Program-Pageant Book: 250th Anniversary, Old Mines, Missouri*, Natalie Villmer; Wikipedia: Our Lady of Fatima; The Historic Iron Mountain Route, Rick Sprung, *The Midwest Challenger Special*, Nov. 8, 1992.

30

Old Mines Today (2021)

TOUR

If the original founders were to come back today to see the mining camps for lead and barite that they left many years ago, they would be startled. They would not only not find hand picks and shovels, but they would not find any mining. The small village that began small along Old Mines Creek has both become smaller and larger. It is smaller, as many of its businesses have disappeared; it is larger, as the speed of automobile travel on Missouri Highway 21 and 47 has made it easy to access businesses spread over the distance from one end of the Old Mines Concession to the other end.

If one enters the Old Mines Concession coming from the north and heading south, immediately inside the southern border on the right side of Highway 21 and 47 (hereafter referred to as only Highway 21) is K(ingston)-14 School. At one time it was Cruise School, one among fourteen other one-room school houses scattered around the Old Mines area. Now, it contains pre-school, elementary school, and high school.

Then, one crosses Old Mines Creek, which meanders through every one of the thirty-one tracts of land that form the Old Mines Concession. The creek crossed here is a multi-spring-fed and multi-branch-fed creek originating in Frogtown south of Old Mines proper (referring to the area between the two speed zone signs). Old Mines Creek travels for about eight miles before emptying into the Mineral Fork, which in turn empties into Big River, which in turn empties into the Meramec River, which in turn empties into the Mississippi River.

Continuing south on Highway 21, on the left side of the road is Lawson Veterinary Clinic. After originally opening in a new section attached to the old Brown's Store (now razed), the owners built a new clinic on Highway 21 between K-14 and Brown Hollow Road.

Past Brown Hollow Road on the right side is All Aboard Marine, a boat accessories store. All items for sale are produced in the shop by the owners.

Not far from the Veterinary Clinic and All Aboard Marine on the same side of the road is the tin building (Old Mines Manufacturing) that sat empty for many years. Originally built in the hope of attracting a business to the area, it did become a place for a group of young men to play roller blade hockey before being used to make windows. Now, it houses The Vinyl Shop, owned by Joe and Diane Valle of DeSoto, where vinyl fence has been manufactured since 1997. Will Allen and Karrie Boyer, employees, make custom vinyl and aluminum fencing.

Past The Vinyl Shop on the right side of the highway is Ambulance House 2, which provides space for Washington County ambulances. When patients need critical care in a St. Louis hospital, Air Evac helicopters are able to land in the field next to the shed to have patients loaded and flown to St. Louis.

Past Ambulance House 2 on the right side of Highway 21 is Brown's Market. After Roy Brown died in 1991, his widow, Regina (Bequette) Brown, built a new modern convenience store with a modern façade. Modern conveniences, such as a deli, liquor, lottery tickets, newspapers, etc. can be found inside, in addition to usual market fare, and modern gas pumps are located in a row outside. After the new store was completed, the old store was razed. To the north of it still stands the addition that had been made to the old store, but none of its spaces are occupied. At various points over the past fifty years, it has been the home of Richard Juliette's Barber Shop, a Laundromat, and Lawson Veterinary Clinic.

On the left side of the highway almost directly across from Brown's Store is a satellite Firehouse for the Potosi Fire Protection District, manned by volunteers. This facility reduced the cost of house insurance for the whole area. Along with the firehouse came 911; all roads were mapped and given names. Some familiar names were retained, some were given the names of some of those listed on the Old Mines Concession, and some were merely named.

Eagle Cabinet, owned by Brian and Julie Brown, is located on the left side of Highway 21 south of the Firehouse. Doug Short and Tony Brown are employees, who make cabinets for kitchens, bathrooms, and more. Employees custom design, manufacture, and install cabinets and shelves. Further south on Highway 21, on the right side of the road is Custom Cabinets and Furniture, usually referred to as Fran's Cabinet Shop. The owner, Fran(cis) Pashia and his employees make custom kitchen cabinets and accessories, along with furniture. Pashia made the liturgical furniture (altar, ambo, and cabinets) that can be found in St. Joachim Church. He also made the cabinets that were installed in the Incarnate Word Center.

Continuing south on Highway 21 on the left side of the road is Wilson Truck Service. Founded in 1956 by Norman Wilson, it is run today by his son, John L. Wilson, who is expanding his facilities to the north with a new office building to replace his mobile home office. Wilson Truck Service provides heavy and light hauling of freight, building materials, paper products, grain, feed, hay, and construction materials using fifteen trucks, thirteen tractors, thirty-four trailers, and seventeen drivers.

After passing Wilson Truck Service, one sees a sign on the left side of the road for E & J Auto Salvage, an auto parts store located a short distance from Highway 21 off a gravel road up on a hill. The car graveyard can be seen from Highway 21.

Next, the driver passes through the unmarked village of Racola. On the right side of the highway are the ruins of the Peter "Paco" Boyer general store that are gradually caving in and falling down. On the left side of the highway there used to be a barber shop, but that was washed away in the flood of 1957. Further south on the left side of the road there used to be a tavern—damaged by the 1957 flood—called Racola City, gas station and a Western Auto store, but those two buildings closed and disappeared a long time ago. In place of the gas station and Western Auto store is Bills Automotive and More, an auto repair shop.

Continuing south on Highway 21 one comes to the village of Old Mines proper, indicated by a sign—Old Mines—attached to a speed-zone sign of 50 miles per hour. On the right side of the road, Thomas Paul operated a wild game farm in the 1970s and 1980s. He raised chuckers and quails, which he sold to places hunting them all over the midwest.

Next, on the right side of the highway is the Old Mines Old Baptist Cemetery, and behind the house to the south of it is Mineral Area Garage in what used to be the bus shed for St. Joachim School buses, owned and operated by Vincent Paul.

On the left side of the road are the remains of the Bud Nephew Store and home below the store. That general store, previously known as Crystal Spring, closed within the past fifty years; for a while in the early 1990s, it was known as Cousins, a pizza and video rental place. Now, like Boyer's general store in Racola, it is in ruins.

Almost directly across from the Bud Nephew Store on the right side of Highway 21 was a school for the severely mentally handicapped (a light pink home), referred to as the Washington County Trainable School for the Mentally Retarded. The school was opened around 1961 and continued through the 1970s for six to eight Down's Syndrome students, who could attend the school until they turned 21 years old. Some of the organizing members of the school included Howard C. Higginbotham, Verna M. Boyer, and Clarice Koch.

On the right side of Highway 21, the Incarnate Word Center and St. Joachim Church's steeple come into view. The remnants of the lead and barite mines disappeared long ago and the land was reclaimed. Old Mines Creek can be seen on the left side of the highway. When Old Mines was a working village with shops, this is where it was located. Father Henry Pratte built a log church here in 1820. St. Joachim was established as a parish by Father John Boullier in 1829, and from 1829 to 1831 the current brick church was built, dedicated, and consecrated. To the right of the church sits the Incarnate Word Center, a former red brick convent that was renovated and turned into the parish offices and meeting rooms. To the left of the church sits the red brick rectory. Not visible from the highway is the school, which was erected behind the church in 1949. A large sign in front of the wrought-iron fence indicates that it is St. Joachim Church and School.

Immediately south of the church, right along Highway 21, was the Pat Daly Store, and just a few steps up the hill was the Pat Daly house. Patrick and Marie Daly built and operated the general store, while building and living in the home they constructed only a few steps away from the store, after signing a lease on January 1, 1938, with the Archdiocese of St. Louis. The April 29, 1946, *Independent-Journal* reported that the Daly family was driving a new two-tone blue Chevrolet purchased in DeSoto. Upon their deaths, the store passed to their son, Maurice, who ran it until he died in 1972. Father Richard Suren (1970–1975) renegotiated the extension of the lease (sublease) for ten years with the Daly family from 1972 to 1982, when the store, house, and property were returned to St. Joachim Parish. The house was rented for a time, but the store sat empty until Father Robert Johnston (1981–1987) gave it to La Brigade a Renault as a storage building. The house was razed in 2018, and the store was razed in 2019. All that remains of the Dalys is the road to the south of the location of the store and the house now named Pat Daly Road.

After passing the entrance to Pat Daly Road on the right side of the highway, one sees a white-sided house sitting on the hill close to the highway. That is one of the oldest homes in Old Mines. Originally built by John Smith T in the early-1800s, it was purchased by Etienne and Marie-Louise Lamarque, who used property and funds to support the Catholic Church. Almost across from the former Lamarque home, on the right side of the highway, is Wallace Road with a bridge over Old Mines Creek. Wallace Road leads directly to the Homestead, the offices and museum of the Old Mines Area Historical Society currently under development. Fifty years ago, the George Wallace General Store and Post Office occupied this area before they burned. After purchasing the Wallace property, Richard (Dickie) Juliette built a Barber Shop and a home on it.

On the left side of the highway is found the Washington County Knights of Columbus Hall. Over the past fifty years, the KC Hall has been expanded several times, and the grounds surrounding it have been improved. The Knights of Columbus council was begun March 12, 1967.

To the south of the KC Hall on the same side of the highway, right at the junction of Highway 21 and Highway 47 (which continues east), there used to be Bill Polhemus's Liquor Store, Ozark Gas Station, and the Shamrock Restaurant. In the past fifty years, all of those have disappeared. At the time of the writing of this book, plans are for a Dollar General Store to be erected there. If one were to turn left onto Highway 47 and travel a few miles to Tiff Road, he or she would find Buckman Laboratories, built in 1961. Originally founded to work with barite, the plant now makes chemicals used in paints and other products.

Continuing south on Highway 21, on the right side is ZAM Storage, a three-section set of buildings owned by Zach Politte. Different sizes of units are available for rent. Originally built by James and Carolyn Politte, ZAM stands for **Z**ach **A**nd **M**erideth. A little further south there used to be a Zephyr Gas Station on the right side of the highway. On the left side of the highway was located a Western Auto store, which, after it closed, became the Christmas House, which burned. A new Christmas House was built, but it is now closed. Next to it are the ruins of the Union Hall. In the late 1930s, the Miners, Haulers, and Mill Workers Union was formed. The workers went on strike demanding an increase in the price paid for tiff from $3.50 per ton to $5.50 per ton at the processing plants. The strike lasted for three months.

After ZAM Storage, there is Arnault Branch Road. About a half of a mile on that road was Portell Brothers Hauling. Donald Lynn, Tom, and Ronnie Portell ran a hauling business well into the 1970s.

Further south on the right side of Highway 21 is the Starlite Drive-In, which has been in continuous operation since 1952. In 2013, it won one of nine digital projectors in a contest sponsored by Honda. Kevin, Doug, and Rob Mercille own and operate the two-screen, 500-car drive-in April through October. The Starlight Flea Market used to be held on the same property.

On the other side of the highway is Hoot's Convenience Store; fifty years ago, it was known as Mercille's Grocery. Aloysius A. Mercille was known locally as Hoot. After he died in 1988, his son, Doug, continued to sell groceries, liquor, and gas, but renamed the store Hoot's. Years ago, next to Hoot's was Roy Boyer's Barber Shop and Tavern.

After passing Hoot's, there is a speed zone sign announcing that one can resume the standard 55 miles per hour on Highway 21, because Old Mines village is now in one's rear-view mirror. However, while one is leaving Old Mines proper, on the left side of the highway there are two more businesses: Steve's Place Bar and Grill and Osia Automotive. Steve's Place features a full bar with restaurant food to go with a drink. One can order snacks, soups, a light lunch of quiche, fruit, salads, etc., turkey, meatloaf, fish, chicken, and spaghetti and meatball dinners, all kinds of burgers, gourmet sandwiches, desserts, and more. Soft drinks are also served.

After Steve's Place on the left side of the highway is Osia Automotive, an automobile repair shop in Old Mines. On the right side is Eckhoff Excavating.

Highway 21 continues out of the Old Mines Concession and onto Potosi, the seat of Washington County. Unlike the miners of lead and barite of the past, Old Miners, who are not retired, today work in Potosi or drive north to DeSoto, Festus, St. Louis, or elsewhere.

In General

In general, if one travels the backroads, lanes, and byways or walks through the woods in the early spring, one may find indications of the site of a log cabin or farmhouse. The evidence consists of the blooming jonquils, iris, and yucca. The French settlers love flowers, which were protected by a fence built around their homes. Inside the fence line they planted lots of flowers.

Forgotten stores and post offices used to be found in small villages in the nineteenth and early twentieth centuries. Among them were the settlements at Middle Branch, Aptus, Thebeau Town, Cannon Mines, Kingston, Shibboleth, Fountain Farm, Happy Hollow, Cadet, etc.

HERITAGE OF FAITH

It is easy for the members of the older population of Old Mines driving along Highway 21 to remember the homes of the pillars of St. Joachim Parish. Junior and Celeste Bone, Albert and Adele Coleman, Roy and Regina Brown, Kernan and Marie Paul, Bill Coleman, Vincent and Marie Paul, Bud and Lucille Nephew, Lawrence and Ann Pashia, Oliver and Lucille Osia, Vince and Anna Thebeau, Paul and Ina Mae Boyer, Jack and Kathleen Juliette, Jesse and Mary Catherine Bone, Edwin and Catherine Politte, Max and Eileen Villmer, Genevieve and George Hill, and many more planted and nurtured the seeds of faith in Old Mines. Their homes still stand, but a new generation has moved into them.

Those of the past sacrificed for the common good of the community. They used their talents, and they worked hard. All of it was a testament to how they were brought up and what they believed. They planted the seeds, passing on God's word to others so they could absorb it and put it into practice in their own lives.

Around 2000, an influx of families from other places began in Old Mines. The old predominant family names of Boyer, Thebeau, Politte, Portell, Coleman, Robart, Sansoucie, Pratt, Bone, Bourbon, and Bourisaw gave way to Cusamano, Jacobsen, Campisi, Barber, Brueggen, Palazzolo, and Thornton. Families came to Old Mines because of employment opportunities in the prison, hospitals, and schools. Land could be purchased cheaply—the lead and barite companies that owned large tracts of land were selling it because lead and barite no longer had a market. Furthermore, the tax rates were lower than elsewhere, and lower-income families could find access to health care and other resources.

While there was a rise in the number of practicing Catholics in St. Joachim Parish, Old Mines, in the previous century, there has been a decline in the current century. The decline has also been noted in the corresponding decrease in the number of priests; there used to be two in St. Joachim Parish, and now there is but one. The number of Incarnate Word nuns increased from the first four in 1924 to ten or more from the 1950s to the 1960s and decreased to none by 1996. In the twentieth century, St. Joachim Parish was the religious and entertainment hub of the community, but with an ever more mobile culture, people not only neglected religion, but they turned to other forms of entertainment and social venues. While the older generation, the faith keepers, were dying, the next generation no longer looked to the parish as the center of the community and their lives. Only a few remain who identify their faith as the most important aspect of life in Old Mines. This is a phenomenon that is universal.

Once the elementary school was established in 1924 and a high school in the 1950s, the new school building was the realization of a communal vision of families with children in St. Joachim Parish. It was a vision they had for the religious education and formation of their growing families. The new school became the hub around which both the school and the parish community gathered. They saw the expanded elementary school and high school with pride. It was a testament to their faith, their generosity, and their love of education and religious formation. With the close of the high school in 1972, the gradual loss of Incarnate Word nuns as teachers and principals, and the corresponding rise in popularity for public education, the decrease in enrollment in the elementary school was a logical consequence. However, the school remains because of the dedication of Catholic families and their commitment to Catholic education and formation. Through the years, enrollment of non-Catholic students has increased; there are families who value what the Catholic school has to offer. Nevertheless, the cost of education due to the ever-developing technology needed is a financial burden on a small, Catholic school, especially rural schools, like St. Joachim.

Because of the Old Mines Area Historical Society and the La Brigade a Renault, there has been a resurgence of awareness of French heritage. The annual Fete of the Old Mines Area Historical Society and the bi-annual Rendezvous by La Brigade a Renault remind people of their origins as a French lead-mining community, even though Old Mines French has just about become extinct. Even though families are separated by miles, many return to participate in the Fete through food and genealogy, to participate in the Rendezvous through costume, food, and musket skill, and many return to reconnect with family and friends at the annual September St. Joachim Fall Festival.

In summary, there remain a few who think St. Joachim Church is an integral part of their lives. They do not see the practice of their faith disappearing anytime soon. The faith that has been will still be many years to come. There is a melding that has taken place between French heritage and French Catholicism; one insures the existence of the other. In other words, the people who live in the Old Mines area work together to preserve their past so it is not forgotten, while forging ahead to meet their future.

For Further Reading: *History of St. Joachim Parish: 1822–1972; 1723–1973*, Mark G. Boyer; *Historical Program-Pageant Book: 250th Anniversary, Old Mines, Missouri*, Natalie Villmer; Excerpts from History and Customs of Washington, Iron, St. Francois, and Ste. Genevieve Counties, J.T. Miles, *The Diggin's* 6:1.

Conclusion

In the *Historical Program-Pageant Book* of 1973, on page 22 Natalie Villmer wrote: "All the old customs, the French customs, are gone. But remembrance lingers on, and those who loved them fill their children with pride in the heritage. Many hand on to their children respect, love, and honor of God and family and country." She continues: "Old Mines sons and daughters return. Modern in every way, they love the old home ties, the peace and quiet, the beauty of woods and farmland. Newcomers buy property and fit into the social patterns of Old Mines. Land development is increasing. A few miles north of the former Old Village fifty lots are sold. The search for varied industry goes on."

In the next paragraph, Villmer writes: "Life in Old Mines is a good life. Perhaps in days to come the descendants of early settlers along with the newcomers will make a modern town or city of *La Vielle Mine*. Maybe Old Mines in the jet and space age will become a suburb of St. Louis, that city which so many years ago supplied a link in the lead trade originating in Washington County soil, which sent a son, Auguste Chouteau, to claim a grant in the Old Mines Concession." Villmer continues: "Perhaps! Anything can happen. Old Mines for various reasons has lured men [and women] for over 250 years. And even today her visitors and her families still feel her charm, her lure of life, the good, the simple life. Almighty God has truly blessed the Village of the Old Mines!"

On page 159 in the conclusion to *History of St. Joachim Parish: 1822–1972; 1723–1973* in 1972, I wrote about life continuing in Old Mines. "We are aware that we are a people with a history. We have it written and unwritten. We have it as part of us. We have it deep in our hearts because it is us. It is a history of people. St. Joachim would have no history without the people to make it." I continued: "That part of us which is written here is only the outside of us. What is inside cannot be expressed in words, but can only be lived. We are the living history now. Let us never forget that history of the far past, for from it we grow into the future. We are the present history of St. Joachim now, while we are at the same time past and future. Each of us is at the center. Each of us has a part. Each of us must be what we are, and each of us must contribute to that totality which is the church, for it is from her that we receive our life and spend that life trying to give it in return." I concluded: "It is only because of this that we can close

Conclusion

this book, make the past a part of us, make the present our now, and make the future our goal, while we continue to live. We are a people with a history."

Villmer's words and my words of fifty years ago are an appropriate way to close this new edition of the history of Old Mines and St. Joachim Parish and all else within the boundaries of the Old Mines Concession. In the area of Old Mines, we live our French heritage; it was and is the way we are. We adapted the old customs to meet the present time over and over again. The once interrelated and isolated community made way for the new families and ways of life that connected us to the rest of the world. Once we lived in the woods in a log house; now we live in the world through radio, TV, and internet. According to Jason BeDuhn, professor of Comparative Study of Religions at North Arizona University and writing in the September-October 2020 issue of *The Fourth R*, "We have to let the past be the past, with its own terms, concepts, and ways of seeing things, and at the same time realize that there was nothing inevitable in how things ultimately turned out today." He continues, "For many people, recovering an accurate picture of early [Old Mines history] provides an opportunity to critically assess the choices made along the way of [Old Mines] history and to reconnect with lost aspects of the past that, surprisingly, speak to people today."

The French did not disappear from Old Mines once they got here before 1723. The twelfth-, thirteenth-, and fourteenth-generation continue to express their French heritage today in some ways. And some continue to express their Roman Catholicism today in some ways. Nevertheless, we let the past be the past, with its own terms, concepts, ways of seeing things, and ways of living and at the same time realize that there has been and will continue to be a future which no one can accurately predict. This book has made an attempt to recover an accurate picture of Old Mines history over the past three hundred years, while critically assessing previous histories and the choices storytellers and writers made along the way to narrate Old Mines history. Hopefully, this book has enabled the reader to reconnect with lost aspects of the past that, surprisingly, speak to him or her today.

Mary Ann (Politte) Pratt is one of those lifetime Old Miners who has reconnected with lost aspects of the past that continue to speak to her today. "Something important about our church is something you cannot see or touch," she writes. "[In 2013,] I started opening the church for morning Mass and setting out the wine and the hosts. Many mornings I came out of the sacristy and encountered the morning sun gleaming through the colored-glass window in the choir loft. Those sun rays landed on the tabernacle each morning. Every morning I knelt on the lower step and thanked God for the day and the gift of faith that has sustained me throughout my life. Whenever visitors come to visit the church, they always make a point to say that our church was a holy place." Indeed, two hundred years of St. Joachim Church history set within three hundred years of Old Mines history makes the whole area a holy place!

Index

Adrian, Louis O., 39
Ammon, Ulrich, 167
Aubuchon, Andrew, 211
Aubuchon, Harry, 211
Aubuchon, Lucian, 211

Barbier, Francis, 32
Baron de Carondelet, Hector, 18
Bartin, Joseph, 42
Beil, Joseph A., 39
Bequette, Doris Ann, 83, 117, 120–21, 127
Bliss, Philemon, 53
Bohn, Earl, 211
Boilvin, Nicholas, 18
Bolderson, John, 46, 77
Bolduc, Louis I, 23–25
Bolduc, Louis II, 23–25
Bolduc, Louis III, 23–25
Bone, Kent, 37, 67, 69, 71, 147, 153, 167–68, 187, 193–94
Borgna, Philip, 30–31, 70
Boullier, John, 28–33, 35, 37–38, 41, 43, 57–58, 70, 95, 217,
Bourisaw, Henry, 211
Bourisaw, Loraine (Catherine Rose), 100, 102–3, 126, 145
Boyer, Charley, 211
Boyer, Donald, ix, 63, 75, 83, 92, 114, 146
Boyer, Edward, 127
Boyer, Elmer, 211
Boyer, Mark G., xiv, xvi, xvii, 26, 45, 56, 65, 69, 92, 94, 105, 114, 124, 127, 133, 137, 143, 145, 148, 194, 212, 214, 221
Boyer, Mary Febronia (Theresa Rosalie), 125, 129
Boyer, Mary Herman (Edna Frances), 125
Boyer (Lynch), Mary, 80
Boyer, Ronald, ix, 60, 75–76, 86, 92, 104–5, 108, 114, 146, 200
Boyer, Steve, 211
Boyer, Wallace, 211
Brands, John, 31, 70, 106

Bruemmer, Edward, 42–44, 61, 71, 115–16, 119, 192
Brug, Theodore, 32
Burke, Raymond J., 48
Burke, Theodore, 32
Burke, Thomas, 32–34

Caffrey, John J., 34, 68
Calvert, Neva, ix, 121–23
Capizzi, Joseph A., 42, 192–93
Carberry, John J., 45–46, 144
Carriere, Joseph Medard, 165, 167–68
Carter, William, 52
Cartier, Jacques, 1–2, 5
Casey, Mary Dorothy (Rose), 125
Casey, Mary Georgiana (Louise), 125
Cavelier, Rene-Robert, 2
Cellini, Francis, 30
Clark, P.J., 37
Cole, George B., 51, 53–55
Coleman, Adrian, 29, 35, 51, 107
Coleman, Kathy (Thebeau), ix, 78–79, 114, 147
Coleman, (Finian) Marie (Mary), 126
Cook, John, 211–12
Cooney, P.F., 37, 106
Cotter, John, 32, 34, 106
Crozat, Antoine, 3–5

Dahmer, Francis Xavier, 28, 30
Daly, John P. (pastor), 39–41, 66, 71, 108, 196, 211
Daly, John P. (son of Patrick), 127
Daly, Patrick, 40, 49, 58, 63, 66, 68, 110
Daly, Thomas G., 37
Danter, Albert, 212
Dattilo, Anthony, ix, 49, 63, 79, 200
Daugherty, Marie (Margaret Mary), 126
Daugherty, Tom, 211
Dean, Mary Jerome (Mary Nazarena), 126
Dean, Mary Nazarene (Cornelia), 125
Dean, Nazarene (Cornelia), 125
De Boisbriant, Pierre Duque, 7

Index

De Champlain, Samuel, 215
DeGonia, Yvonne (Helen Catherine), 100, 103, 126
De Granada, Joseph, 27
De La Loire des Ursins, Marc Antoine, 7–8
De La Motte (Mothe) Cadillac, Antoine, 3–5
De La Renaudiere, Philippe, 6–7, 12–13, 20, 147, 154–55
Delassus, Carlos Dehault, 18–19
De Leon, Juan Ponce, 1
De Lochon, Sieur, 4
De Marche, Joseph, 32
De Mont Brun Sieur de La Seaudrais, Therese Boucher, 25
DeMoor, Mary Ann, 120
De Soto, Hernando (Fernando), 2
De Tonti (Tonty), Henry, 2
D'Iberville, Pierre Le Moyen, 2
Donovan, Francis P., 41, 59, 69
Dorrance, Ward Allison, 165
Doutreluingne, Peter J., 31
Dubourg, Louis William, 27
Duggan, James, 35, 38
Du Tisne (Dutisne), Charles Claude, 4–5

Eschen, Frnak, 192–93
Evans, William, 54

Fouquier Von Petre, Jean, 25
Fox, James, 32–37, 41, 43, 45, 51–55, 68, 70, 106
Freeman (Ferguson), Obadiah, 29

Garesch, Alex J.P., 54
Gallagher, E.T., 143
Gallagher, Francis P., 37
Gerst, Larry, 46–47
Gimon, Joseph A., 39
Glennon, John J., 39, 41–42, 108, 210
Gold, Gerald L., 166, 168
Gossett, Scott, 168
Gravier, Jacques, 3, 5, 27
Grugan, S.A., 34

Hamilton, George, 30
Hanson, James E., xiv, 83, 110, 127, 129, 144
Helfrich, Joseph, 42
Helmsing, Charles H., 72–73
Hermann, LaDonna, 48, 115–19, 121–24, 128, 137, 149, 152
Hogan, John J., 33, 38
Hoormann, Alphonse, H., 42–43, 61, 73, 144, 212
Hynes, Andrew M.J., 37

Jansen, Anthony J., 42–45, 101, 144, 212
Joliet, Louis, 2
Johnston, James, ix, 78, 85, 92, 131, 133
Johnston, Robert, 46, 59–61, 63, 75, 77, 155, 218

Kain, John J., 39
Kalter, Roy C., 41
Kane, C.J., 39
Keller, Doris Ileen, 120
Keller, Dorothy Irene, 120
Kernan, Luke J., 39, 210–11
Kincaid, Mary Antoinette (Marie), 125
Koester, Charles K., 145, 212

LaCroix, Francois, 24
LaCroix, Marie-Louise, 24–25
Lamarque, Etienne, 22–25, 28, 33, 37, 56
Lamarque, Marie-Louise, 22, 24–26, 28, 33–37, 40, 43–44, 51–56, 66–68, 70–72, 96, 106, 141, 147, 182, 218
Larche, Louis Napoleon, 39
Laucier, Frederick, 30
Law, Bernard F., 127–28
Law, John, 3–4, 9
Le Sueur, Pierre-Charles, 3, 5
Lobyn, Myles W., 37
Loisel, Regis, 30

Maddin, Thomas, 18–19
Maher, Philip, 39
Marquette, Jacques, 2
Mascaroni, Angelo, 30
Maxwell, James, 27
May, John L., 46, 121
McDonald, O.J., 38
McMahon, J., 39
Mignard, J.M., 32
Miles, J.T., 165, 187, 221
Miller, William Marion, 165
Moll, James, 45–46, 111, 129, 145, 212
Mullanphy, John, 34
Murphy, Henry B., 35–36

Naes, Vincent L., 41–43, 45, 48, 58–59, 61–62, 69, 72, 101
Native Americans, xii, 2–4, 7, 9, 14, 199
Nixon, Pat L. ix, xvi
Noonan, William, 39
Norris, John, 211

Odin, John, 30–31, 38
O'Donnell, Edward J., 121
Oliva, Angelo, 30
Orfei, Nazareno, 38–39, 107

Index

Pace, Miriam (Valerine Boyer), 126
Paris, A.S., 34
Pashia, Fran(cis), ix, 49, 60, 110, 149, 152, 216
Pashia, Lawrence Z., 40, 139–40, 145, 187, 196, 201
Pashia, M. Bertille (Mary), 126
Pashia, Monica, 83, 94, 122–23, 136, 145–46, 199, 208
Pieper, Theodore, 47–48, 60, 68–69, 93, 104
Politte, Dorothy Mary (Catherine), 126
Politte, (Evangelista) Rosemary (May Rose), 100, 103, 126
Politte, Joyce (Daugherty), ix, 74–77, 80, 91, 94, 103, 114, 145, 147, 213
Politte, Marvin J., 63, 145, 208
Politte, Stephen, 85, 91, 94, 127, 213
Portell, Edward Aloysius (Viola Rose), 126
Pratt, David, ix, 152
Pratt, Mary Ann (Politte), ix, 60–62, 76–77, 79, 94, 104, 143, 223
Pratt, Monica, 79, 81
Pratt, Rose E., 75, 61
Pratte, Henry, 27, 29, 217

Quinlan, John I., 37

Recar, Mary Alda (Maryrose), 125
Reichling, Richard, 41
Renault, Philippe Francois, v, xii, xiii, 1–2, 7–14, 17–18, 20, 146–48, 153, 157
Richards, Kris, ix, 152
Rigali, Justin F., 48
Ritter, Joseph E., 42–43, 115, 119
Rolando, Bart, 31
Rondeau, Marie Anne, 12, 27
Rosati, Joseph, 28–32, 35, 38, 57, 70, 95
Rosebrough, Robert, 45–46, 94
Rosi, Louis, 33, 51
Roux, Benoit, 30–31
Rozanski, Mitchell T., 48–49, 137
Ryan, Joseph J., 42
Ryan, Patrick J., 38–39, 107

Saffa, Mary Catherine, 121
Saint-Cyr, John, 31–32

Ste. Jeme dit Beauvais, Jean-Baptiste I, 24–25
Ste. Jeme dit Beauvais, Jean-Baptiste II, 25
Ste. Jeme dit Beauvais, Marie-Louise, 23–25
Schloemer, Bernard, 46
Schramm, Edward, 44, 131, 144
Shannon, John, 30
Shea, Edward J., 37
Siegel, Robert, 167–68
Siegfried, Mary Margaret, 118, 121–22
Smith, Erastus B., 51–52
Smith T, John, 21–22, 26, 30, 182, 218
Stroughmatt, Dennis, 150, 167–68, 193, 199
Suellentrop, Bernard A., 41–45, 48–49, 59, 68, 71–72, 101, 115–17, 122, 129–31, 144, 212
Suren, Richard H., 45, 59, 69, 73–74, 101–2, 128, 144–45, 217–18

Thebeau, Helen, 68, 80
Thebeau, Neil, 62, 80
Thogmartin, Clyde O., 166, 168
Thomas, Rosemary Hyde, ix, 13, 149, 166, 168, 187
Tillman, Richard, 213
Tornature, J.B., 32
Trumm, P.A., 37–38
Tucker, Hilary, 30
Tucker, Louis, 30, 32

Valle, Francois, 18–19
Villmer, Natalie, ix, xi, xiv, 5, 13, 20, 46, 69, 73, 77, 83, 90, 105, 110–12, 114, 118, 121–24, 126, 133, 137, 144–49, 152, 162, 187, 193–94, 199, 214, 221–22
Vivarenne, Pierre, 12, 27

Wagner, David, 55
Walsh, John F., 41–42, 68, 108
Watrin (Vattrin), Philbert Francis, 27
Widmer, Alice, 115–19, 121–24, 147, 149, 152
Winkelmann, Christian H., 41
Winter, Joseph B., 212
Wiseman, Joseph V., 32
Wurm, John, 45

Recent Books by Mark G. Boyer Published by Wipf & Stock

Nature Spirituality: Praying with Wind, Water, Earth, Fire

A Spirituality of Ageing

Weekday Saints: Reflections on Their Scriptures

Human Wholeness: A Spirituality of Relationship

A Simple Systematic Mariology

Praying Your Way through Luke's Gospel and the Acts of the Apostles

An Abecedarian of Animal Spirit Guides: Spiritual Growth through Reflections on Creatures

Overcome with Paschal Joy: Chanting through Lent and Easter—Daily Reflections with Familiar Hymns

Taking Leave of Your Home: Moving in the Peace of Christ

An Abecedarian of Sacred Trees: Spiritual Growth through Reflections on Woody Plants

Divine Presence: Elements of Biblical Theophanies

Fruit of the Vine: A Biblical Spirituality of Wine

Names for Jesus: Reflections for Advent and Christmas

Talk to God and Listen to the Casual Reply: Experiencing the Spirituality of John Denver

Christ Our Passover Has Been Sacrificed: A Guide through Paschal Mystery Spirituality—Mystical Theology in The Roman Missal

Rosary Primer: The Prayers, The Mysteries, and the New Testament

From Contemplation to Action: The Spiritual Process of Divine Discernment Using Elijah and Elisha as Models

Love Addict

All Things Mary: Honoring the Mother of God—An Anthology of Marian Reflections

Shhh! The Sound of Sheer Silence: A Biblical Spirituality that Transforms

What is Born of the Spirit is Spirit: A Biblical Spirituality of Spirit

Very Short Reflections—for Advent and Christmas, Lent and Easter, Ordinary Time, and Saints—through the Liturgical Year

Living Parables: Today's Versions

My Life of Ministry, Writing, Teaching, and Traveling: The Autobiography of an Old Mines Missionary

www.ingramcontent.com/pod-product-compliance
Lightning Source LLC
Chambersburg PA
CBHW081146230426
43664CB00018B/2822